PENGUIN BOOKS
THE BURNING CHAFFEES

Brigadier Balram Singh Mehta was commissioned on 15 June 1966 in 45 Cavalry. He comes from an illustrious military family. In 1984, he raised the 13 Armoured Regiment, which later participated in Ex Brass Tacks with distinction under his command. Brigadier Mehta attended the Higher Command-18 at the College of Combat in 1990. He has the distinction of having served in command assignments under all the three Strike Corps as also on the staff of the Mountain and Infantry Division, besides being deputed with the Cabinet Secretariat. In 1998, he took premature retirement to serve with the Government of Gujarat till 2001. He organized the first entrepreneurship course for retiring defence personnel at the Entrepreneurship Development Institute, Ahmedabad, in 2000. During the last 15 years, he has served with universities in Madhya Pradesh and Chhattisgarh as Vice Chancellor. He is an Adviser to the Surat-based NGO Jai Jawan Nagrik Samiti, which helps the dependents of martyr families. His other interests include practising transcendental meditation and skill development, and encouraging Gujarati youth to join the defence forces. He can be reached at brig_bsm@yahoo.com.

THE
BURNING
CHAFFEES

A Soldier's First-Hand Account of the 1971 War

BRIGADIER B. S. MEHTA

PENGUIN BOOKS

An imprint of Penguin Random House

PENGUIN BOOKS

USA | Canada | UK | Ireland | Australia
New Zealand | India | South Africa | China | Singapore

Penguin Books is part of the Penguin Random House group of companies
whose addresses can be found at global.penguinrandomhouse.com

Published by Penguin Random House India Pvt. Ltd
4th Floor, Capital Tower 1, MG Road,
Gurugram 122 002, Haryana, India

Penguin
Random House
India

First published in Penguin Books by Penguin Random House India 2021

10 9 8 7 6 5 4 3

ISBN 9780143454656

Typeset in Adobe Garamond Pro by Manipal Technologies Limited, Manipal
Printed at Replika Press Pvt. Ltd, India

www.penguin.co.in

MIX
Paper from
responsible sources
FSC® C016779

In memory of my parents, sister and brother,
who now reside in the timeless

CONTENTS

A MESSAGE OF THE CHIEF
OF DEFENCE STAFF

The Burning Chaffees is a first-hand account of a very significant tank battle won by the Indian Army in the 1971 Indo-Pak War. The author had the unique distinction of commanding the PT-76 Tank Squadron of 45 Cavalry as a young captain after his Commanding Officer was martyred. Brigadier B.S. Mehta's writing has highlighted the patriotism and bravery of the Indian soldiers whose selfless sacrifice won India the war through these small but vital battle victories. He has also brought to life the esprit-de-corps and the bonhomie that exists between our services. It is essential to record such important events of India's contemporary military history and the author has done full justice to the subject. I congratulate Brigadier B.S. Mehta on presenting and documenting the battle of Garibpur, the way it was.

Jai Hind!

(Bipin Rawat)
General
Chief of Defence Staff

PREFACE

The military literature of the subcontinent is packed with the writings and musings of venerable flag officers of the three services on 'war as they saw it' and their invaluable impact on military history. Rarely do the words a young officer—the 'cutting edge' of the nation's military power—reach the print stage to share the actual combat experiences of his sub-unit and the personnel he commanded. The junior officer, blooded in battle, leads, performs and accomplishes, sometimes dies, to bring victory and glory to his unit. How, in spite of contrary orders, deficiency in planning and paucity of logistics, the miracle of success is achieved remains covered under a veil of secrecy. This book lifts the veil to present an accurate and unbiased account of how 45 Cavalry, the only regiment raised post-Independence, with a class composition of Other Indian Classes (OICs) and South Indian Classes (SICs), led the Indian advance into erstwhile East Pakistan during the 1971 War.

The book is a first-hand account of a frontline combat soldier who led India's tank column into East Pakistan

(now Bangladesh). Providence led to his taking over command
of 'C' Squadron, which completely destroyed the Pakistani 3
(Independent) Armoured Squadron and badly mauled two
infantry battalions and a company of the reconnaissance and
support battalion, after the officer commanding was killed in
action in the midst of the tank versus tank battle at Garibpur
on 21 November 1971. The squadron then led the advance of
HQ 9 Infantry Division through Burinda–Jessore–Ramnagar–
Daulatpur–Khulna until ordered to halt the tanks from
assaulting across River Bhairab for the capture of Khulna on the
afternoon of 16 December 1971. Unlike other battle accounts
of senior officers discussing strategy, tactics, personalities and
damaged egos, this narrative is different. It brings out in bold
relief the courage and character of the so-called non-martial
races, represented as the OICs and SICs in the Indian Army.
The bravery and sacrifices of the rank and file and the immense
camaraderie that prevailed at the regimental level outclassed
many older cavalry units, stiff with battle honours. The
sacrifices of junior leaders at the executive level are the backbone
of national defence. Be it Kashmir, Kushtia or Kargil, the truth
lies interred with their bones and is rarely reflected in official
accounts or faithfully recorded in regimental history and war
diaries. War brings out the best but also the worst of double
talk, duplicity and deception, practised at the higher echelons.
At the unit level, there is no myth or mystery as every action
is transparent and every officer an open book, accepted for
the true worth of his merit, professional integrity and, above
all, character. This reputation precedes the officer during his
postings while in service, and is subsequently recalled with pain
or pleasure long after he hangs up his uniform and sheds his
rank. The higher command, consisting of honourable men,

above reproach, has been under the media glare. Even the tallest amongst the shining brass has chinks in their armour and feet of clay. Invincibility dwells at the unit level and this fortress will remain impregnable to all outside influences. Therein lies the strength of the Indian Army.

This battle account is noteworthy for the wide range of combat situations experienced by the tank crews. For instance, destruction of enemy tanks at a range of 30 metres on a foggy winter morning or the reactions of tank crews trapped between *khaji* (date) trees while under rocket attack by F-86 Sabre jets. Driving through 800 metres of an anti-tank minefield to find that the trailing tanks have become mine casualties. Floating down a tidal river in an amphibious tank, with jammed water propellers, and enemy 6 pounder coastal guns coming into full view—a nightmare personified. The machinations of a company commander to derail a brigade river crossing operation because of the All-India Radio broadcast that a ceasefire was imminent. The ambush and massacre of the Indian tank column at Kushtia, resulting in derailing of 2 Corps' plan. Whenever troops are deployed, young officers and soldiers will encounter such battle-related incidents woven together. The combat experiences provide valuable lessons to those serving and are a reminder to those who may have crossed the Rubicon. To that extent, the book not only informs and instructs but also entertains and educates the reader about the brass tacks of the men in combat.

The unit was amongst the first to be moved to the Western Sector immediately after victory in the east and redeployed near Ganganagar, Rajasthan. The desert provided the time and inspiration to record the grit, courage and sacrifices of subordinate commanders, not mentioned in published war accounts or logged in war diaries. Unlike other war records, written at home or in the office on computers, this was written in longhand, under a 'forty-pound tent', sitting by a 'lamp hurricane' on a 'table folding IT (Indian Troops)' and 'stool folding' issued by the ordnance corps to young officers awarded parchment commissions by the Rashtrapati. Oblivious of the dust, heat, mosquitoes and desolation of the drifting sand dunes of the desert, the author put pen to paper to record the courage, bravery and conduct of comrades in combat. The unvarnished account represents the truth, as the author had no axe to grind and no reputation to protect. Some regimental officers and the batman, Massey, were privy to the manuscript, running into over 400 handwritten pages.

C/o 56 APO
7 March 1972

1

9B HOPE ROAD

My name is Mehta. Balram Mehta. I also have a middle name—
Singh. This is reminiscent of earlier generations, when the eldest
male child in the family was anointed as a Sikh—Defender of
the Faith. The surname—Mehta—is actually a title granted
to the more erudite and better educated amongst the Mohyal
community, originating from the Gandhara region. The Mohyals
developed a war-like culture and reputation, comparable to the
Pashtuns and Rajputs. In 1971, dozens of Mohyals were one-,
two-, and three-star Generals, Marshals, and Admirals, and were
leading Indian troops into Pakistan.

My father was born in village Bhaun, district Jhelum, the
cradle of military warriors of undivided India. After the Afghan
War, in which he was commended for gallantry, he joined the
Indian Audit and Account Service. He was Deputy Controller
Defence Accounts (CDA) at Jabalpur when he died while on
a tour of East India, in December 1953. Prior to his death,
he had confided to our mother that he wanted his children
to join the defence forces as he admired the discipline, sense

of duty, dedication, and patriotism of Army officers. Father's wish, monetary considerations and Mother's determination combined to steel her resolve and our destiny. As a young girl, Mother was discouraged from pursuing higher education and thrust into wedlock by her parents. She was determined, therefore, to not only make us boys stand on our own feet after completing schooling but also to live her dream by encouraging her daughter to pursue a career path.

Death can bring disaster to families. Ours was no different. In those days, the pension awarded was a measly Rs 150 per month for a five-year period. Family assets at Rawalpindi could not be reclaimed due to the partition in 1947, except some meagre compensation provided subsequently. The family moved to Lucknow where an uncle, K.D. Dhawan, helped as a mentor and motivator. Mother was educated and had some sterling qualities of head and heart. In spite of financial stringency, she was clear-headed and uncompromising and ensured the best for, and from, her children. Her first priority on arriving in Lucknow was to admit her two elder sons, aged nine and seven, into the best school, St Frances High School, and her five-year-old daughter to Loreto Convent.

In 1958, the eldest son, Shamsher, qualified for the National Defence Academy (NDA), Kharakvasla, Pune. I followed the same route and joined the NDA in January 1962. During the second term, I broke a bone in my left leg playing football and spent twelve weeks in a sick bay.

During this period, an epidemic broke out in the academy, resulting in my being shunted to the isolation ward, along with another cadet. It was during this period that the war with China started. With no radio or transistor, our only source of information was the nursing orderly who brought our regular supply of meals and tales of massacre of Indian troops. Then, one day, he announced at breakfast that Brig Hoshiar Singh, the deputy commandant, had been posted out to command a brigade. Brig Hoshiar addressed the cadets and staff before leaving for his new assignment. That evening was special and remains embedded in my memory as the thunderous applause and ear-splitting sound waves of 'Brig Hoshiar ki jai' (Long Live, Brig Hoshiar) reverberated from the academy auditorium to the isolation ward over two kilometres away. That sound still rings in my ears. By the time the academy closed for the term break, the war was over and Brig Hoshiar was no more. I was deeply saddened.

With my leg in plaster, I proceeded on term leave to Lucknow to learn from the newspapers, radio, and friends about the humiliating defeat suffered and the shame that the Chinese had cast on a nascent nation. I visited the Military Hospital and met many of the wounded to hear their tales of defeat and death of comrades. Dejected and saddened, I set out in search of my school friend, Ching Kong, the son of a prominent dentist. It would be the last time we would be meeting as his father sold his shop when it was ransacked. I returned home to meet a smart, debonair Shamsher, decked in his cavalry uniform and black beret, surrounded by siblings and a proud mother, admiring the single pip on his shoulder. His training at the Indian Military Academy (IMA) had been reduced by six months due to the Indo-China War, resulting in his being awarded permanent commission at the age of eighteen years and six months. A small prayer, followed by a thanksgiving function, was organized by this united family, under the watchful eye of our favourite uncle at 9B Hope Road, Lucknow. It signified a return to happy times.

The NDA site in Pune was chosen due to the Pashan Lake, the suitability of the neighbouring hilly terrain, the proximity to the Arabian Sea, an operational air base at Lohegaon as well as the salubrious climate. The location formed part of the hunting grounds of the legendary Shivaji, with the Singhgad Fort as a panoramic backdrop. A new batch of cadets would arrive after a tough selection process. The cadets—belonging to the Army, the Navy, and the Air Force—trained together before getting pre-commissioned in their respective service academies. It was where they were taught diverse subjects and imparted a blend of outdoor and indoor training.

Adjusting to the academy's regimen was an uphill task. This 'cradle for leadership' transformed cadets, wearing khaki uniforms and blue berets, from boys into men. The training moulded our overall personality, while all the sports that we played instilled team spirit. An immaculate sense of dress and deportment, upright bearing, and etiquette set us apart from the crowd.

In June 1965, I reported to the IMA at Dehradun after three years at the NDA, and was assigned to Alamein Company. The major change was our newfound status of being Gentlemen Cadets (GCs). At the time, rumours were afloat that the training period at the IMA would be curtailed as Pakistan had attempted a limited offensive in the Kutch sector. Reports of Pakistan receiving massive military aid from the USA, including tanks, armoured personnel carriers, guns, and aircraft were spoken about in whispers. The 1962 debacle had given the Army a bloody nose and muddied its reputation as an effective fighting machine. The press and media were beginning to highlight the tension along the border, soon followed by reports of mass scale infiltration into the Kashmir Valley. The IMA, impervious to these developments, issued instructions for night patrolling by GCs in the Tons valley of Dehradun. While we were not easily convinced about the likelihood of Pakistani infiltrators ever entering the Tons valley, the nocturnal exercise did add to the excitement of GC footsloggers. It was not long before Pakistan declared war on India.

The training of my batch at the IMA was not curtailed in spite of the 23-day war with Pakistan. For the young GCs, it carried a tinge of disappointment at missing the opportunity of receiving early commission and participating in the war. The drubbing received from the Chinese Army in 1962 was a wake-up call for the nation's political and military leadership. In 1965, it was evident to the citizens of India that a radical change in the political leadership and organization of the defence mechanism had taken place within the country. This lesson of defence preparedness was not lost on my generation, born prior to the partition, especially those who survived the holocaust of wanton killings and bloodshed in 1947–48.

2

ROARING FORTY-FIVE

The 1965 War with Pakistan was limited to the Western Wing only. Had India displayed strategic sense by refusing to open a second front in spite of public pressure? The hard truth was that India did not have the troops or the military hardware to wage war on both fronts. No major action was initiated other than mobilization and deployment of troops of HQ Eastern Command, earmarked for the East Pakistan border. This operational deficiency must have forced the mandarins in the Ministry of Defence to do some hard thinking on raising new units, and acquisition of military equipment for deployment in the riverine terrain of East Pakistan in the future. The armoured corps was then equipped with vintage Sherman and Centurion tanks and one regiment of AMX-13 tanks, none of which was suitable for deployment in the terrain pertaining to East Pakistan. Prior to the commencement of the 1965 War, some Russian tanks had been inducted but allotted to 7 Light Cavalry, deployed in the Western Sector.

The Armoured Corps Directorate had recommended re-raising of 45 Cavalry. This regiment was originally raised in

1916, during World War I, and then re-raised during World War II. It became a prominent member of a group of regiments that had earned the sobriquet of 'Roaring Forties'. The regiment was deployed in Burma and was known to have performed creditably, winning a number of gallantry awards. Thereafter, it was re-raised by Lt Col S.K. Candade at Delhi on 15 May 1965, with a class composition of Sikhs, Rajputs, and Jats. The raising process was subsequently altered due to manpower and equipment problems; further compounded by developments on the Rajasthan border where Pakistani troops had launched a limited offensive in Kutch in the Barmer sector. Prior to the start of the 1965 War, the regiment was re-assigned the role of the Armoured Delivery Regiment (ADR). Due to shortage of trained manpower in the original class composition, it was changed to two-thirds South Indian Classes (SICs) and one-third Dogras. Officers and men, milked at short notice from existing regiments, were grouped into squadrons/detachments, and spread across the Western Sector to perform the duties of the ADR. The basic role involved forward supply of tanks and recovery vehicles to armoured formations on mobilization for war. Many of the detachments were in the battle zone and would have qualified for the award of Theatre Honour 'Punjab 1965'; however, the Battle Honours Committee formed after the ceasefire turned down the claim as the Regimental Headquarters had remained in Delhi for close coordination with the Armoured Corps Directorate and Army Headquarters.

Notwithstanding the honour withheld on technical grounds, it won approval for being re-raised as a light armoured regiment equipped with the Palavushi Tanka-76 (PT-76), an amphibious tank of Russian origin. Field trials of the PT-76 tank had earlier confirmed its suitability for deployment in the riverine terrain of West Bengal. A small consignment of these tanks, received for trial by 7 Cavalry, was taken over for conversion training. The regiment moved to Babina in central India in January 1966 where there were facilities of open ranges for training of the gunners, drivers, and operators. Babina or Babs was a popular military cantonment with cavalry units. This was the best laid out and modern military station of its time which had the entitled scale of married, single, and institutional accommodation. The regiment moved to Bagrakote, West Bengal, in July 1966. In 1967, its class composition was changed once again, with the Dogra squadron being replaced by a squadron of Other Indian Classes (OICs). OICs implied that all castes, tribes, communities not represented in the Army could enrol in this squadron/regiment. That this twice raised 'Roaring Forty-Five' light-armoured regiment, equipped with PT-76 tanks, would become the battle-winning factor in the creation of Bangladesh was never visualized.

The 28 NDA/37 IMA cadets earned their first pip on 15 June 1966, after an impressive passing out parade held at the IMA in Dehradun. I had received my Parchment Commission signed by the then President of India, Dr Radhakrishnan, and had been assigned to 45 Cavalry. On 7 July 1966, I arrived at Babina railway station and was received by Lt Maruti Rao Bhonsle and driven straight to the Officers' Mess, where an enjoyable breakfast, a glass of cold coffee and a short briefing on the history of the regiment followed. The unit was preparing for the move by special trains that would start rolling within a fortnight. During this transition phase, prior to the move, soldiering duties were effectively suspended, and the opportunity ceased to 'make much of your horses' in which all joined with full gusto. Farewell parties by other units in the station were a daily feature amidst late night merry-making, rich food, and music. The Babina parties attracted young women from the nearby colleges and the railway colony, Jhansi. The pleasurable stay did not last long as Major Balwinder, my first squadron commander, announced one fine morning that I would leave with the first military special for Bagrakote, West Bengal. I was soon to learn that life at Babina was like the proverbial trailer of a Bollywood movie.

The reality started unfolding soon after the train steamed out from Babina where the pipe bands, flowers, goodbye kisses, handshakes, and *jhappies* (hugs) would dissolve into dreams and memories of yesteryears. Travelling with a military special tank train of an armoured regiment was an extraordinary, spell-binding experience. Heavy chains fitted on flats were utilized to anchor the tanks so that they remained immobilized and stable during the long rail journey. As the crew preferred to travel with their tanks, they had designed bivouacs to sustain them during the long haul. To answer the call of nature or catch up with friends for a game of cards, the crews would utilize the passenger bogies attached to the train. A separate kitchen car served as a langar on wheels. The tank crews were authorized ice, mineral water, and lemonade during the journey. All requirements projected would be delivered by the local military station headquarters and station marshalling staff would receive generous doles of the magic potion called rum that provided easy access to most facilities, including the communication network of the railways. At the end of the journey, a report would be filed on the quality of the services provided by the railways during transit. As the railway authorities viewed this report with seriousness, it served as an effective handle to obtain local cooperation. These military special trains allowed halts for meals mutually agreed on—speed was not a priority unless the military authorities, for operational moves, had assigned red-hot or white-hot priority.

The long journey from Babina to Bagrakote was a logistical nightmare. At Farakka Barrage, en route, the special train had to switch from broad gauge to metre gauge for completion of the onward journey. Tanks, vehicles, military stores had to be unloaded and trans-shipped in barges across the mighty Ganges. The railway marshalling yards were at some distance from the riverline at the far bank, necessitating movement of tanks under their own steam. The railway infrastructure to support such movement was vintage and old-fashioned. The willing cooperation, grit and fortitude of railway officials, coaching staff, train examiners, and other railway employees made our task manageable. It was with a sense of relief that we steamed out from Farraka Barrage, imagining a comfortable ride into Bagrakote. Midway, we learnt that due to non-availability of a railway ramp at Siliguri, the tanks would be unloaded at New Jalpaiguri, and this was further compounded by the unavailability of the desired number of tank transporters, splitting the road movement of tanks into three phases.

As a subaltern, the one word repeatedly heard was 'security'— it encompassed physical security, security of information relating to personal particulars, unit identity, safety of equipment and, above all, of the recently acquired PT-76 tanks. The tanks were loaded at night, covered by tarpaulins, and secured by ropes and chains. At every halt along the route, the sentries would dismount to patrol the length of the train to keep curious civilians with prying eyes away. Photographs or queries regarding the technical details of the tanks were not permitted. By the time we reached Siliguri, however, the security balloon had burst. The tanks were dismounted and reloaded onto tank transporters for the road journey to Bagrakote. En route, while crossing the Teesta bridge, the column of tanks halted temporarily due to a traffic jam. The induction of tanks into this part of the country for the first time aroused great curiosity amongst the citizens, driving past in buses and cars. Their anxious queries remained unanswered till a couple of tea planters exposed the hollowness of our misplaced emphasis on physical security. A young planter gave us the particulars of the tank, gun calibre, ammunition, etc., to our complete surprise. When questioned, he was frank enough to admit he had read about the import of PT-76 tanks from Russia in one of the magazines! The local media, however, continued to treat this as confidential under the Official Secrets Act and, therefore, subject to government protocol.

The Siliguri corridor is a narrow stretch of 40 km linking West and North Bengal with the seven north-eastern states of India. The corridor is a high value communication bottleneck of strategic, political, and military importance. Any military threat to the corridor, through any of the neighbours, in conjunction with China, could fragment the sensitive north-eastern states. The location of an armoured regiment at the mouth of the corridor appeared to be a careful and well thought out operational decision. While operational compulsions justified locating the regiment at Bagrakote, I was horrified by the complete disregard of the military establishment, not providing even basic creature comforts for the officers and men in uniform. The primitive infrastructure was a sad reflection of the neglect and complete indifference of the higher command. The excitement of guarding the corridor evaporated as we battled the mosquitoes, leeches, and humidity of the area. Bagrakote was devoid of basic infrastructure and amenities, including electricity. The exquisite flora and fauna and awe-inspiring sunsets over the tea gardens were wasted on us as we struggled inside a dormitory, consisting of a bamboo hut, with a thatched roof and rusted, corrugated iron sheets, and a dilapidated, common bathroom, without piped water and WC. A few temporary huts and bashas constructed by the previous unit comprised all that was available. There were no garages for the tanks or vehicles. The unit, carrying crores worth of battle-worthy equipment that was sensitive to the vagaries of the weather, had been inducted into a field area without due thought about infrastructure and amenities. Babina was indeed a trailer to suck you into this neglected corridor now renamed as Buggerkote. The collective effort of the officers and men transformed the environment within a few weeks to make the unit area habitable. Veteran Junior Commissioned Officers (JCOs) invoked the 'beg, borrow, steal' approach, while the officers put their heads together to exploit contacts and ex-regimental officers for release of tents, tarpaulins, stores, and funds. Before long, we were able to invite commanders of local formations and managers of neighbouring tea gardens to our modified Officers' Mess. Some of the more adventurous also ventured into the border town of Dhulabari to buy smuggled imported goods from Indian traders operating from Nepal.

Until the induction of the PT-76 tanks from Russia, the tanks held on the inventory of the Army carried heavy armour plating and weighed over 30 tons. While the heavier tanks could wade through water, the PT-76 was a light tank and amphibious! The training modules, therefore, were at total variance with the existing ones. Officers who had joined from older regiments found it difficult to accept the fact that this tank was designed to operate with a crew of three, as opposed to the Centurion and Sherman tanks, which needed four tradesmen. The senior lot of Majors had mentally written off this tank and their attitude and constant bickering during training was a dampener on the younger Captains. The other sore point was the organization of a light regiment with 35 tanks instead of 45 tanks authorized to armoured regiments. For the new inductees, who were to learn the basics of tank troop leading, the tank held out a promise and a challenge. While as young officers we were appreciative of its ability to overcome minor water obstacles and boggy patches, the veterans viewed it as a poor relation of the armoured corps. Their minds were conditioned by their early experience and training. The one-point agenda to revert to their parent regiments was uppermost in their minds. That so many of them succeeded in returning to their parent regiments speaks for itself.

Loyalty to one's regiment was a lifetime commitment. In those days, getting posted out from your regiment was viewed as a punishment. The bonding was so strong that many were ready to sacrifice their careers and forgo promotions. The record of officers posted to 45 Cavalry was no different. Major[s] Chibber, Chengappa, Mahinder Singh, Namjoshi, Randhwa, Manmohan, Balwinder, Bakshi, Pitre, Amrik Virk—most found their way back to the same or similar regiments. Others who stayed on fell into two categories—some who willingly accepted the change, like Chaks, Inder, Bantu, Gulati, Devindar Virk while the others realized they were nominated out by design and not default. Those commissioned directly into 45 Cavalry would become the core foundation to serve the longest in the regiment. By 1971, the more determined had found their way back to parent regiments. Those left behind lived to tell their tales in the days ahead.

Armoured regiments operate in close cooperation with infantry, engineers, signals, and artillery. Induction of the newly acquired tanks entailed holding of a number of demonstrations and field exercises so that their capabilities and employment could be better understood by the commanders of all arms and services, at all levels. A large number of demonstrations were organized for commanders of other arms and services, particularly the infantry with which we would be working in close cooperation not only for crossing water obstacles but also in different operations of war. During one such demonstration, one of the Punjabi JCOs, having sat through the entire 90-minute demonstration, was astonished to see the PT-76 entering a lake to float on water. He could not control his amusement at this strange phenomenon of an armoured fighting vehicle bobbing in the water. Wondering at this unusual spectacle unfolding in front, he could, by association, correlate this with a tin can floating in water, a common sight in villages. Without realizing that the mike was on, he blurted out his amazement with the words *Pippa tair rehya hai* (Pippa or Peeppa is afloat). Pippa is a common word for a *ghee* tin. The troops watching the demonstration burst out laughing, soon joined by the officers present. The colourful Punjabi description caught the imagination of the troops and the Russian PT-76 was re-christened with the Indian equivalent of Pippa on that eventful day. It soon got embedded into the military lexicon of the Indian Army.

In addition, the regiment participated in a number of formation level tactical exercises—exercises that helped build confidence amongst the commanders that the tactical and logistic plans of the battle groups were sound and executed efficiently on mobilization. The training areas were essentially large riverbeds during the dry season, which provided unrestricted movement and deployment of tanks while practising battle drills. The troop leaders had ample freedom to camp out with a full complement of tanks and to mould their tank troop and crews. These troop training camps were great opportunities to live, work, and train alongside the crews. We got to know each other more intimately and developed comradeship, mutual respect, and understanding, with the formality and mental barriers of rank and age melting away, permitting everyone to be their natural best. The majority being in the age group of 30 and below made mixing and sharing and growing up in the same unit a wonderful experience.

The regiment gained respectability as we trained along with other arms in the riverine terrain. The amphibious potential and ability to carry tactical loads of infantry across water obstacles provided speed and momentum to the operations. The semi-gyro and infra-red facility for night movement gave great confidence to the troops to undertake missions at night. Gradually, the unit gained a reputation for being thoroughly professional and battle-ready. Ex Scimitar, a test exercise, conducted under the aegis of HQ 20 Mountain Division, declared the regiment fit for war. Joint training gave Pippa a respectability, and its officers and men a sense of pride and recognition.

Four years of service in this field area, with brief interludes to undergo courses helped gain confidence and learn the art and science of leadership at the regimental level. While the senior Majors reverted or moved out on posting or retirement, many youngsters from the Short Service Commission or IMA joined the unit. They included Suri, Arun Uttam, Satish Gupta, R.S. Tiwana, Kocky Kochhar, Ravi Bains, Ravi Bhandari, Sidhu, Harshvardhan, Rekhi, Chandravarkar, Chhabra, Narain, Mishra, and many more. A well-knit team of spirited and talented officers formed the backbone of the regiment. Each officer found an opportunity to function as a troop leader and then hold regimental staff appointments. Many had served with both the SIC and OIC squadrons to cultivate a bond of affinity and compassion with the troops. Having arrived as a Second Lieutenant (2 Lt) to learn the ropes under a senior subaltern, one gradually moved up the ladder to add another star to the lonely pip on the shoulders. The lucky ones picked up the third star early, depending on local vacancy, to finally gain stability and acceptance as a hardcore member of the regimental fraternity.

The policy of rotation of units between field and peace stations was not transparent in those days. Regimental ties and the influence of the Colonel of the Regiment sometimes determined the peace location of the regiment. As per rumours, one regiment had transformed Ambala into a semi-permanent home for itself for over ten years. Others changed location sometimes to meet operational compulsions or the whims of the Colonel of the Regiment if he was powerful and influential enough. The special nature of our equipment further narrowed our choice of stations as the armoured brigades and armoured divisions had no need for an amphibious tank regiment. Our first peace station was Ramgarh, a glorified village in Bihar (now Jharkhand). Though not a popular choice, it fitted the logic of operational compulsion due to the category of our equipment. Basic facilities and accommodation were available and soon the regiment and the families settled down to enjoy Army life in a regular cantonment. An infantry brigade was co-located, with the Divisional HQ approximately 30 km away at Ranchi. While the married ones settled down to domestic life with the families, the young officers looked forward to weekends in Ranchi. The distance, lack of transport, regimental routine, and social engagements within the regiment/station limited the scope of frequent excursions into Ranchi. Ranchi appeared as the only oasis for hard up bachelors to establish some contact with girls, away from the prying eyes of overzealous wives of married officers. Teji Sidhu, a handsome, broad-shouldered tall Sikh officer, was my constant companion on these weekend trips. This drew the attention of the more domineering wives who did their best to elicit details of the goings-on in Ranchi but, alas, Teji, under the garb of being shy and innocent, would just smile and leave them speculating. Some of the other bachelors were happy shagging in bed or playing rummy/bridge in the Officers' Mess. Others, under parental guidance and the advice of regimental ladies, took leave to tie the nuptial knot, discarding the bachelors' belief that a 'married soldier was a dead soldier'.

Col R.N. Madan, having completed his tenure, was posted out on staff, a few months after our arrival in Ramgarh. He was professionally competent and had put the regiment on a firm footing, both administratively and operationally. He devoted time to put the regimental history together as also recast standing orders for peace and war, along with a wide range of Standing Operating Procedures (SOPs) to meet different contingencies. Regimental institutions were strengthened and guidelines established for financial management. A dress code for officers, mufti for the rank and file, approval of the regimental crest, badge, etc., were undertaken by him. He took special interest in the officers' training, and encouraged them to prepare for staff college so that the need to induct officers from other regiments for command could be eliminated. The regiment and station units gave him an affectionate and fitting farewell.

The officer appointed to command the regiment was Col D.S. Jamwal, Digby to his friends. Digby apparently sought an interview with the Military Secretary to claim command of his parent regiment, 14 Horse (Scinde Horse) but was turned down. Once in the saddle, he took charge to establish effective control and command. He exuded confidence and was professionally competent. He also enjoyed his whiskey, which made him garrulous and long-winded. His frustration at having missed command of his original regiment remained hidden from the troops. He started off on a positive note by undergoing a short conversion course on the PT-76 but rarely mounted one during the rest of his tenure. His tenure is remembered as one of frequent mobilization and movement and, finally, war. Within a few weeks of taking command, state elections were announced in West Bengal. The services of the regiment were requisitioned 'in aid to civil authority'. Translated at its most crude, practical level, it implied 'Keep the Naxalites off our back, while we vote ourselves to power'. Employment on Internal Security (IS) duties entailed the move to Kanchrapara, a suburb of Calcutta (now Kolkata) and the squadrons spread in different districts. The likelihood of violence by miscreants or misguided groups was a rare event as the 'IS duty columns' were armed and invariably accompanied by a local magistrate who was empowered to meet all contingencies.

Siddhartha Shankar Ray, a close confidant of Shrimati Indira Gandhi, was the Congress candidate chosen to lead the party to power in the elections in West Bengal, until then ruled by the communist parties. In those days, an entire generation of young men and women was roaming the streets, talking about the lofty ideals of communism. The Naxalites had become a force to contend with in West Bengal. Fear of violence, death, and intimidation had become widespread, especially in the countryside. The civil administration had been overwhelmed and petrified by the fear of a Naxalite hiding behind every bush. Daily reports of firing, killing, kidnapping, riots, and police high-handedness were splashed all over the English and regional newspapers. The deployment of an armoured regiment in aid to civil authority gave us some insight into the working of the civil administration. The police atrocities, the unquestioned powers of search and arrest, the treatment meted out to those unfortunates labelled as Naxalites, the horror stories of jails in the countryside remain embedded in one's memory. The unbridled powers of the politicians, the cussedness and complicity of the senior leadership came as a culture shock. In the words of Gen J.F.K. Jacob, Chief of Staff HQ Eastern Command, 'From October 1969 to the middle of 1971, we broke the back of the Naxalite revolt in West Bengal' (*The Blood Telegram* by Gary J. Bass, 2013, p. 44).

The Army list of 1971 recorded my name under 45 Cavalry as substantive Lt/Acting Capt B.S. Mehta; date of commission: 15 June 1966; date of birth: 16 April 1945. By June 1971, I had completed five years of military service, mostly in the Eastern Sector. I had read reports and books on the partition and military operations undertaken by our Army post independence. The mind stood conditioned by stories one had heard from elders sitting around the family fireplace, describing eyewitness accounts of murder and mayhem, my own recall of the NDA/IMA days and the stories of valour and glory of serving and retired officers and jawans. While it did not make one a war-monger or create a pathological hatred for any class or community, it was evident that I would rejoin my regiment if ever a shooting war was announced. As a family, my mother's dream stood nearly accomplished. My younger brother Rajendra, had been commissioned into 16 Light Cavalry. Narinder had joined the NDA in 1968 and would earn his Parchment Commission in December 1971. The youngest, Surinder, on completing his Senior Cambridge from St Francis with a first division, had sat for the examination conducted by the UPSC for entry into the NDA. Kusum, our only sister, on completion of her college education from Loreto, had appeared for the pre-medical test and been cleared for admission into King George Medical College, Lucknow, in the Dentistry Department. Mother had devoted her life to her children in spite of all odds, and a mountain of difficulties that a widow has to face in society. The courage and character she displayed during those challenging years, gave her a new iconic status within the family, with friends and in the neighbourhood.

3

THE MELTING POT

1971 was a significant year for South Asia. In India, Prime Minister Indira Gandhi had been elected to the office of Prime Minister with a commanding Parliamentary majority. In Pakistan, Gen Yahya Khan had held the first national election on the basis of universal franchise which would divide, instead of unite, the country. Before the end of the year, two wars had been fought, one internal in Pakistan and the other with India. The first led to millions of refugees, mostly Hindus, from East Pakistan, seeking refuge in the economically impoverished eastern Indian states of West Bengal, Assam, and Bihar. The second was the onset of a military campaign which lasted less than a month, starting on 21 November 1971, and ending on 16 December 1971. By the end of the year, the political contours of South Asia had been redrawn, Bangladesh had become a reality, and Pakistan dismembered forever. India emerged as a significant regional power in the subcontinent.

The Pakistani military establishment has the unenviable record of seizing power through military coups. It achieved further disrepute when Gen Yahya toppled his military superior, Field Marshal Ayub Khan, President of Pakistan, by planning a 'silent' coup. Little did Gen Agha Mohammed Yahya Khan realize that in a couple of years, this would lead to civil war in Pakistan, war with India, and the emergence of Bangladesh in 1971! Gen Ayub Khan had ruled Pakistan for 14 years as the Chief Martial Law Administrator and then as President. However, by 1969, political unrest led to street agitations and Gen Yahya Khan, who was heading the Army, started plotting against his superior. In secret meetings with Mujibur Rehman, he encouraged him to press on with his 'Six-Point' demand for East Pakistan. They assured Mujibur Rehman that 'he could go ahead with his anti-Ayub campaign without any let or hindrance from the Army'. Yahya cunningly enlisted the support of his old friend and drinking partner, Interior Minister Admiral A.R. Khan, who persisted in presenting highly pessimistic daily briefs to undermine Ayub. With law and order getting shoddier and the political parties creating civil unrest, Ayub called for the Army commanders to devise a plan to quell the unrest. Finally, in middle of March 1970, Ayub asked Yahya to come to the aid of the civil administration. Yahya asked Ayub to abrogate the Constitution and impose Martial Law. A frustrated Field Marshal Ayub, who had recently suffered a heart attack, ordered the military on the evening of 25 March 1970 to impose Martial Law and assume power. Thus, Yahya had conducted a 'silent' coup while the outside world and media believed that Ayub had handed over power of his own free will.

Gen Yahya Khan, having assumed the powers of Chief Martial Law Administrator, started a series of consultations with the political parties to introduce electoral reforms as also a revision of the Constitution. Amongst the first major changes he introduced were disbandment of the military council and appointment of a civilian cabinet in August 1969. A committee was set up to establish electoral reforms and also revise the Constitution. Within two decades of the creation of Pakistan, the differences between the Punjabi-dominated West Wing and their Bengali brethren in the Eastern Wing were beginning to tear the country apart. At the time of partition, Maulana Abul Kalam Azad had forecast that Pakistan would disintegrate within 25 years.

Gen Yahya was true to his word and announced in March 1970 that the national and provincial elections would be held in October 1970. It was these elections that provided the spark for the split. He issued guidelines for the conduct of elections published under the Legal Framework Order (LFO). The LFO set forth a number of basic principles and arrangements that would have to be honoured in the new Constitution. It stipulated an Islamic Republic in which laws repugnant to the Quran and Sunnah would not be admissible. The Constitution would provide for fundamental rights to the citizens and an independent judiciary. Provincial autonomy, administrative and financial powers, and removal of economic disparities between the two wings, as demanded by the people, were to be undertaken. The major change from previous Constitution was removal of the 'principle of parity' and bringing in direct elections on the principle of universal adult franchise which favoured the Bengalis of East Pakistan due to the higher population ratio.

The problems between the Western and Eastern Wings of Pakistan were deep-rooted—physical separation, different languages, and lack of trust being the fundamental ones. The popular joke in the subcontinent used to be that the two wings of Pakistan, separated by a thousand miles, were united by three things: Islam, English, and Pakistan International Airlines, the last being the most important. The 1965 War had created the perception in Bengali minds that they had been left to the mercy of India. Only one division was deployed to defend East Pakistan against India, and the assurances that China would intervene in case India attacked sounded hollow. The long-standing discriminatory and exploitative policies, the sense of alienation, and the Bengali grievances since the formation of Pakistan in 1947 had created a sense of victimization. The Bengali representation in the civil services, defence forces, and managerial positions was relatively low. Economic disparity was evident as also the lack of autonomy. At partition, Urdu-speaking Biharis, who migrated to East Pakistan, did not feel the need to merge with the local Bengali population. They generally settled close to the seats of civil and military concentrations manned by the West Pakistanis. Language and cultural affinity led to closer relations between Biharis and West Pakistanis, to the exclusion of the Bengalis. To make matters worse, the West Pakistani scorned the Bengali 'Bingo' as weak and unmartial, unfit for soldierly duties. No discernible effort was made to eliminate friction and promote cohesion.

All these factors combined to unleash the Bengali angst against West Pakistan. The year-long political campaign of Sheikh Mujib, that had been vitriolic in many ways, invoked a sense of hatred. On 13 November 1970, East Pakistan was lashed by a severe cyclone and heavy floods, resulting in the election being deferred to December 1970. Death and devastation were widespread. As per some estimates, over two lakh people or nearly 1.5 per cent of East Pakistan's population ended in a watery grave. The lukewarm response of the Western Wing to the abject misery and suffering due to the floods and cyclone suffered by East Pakistan during 1970 had further hardened attitudes towards cooperation. The Awami League leadership was agitated and converted this widespread negative disposition amongst the Bengali population into a mass movement. The clash had virtually become 'civilian vs military', 'Bengali vs West Pakistani', 'popular democracy vs military dictatorship', 'non-violent vs violent'. The alienation was reflected in the 'Six-Point' formula proposed by Sheikh Mujibur Rehman and the Awami League Manifesto, demanding major constitutional changes.

While the East was immersed in fighting death, disease, epidemic, and starvation caused by the vagaries of nature, the Western Wing was toasting the emergence of Zulfiqar Ali Bhutto as the leader of a newly formed political party, Pakistan People's Party (PPP). Bhutto had served as erstwhile Foreign Minister under Gen Ayub Khan. He belonged to the landed gentry of Sindh and was considered a heavyweight politician, with a strong base in West Pakistan. He was a strong votary of close relations with China. He was also identified as a Mujib baiter. By the time the names of the candidates for the elections were announced by the political parties for the December elections, it was evident that the PPP and Awami League were the main contenders. The PPP did not field any candidates for the 162 seats in East Pakistan, while Sheikh Mujib contested only 7 out of 138 seats in West Pakistan. Party workers and leaders concentrated only in a single region, thus, converting the national elections into provincial elections. The results had the Awami League winning 160 of the 162 seats in East Pakistan, while Bhutto's PPP won 81 out of 138 seats in West Pakistan. The National Assembly of 300 seats confirmed the predictions of a vertical split: 160 seats from East Pakistan represented

53 per cent of total seats whereas the PPP's share of 27 per cent of the seats and the balance divided amongst the minor parties, stood at a poor second.

The major political figures represented a cocktail of irreconcilable personalities for which there were no easy solutions. Yahya's power base was the 'military' and the 'economic elite'; both opposed a compromise with Bhutto who, in their view, was a 'leftist and populist leader', wanting to control a strong central government. Yahya and Bhutto, however, had one thing in common—both opposed Mujib who remained steadfast on his autonomy plan and his Six-Point agenda. Mujib, having won the election, was careful, and had abstained from a unilateral declaration of independence of East Pakistan during the election rallies. This provided hope that the differences could be resolved and that Mujib could work with Yahya to find a political solution. The key to the resolution of the autonomy issue lay with Yahya. Bhutto realized that the only way he could get power was if a fragmented Pakistan became a reality. Mujib was unwilling to divide Pakistan. But sensing danger, and due to the reluctance of the military to transfer power to the new assembly and elected government, Mujib refused to go to West Pakistan for talks.

The formal announcement that the National Assembly would be convened on 1 March 1971, was the proverbial last straw. The dam of pent-up feelings, emotions, and disappointment burst forth to cast a spell of gloom and doom. Mujib declared 'non-violent non-cooperation'. Within an hour of the announcement, 50,000 to 60,000 people, carrying bamboo sticks and iron rods, gathered in Dhaka to burn Pakistani flags. Curfew was declared on 2 March, and for some strange reason, the troops were withdrawn into the barracks on 3 March, and ordered not to use force even in the case of curfew violation. A hartal was announced by Mujib wherein he exhorted his followers to make every house a fortress and fight the enemy, as this struggle had become a struggle for independence. The violence unleashed over the next few weeks was uncontrolled. East Pakistan had virtually come under 'Mujib Rule', with the troops confined to the barracks. The loyalty of the East Pakistanis had become suspect, including of the government servants. An atmosphere of suspicion had been created, wherein not even a Bengali in uniform could be trusted. The very look in his eye spelt rebellion. The civil disobedience movement had led to the West Pakistani troops being confined to the cantonments, behind barricades. The situation made it evident that the Pakistan government had lost control of East Pakistan and that a 'parallel government' led by Mujib had taken charge. Arson, looting, attacks on non-Bengali people and properties were rampant. Encouraged, the Awami League organized effective blockades against the Army. Food and fuel supplies were blocked, and local markets would not sell fresh food, fish, meat, vegetables, or even milk for infants. The Army's movement was disrupted. Army personnel were jeered at and spat upon. In many cases, soldiers were attacked and their weapons snatched.

Yahya arrived in Dhaka on 15 March 1971, followed by a belligerent Bhutto, who refused to converse, or even sit face to face with Mujib till Yahya chided them, and told them not to behave like bashful newly-weds but as national leaders. Finally, Yahya took their hands, and asked them to honour the rules of courtesy and shake hands. During the initial talks, Yahya agreed to transfer power to Mujib, if the conditions stipulated in the LFO, 1970, were accepted. Mujib suggested that two assemblies, with members from West Pakistan and East Pakistan, prepare separate draft Constitutions, followed by a joint session of the two assemblies to draft a Federal Constitution. Yahya insisted on convening one assembly only. Bhutto was aware that if Mujib and Yahya reconciled their differing viewpoints, he would end up playing an insignificant role. Bhutto had mustered support amongst senior military officers to serve his cause, which jettisoned progress. Mujib finally understood that Yahya's negotiation to defuse the crisis was a sham; the military had purchased time to deploy additional troops for the planned crackdown. Yahya, along with his top generals, had held a secret meeting towards the end of February 1971 in which the decision to crush dissent with military might had been taken. The deputy chief of Pakistan's intelligence agency S.A. Saud leaked the information to a Bengali officer of the intelligence department who, in turn, informed Mujib. Yahya's return to Islamabad could not have been very pleasant. Questioned by a reporter, he blurted out, 'the people did not bring me to power, I came myself'.

Gen Tikka Khan was appointed as Governor/Chief Martial Law Administrator (CMLA). He issued his first order—'Capture Mujib, dead or alive'. On the night of 25–26 March, the Pakistan government launched 'Operation Searchlight', a military solution to a political problem. The immediate aim was to re-establish the writ of the government in East Pakistan by arresting the leaders, rooting out militant elements, disarming the Bengal Police and Army personnel, and establishing control over the radio and print media. The operation led to the arrest of Mujib but most of the other leaders escaped. The disarming of the Bengal Police and Army personnel turned into a bloodbath in many places, with casualties on both sides. The Army did get control of the entire province but it took several weeks. All hopes of a negotiated settlement evaporated with the military crackdown unleashed by Gen Tikka Khan. Cries of Joi Bangla (Long Live Bengal) and Sonar Bangla (Golden Bengal) rent the air across entire East Pakistan. Large groups of men, women, and children, uprooted due to the military crackdown, started fleeing, seeking refuge in West Bengal. The figure would finally run into millions, forcing India to put up refugee camps. The leaders of the Awami League crossed over into India to form the Government of Bangladesh (in exile) in Mujibnagar, in reality, 7 Theatre Road, Calcutta (now Kolkata).

Once Operation Searchlight commenced, the boast of the Awami League of revolt turned hollow. It appeared that no detailed plans had been prepared. A few World War II rifles and some weapons earlier captured from Pakistani soldiers formed their total armoury. Bamboo sticks and swords could not have stopped a determined Army deployed to quell a revolt. It finally ended as it had begun, best described by Simon Dring when he wrote in the Sunday Telegraph, 'the supporters of Sheikh Mujibur Rehman talked a great deal before the crackdown last month about how they would fight, but they did virtually nothing about preparing themselves. They led noisy and often violent demonstrations, but they had no organization, no training, no weapons, and as the Army proved in Dhaka, no real stomach for war' (*Dead Reckoning* by Sarmita Bose, 2011, p. 52). 'There is among the East Bengali Muslims, a very widespread and acute sense of grievance against West Pakistan, and what is more disquieting, a disposition to accept and gloat on the grievance in self-pity rather than to show a determination to get rid of the grievance by taking practical and energetic steps,' wrote Nirad

C. Chaudhuri. The hijacking of an Indian Airline plane to Lahore on 30 January 1970, and the subsequent blowing up of the plane had forced India to ban overhead flights from West Pakistan to the Eastern Wing. The two Kashmiri hijackers were welcomed by Zulfiqar Bhutto, while the act was solemnly condemned by the Bengalis, including Mujibur Rehman. These contrary reactions were an important indicator of the split between the two wings. Around the same time, articles by K. Subramaniam, India's most influential strategic thinker and head of the Indian Institute of Defence Studies and Analyses (IDSA), a think-tank, funded by the Defence Ministry, encouraged us to believe that India must prepare for the worst as the differences between the two wings of Pakistan were not likely to be resolved. As junior officers, we heard rumours of violent agitations in Kashmir and a likely military adventure by Pakistan, with the support of China. As per some reports, the military displayed stark cruelty, more merciless than the Jallianwala Bagh massacre by the British Gen Dyer. Stories of rape, torture, arson, and targeting of Hindus came with every fresh batch of refugees pouring into India. Imagine a Pakistani General asking his soldiers, 'How many Bengalis have you shot?' Infrastructure destroyed, villages razed, Awami League workers and Hindus targeted—all left a blaze of devastation across the length and breadth of East Pakistan. This was how an army of 30,000 troops could silence and control 75 million Bengalis. The civilized world simply ignored the atrocities in East Pakistan, viewing this man-made crisis as 'an internal affair' of Pakistan.

The flow of refugees was unstoppable and they came in rickshaws, bullock carts, and country boats. It brought to mind pictures of the murder and mayhem of the 1947 partition.

Forcing people of every religious persuasion—Hindu, Muslim, Buddhist, Christian—to leave their 'home and hearth' and pour into India was no different from the carnage and genocide of the Holocaust.

4

TURMOIL IN THE EAST

The military crackdown by the Pakistan Army became breaking news on All India Radio. All national dailies carried headlines of this serious development. Headquarters Eastern Command, located in the famous Fort William in Calcutta (now Kolkata) and responsible for guarding our eastern borders with neighbouring countries had been closely watching the gradual slide, leading to anarchy, in neighbouring East Pakistan. It had earlier issued a warning order to the regiment to relocate at Kanchrapara, near Kolkata, capital of West Bengal as the 'aid to civil authority phase' ended. Kanchrapara and Kolkata are connected by road and rail. Kanchrapara boasts of an old, unused airfield of World War II vintage. An Air Defence (AD) missile unit of the Air Force and an engineer bridging unit of the Army were located there. Midway on this 70-km stretch, one crossed the more easily recognizable Barrackpore military garrison where an infantry brigade with ancillary units was permanently located. The regiment would remain in the orbit of Headquarters 9 Infantry Division located at Ranchi, indicating that our move was only a precautionary measure and not part of general mobilization.

Many of us who had had an opportunity to study the prevailing situation in West Bengal fully understood the implications of the mass exodus of men and women from East Pakistan. This region was already in a state of political turmoil due to the Naxalite movement, inter-party rivalry, unstable government and labour unrest. The recent elections had once again put the Congress in power but it would take considerable time before the law-and-order machinery of the government was made effective in the state. I remember leading a column of 80 men on a flag march through the narrow lanes of Midnapore, staring at a tense but friendly population. Living like nomads, constantly on the move, shifting camp from one government school building to a well-equipped rest house of some jute mill owner brought us in contact with the local *bhondoos, badmash, banias,* and bureaucrats ruling the countryside. Into this cauldron was now pouring in a sea of humanity from East Pakistan, looking for food, shelter, and sustenance, already in short supply.

The only course open was to provide shelter to the refugees and hope that sanity and stability would prevail in Pakistan and steps would be taken for their return. In the meantime, however, the nations of the world were expected to be generous with their aid, and accept substantial economic responsibility to help the country tide over the influx of the refugees. Two important factors, difficult to comprehend at that early stage, were that the refugees would eventually add up to a figure of 10 million; and some of the world powers would be reluctant to shoulder the economic responsibility for these unfortunate people, who would remain homeless. The central and state governments prepared to marshal all the resources at their command to overcome this man-made calamity with grim determination.

The civil services had geared up to cope with the migrant crisis. Refugee camps were set up all along the border. With the help of some aid coming in from some countries, the necessary arrangements were made to provide at least the essentials of life to all. Food, shelter, medical aid, and necessary clothing was provisioned. The influx, however, kept multiplying at an unprecedented rate. Infectious diseases spread, demanding added resources and trained medical personnel to fight disease and death. Similarly, stocks of food and clothing were soon depleted, posing fresh problems. Reserves were dug into, and fresh appeals were made to the nations of the world. Finding only a limited response, the country once again coaxed itself into accepting added responsibility. The so-called 'internal problem' of Pakistan had become a national crisis for India and there seemed no easy solution to it. But the country had already committed itself and was now spending a sizable percentage of its own budget for the upkeep and maintenance of the refugees. That this was a big drain on an overpopulated and still developing country was no secret.

Besides the civil services tailored to cope with the ever-magnifying refugee problem, the Ministry of Defence, realizing the inherent security risks of the situation, had redeployed troops in the Eastern theatre. No large-scale movement took place and only the forces under Headquarters Eastern Command were readjusted to keep a close watch on an unfriendly and unpredictable neighbour. Throughout history, India has provided refuge and shelter to the needy. Humanitarian considerations apart, it was virtually impossible to seal the long, porous border, stretching for hundreds of miles. But the country could not possibly welcome them indefinitely, for we had very little to share, except our own poverty and misery.

In the regiment, news about the developments in East Pakistan was read with curiosity and concern. The newspapers and radio were providing comprehensive coverage on the unfortunate plight of the refugees. Gruesome photographs showed the mangled bodies of women and children, and the tales of the Pakistan Army's involvement in the killings, rape, and plunder were disturbing. Gradually, some of this concern started evaporating partly because the overdose of such news was benumbing us and also because we were spending more time fighting the elements of nature to make our own life a little tolerable. Though the living conditions were marginally better than at Bagrakote, one still had to overcome the side effects of poor hygiene and sanitation and erratic power supply. As there was no officers' accommodation, a barrack was converted to provide dormitory type lodgings, with common bathrooms for single officers. In Army regulations, contacting malaria was a military offence, punishable under the Army Act. 'Sun down, sleeves down', regular use of ordnance-supplied mosquito repellent, and a daily dose of a chloroquine tablet before the evening meal ensured a malaria-free life. We received orders for a weekly dose of night training being made compulsory, followed soon after by orders that anti-malaria tablets for the rank and file would be administered 'on parade', in the presence of officers. The married officers and men were worse off as many had to shuttle between the peace station at Ramgarh and the operational base, Kanchrapara, balancing domestic responsibilities with professional duties within their meagre pay. Due to acute shortage of authorized accommodation, many had to hire one-room and two-room tenements in the small civil colonies. The high rent that the soldiers had to dish out was only partially compensated for by the recently introduced scheme titled 'Compensation In Lieu of Quarters' (CILQ).

It was felt Pakistan may attempt an attack on India to divert world attention. India had to mount an all-out effort on the political and diplomatic fronts to bring into the public focus the exodus of refugees into India. Pakistan's claim that the forced migration of refugees was its 'internal affair' had to be contested and world opinion harnessed to apply political and economic pressure on Pakistan.

As regimental soldiers, we were involved in these developments only as citizens and silent observers. Due to our prolonged stay and involvement in aid to civil authority, we had lost touch with active soldiering. Training started in right earnest, for our unstable neighbour had jerked us back into the realization that national security, not elections, was our primary task.

Our daily routine underwent a radical change. Our days, also nights, were henceforth filled with reconnaissance, planning, training, and maintenance of arms and equipment. Drills we had gone over a number of times were rehearsed to perfection.

The thought that war was a possibility, though remote, started shaping into reality with the passage of time. Intelligence summaries and reports received from higher headquarters reflected a changing trend in the Pakistan Order of Battle (ORBAT). They had also moved men and munitions of war closer to the border on the pretext of filibustering off refugees. Their military strength in East Pakistan had multiplied nearly four-fold since the crackdown. There were many amongst us who argued that as Pakistan was divided and in a state of turmoil, India should take advantage of the opportunity and split Pakistan into two by military intervention. They were convinced that it was in the national interest to take the first step to divide the wobbling nation, for the odds were against it.

There were many others who felt that considering our Panchsheel past, it was beyond us to take a bold, imaginative step, and strike when the iron was hot. This group felt convinced that we would continue to follow a policy of ambivalence, of wait and watch, and permit vacillation to overtake our judgment. Finally, we would succumb to the pressure of the world powers and accept a solution, detrimental to national interest, to please the world. For us, the motto remained training, training, and more training. Soldiering is not a world cup match where you shake hands or tear shirts. It is a more serious business where you determine the destiny of nations. The soldier returns from the battlefield to his home and hearth, unhonoured and unsung, to start again at the beginning, without breathing a word about his loss. Neither the government nor society can ever give him enough to compensate him for the precious moments of his life spent preparing for war—not his war—our war, our freedom, our destiny, the nation's destiny!

5

NAGAR FEST

It was under these circumstances that marching orders to return to Ahmednagar were received, as a second batch of Russian experts working on the Tankodrom project had arrived to complete the final phase. I had worked with them during an earlier spell and realized the importance attached to this task. The difference this time was that I would be moving on permanent posting and not temporary duty. On completion of the project, we were to take over and operate the system as a training facility for the armoured corps regiments. The implication of being away from the regiment now when the ominous war clouds were becoming visible on the horizon did rupture one's soldierly instincts. Two years is a considerable period by any stretch of the imagination, especially when the ensuing interval may turn out to be an eventful one. An officer or a soldier cannot do much to change the orders and, therefore, has to accept what comes his way. The Officers' Mess farewell function was lively, with repeated bouts of 'bottoms up' and 'one more for the road'. The farewell arranged by my troop and the squadron was different. It reflected a bondage of trust, a camaraderie, for which no words were necessary.

Ahmednagar is located about 120 km north-east of Pune and 120 km from Aurangabad. Ahmednagar is home to the Indian Armoured Corps Centre and School (ACC&S) and the Mechanised Infantry Regimental Centre (MIRC). Ahmednagar Fort, once considered the second most impregnable fort in India, was used by the British to imprison Jawaharlal Nehru (the first Prime Minister of India) and other Indian nationalists before India attained independence. It is in this fort during his confinement in 1944 that Nehru wrote the famous book, The Discovery of India.

Ahmednagar is a small town also called Armourednagar or more popularly just Nagar by the veteran fraternity. The small town continues to train officers and soldiers on whom the security and good name of the corps depends. The town houses the second-largest display of military tanks in the world, and the largest in Asia.

The centre and school comprise a vast complex subdivided into regiments and wings, and commanded then by a Brigadier. The posting was to the range wing, a small newly raised unit working through the armament regiment. This wing was given the task of making a success of the Tankodrom project. The armament regiment had delegated the responsibility to Major Sabharwal, who had trained on this equipment in Russia, during the procurement phase. Many uncomfortable questions regarding delay in completion of the project were flying between Army Headquarters and the ACC&S. The reality unknown to many was that this imported equipment from Russia had been lying unopened for many years, and was now badly rusted. No heads had rolled. A smart alibi was cooked up that due to the technology gap, only a team of experts from Russia could unravel this high-tech marvel, at some cost to the Indian taxpayer. Phase 1 was completed during the first visit by the Russian team.

Amongst the three trades in the armoured corps viz driver, gunner and radio, the most important undoubtedly is the gunner. Without in any way underrating the contribution or teamwork of the other members, the gunner's ability to destroy is what will finally win the war. From this perspective, the most important battle winning quality of every gunner becomes his ability to get a 'kill' in the first round fired. The range wing imparts training on this on the open ranges.

The tank firing ranges comprise a vast barren area, stretching for miles. Due to the nature of the soil and rocky outcrop, virtually nothing grows except in small low-lying patches where the top soil may have accumulated. The undulating nature of the ground makes it ideal for tactical training at the troop and sub-unit levels by the mechanised forces. Within the ranges, a number of firing points are selected, keeping in view the field of fire, safety angles, and practices specified for the weapon system. The ricochet tables of ammunition fired set the safety template so that the lives and property of the population living on the fringes of the demarcated range remain secure. The Tankodrom provided tank crews the facility of firing both the main and auxiliary weapon systems of tanks from a platform designed to simulate the rolling, pitching, yawing movements of a moving tank, while engaging hard and soft targets at varying ranges and speeds in the stand-up and pop-up modes. Variable programmes could be set through the electronic equipment in the control tower, depending on the grade of the gunner under training. A performance chart showing the record of hits scored by the gunner was provided to the commander conducting the shoot for debriefing of the gunner. The sensors fitted on the targets would provide details of the performance parameters of individual gunners, commanders, and sub-units.

The training facility was designed to bring in innovation, imagination and a spirit of competition, besides providing realism to the training. This equipment was completely alien to us though not as complex or even as sophisticated as our Russian friends would have had us believe. A number of technicians from the Electrical and Mechanical Engineers (EME) were inducted along with one Major Telang, so that they could help in the installation work as also gain on the job experience for the maintenance and repair of equipment after the departure of the Russians. The Russians were a wonderful team to work with. Well trained in their jobs, they never ducked responsibility.

It was common for members of the Russian and Indian teams to have picked up a modicum of common Russian/Hindi words while working together. This made communication easy as also it brought in an element of familiarity and even friendship. While immersed in some talk, Captain Sagar spotted the Range Junior Commissioned Officer (JCO) Bhan Singh escorting two civilians walking towards the Nasheman Camp. The cancellation of firing for the day saw local civilians cutting across the range area. Even at this distance, however, it was evident from their dress and turbans that these two were not locals. Capt Sagar, who was also performing the duties of range officer, signalled to Bhan Singh and directed him to escort the intruders to our location. Bhan Singh, with a mischievous smile, declared that he had caught these two loitering in the range area.

Capt Sagar (CS): 'You are not locals, where are you coming from?'

First Civilian: 'Sir, we belong to Rajasthan.'

CS: 'Therefore, what are you doing on the ranges, collecting fired shells for sale?'

Second Civilian: 'No, we are travelling salespersons. Please do not suspect us for pilferage.'

First Civilian: 'Bhan Singh invited us.'

CS: 'What are you carrying in that bag?'

Bhan: 'I have checked, Sir. There are no fired shells.'

Second Civilian: 'Herbs and berries brought from the Himalayan jungles.'

The Russian who had been listening intently to this exchange broke out in Hindi, '*Dikhao, Dikhao!* Show, Show!'

While the two civilians placed their bags on the ground to display their wares, we heard Bhan Singh whispering to Sabharwal that they were carrying Shilajeet, an Indian aphrodisiac.

Sabharwal: 'He is carrying Indian medicine that can make you more virile.'

The two Indian interpreters, who were in the same age group as Sabharwal, burst out laughing. Soon they were translating the sales talk of the two civilian salespeople as a running commentary in English and Russian for the benefit for all present. The Russian, however, needed confirmation on the herb's effectiveness: 'But is it effective?'

'You are asking me, I have sired four children using this stuff,' Bhan responded in Hindi. The Indian interpreter then translated this into Russian.

Bhan: 'It is excellent. Your wife will thank you, have it regularly.' It was now evident to everyone that the civilian had spoken the truth when he said that he had been invited. It transpired that Bhan was his regular customer. Soon a large assortment of salts and small sized rocks/clays were on display. The moment the elder of the two started his sales talk, the

Indian officers broke out into laughter. Each one of us had heard the name Shilajeet—commonly believed to have qualities to improve male potency. The gaps in the sales talk were filled in by JCO Bhan who claimed first-hand knowledge.

The Russian, initially hesitant to bring up this subject, warmed up to the discussion and admitted that a high-ranking Russian officer had asked him to get some Shilajeet from India as the potency of the Indian variety was supposed to be very high. All differences of rank, class, creed, nationality merged into the discussion on the purity, price, and performance of this magic potion.

The two intruders did good business while our Russian got bargains on behalf of dysfunctional generals. This small event, highlighting the frail vanity, eccentricities, and indulgences of all men, in uniform as well as in all sections of society, only shows that we are but human. On a more positive note, we do know that all the carriers of this magic potion secured their next promotions; no one was reported missing nor was anybody suddenly deported to Siberia to spend the rest of his life in regret because a general officer could not rise in the esteem of his beloved wife.

Aside from work on the open ranges, we found the Russians agreeable and, at times, even humorous. Two things bewildered them most: one, the Indian women, especially the way they dressed in a sari (the hip sari was in fashion then). The other thing they were even prepared to give their right arms for was to see Helen, our dancing star, give a flesh and blood performance.

With the Tankodrom nearing completion, the Russians threw a farewell party for those connected with the project. They were extremely hospitable and treated us to some of the finest vodka and caviar. The Commandant Armoured

Corps Centre and School Brig Arun Vaidya and Col Joshi (both of whom retired as Chief of the Army Staff – COAS), newly posted Chief Instructor, after completion of an overseas assignment, were present. Brig Vaidya surprised everyone by making a very impressive speech in Hindi with a lot of Sanskrit thrown in, justifying his Brahmin antecedents. The painful part came when we heard the speech translated into Russian again. The reverse flow, when the Russian counterpart took the mike, left most exhausted and possibly a little uncomfortable, as the combined effect of vodka and caviar does not sit easy on Indian stomachs.

The Dasvidaniyas (thank you), handshakes, and farewells finally ended past midnight. As junior officers, we had to wait while the customary military departure drill was completed. While members disbursed, a Russian tapped my shoulder, signalling me to accompany him into the adjoining room. Soon another Russian joined us and together we walked towards the guest room where, sprawled on the bed, lay Maj Khanwan (name withheld). The Russian explained that while the chief guest was leaving, a waiter had informed him that this officer had passed out near the bathroom. He, along with the waiter, had helped him into the room. The situation came under control when Mrs Khanwan, on being informed, rushed in. I asked the Russian to call for an ambulance from the Military Hospital using the VIP telephone installed in their guest house. Mrs Khanwan rejected the suggestion stating that it would become the talk of the town the next morning and cause grave personal and professional embarrassment to her husband. As Khanwan was beginning to show signs of recovery from the effects of imbibing vodka vigorously, the Russian complied and called for his staff car instead.

It was well past midnight when we reached the hotel, to find the shutters pulled down and a sleepy clerk managing the reception desk. Between a harassed wife and hassled escort, we managed to haul this otherwise overweight officer to the comfort of his second-floor hotel room, still drunk, and now snoring. I helped remove his shoes while his wife adjusted the pillows to make him comfortable. The Herculean haul had sapped all my energy. I sat down on the nearby sofa to catch my breath and prepare for a quick retreat. Conscious of my parched throat, I waited for the promised jug of water when suddenly she appeared from behind the wall cupboard at the far end of the room, holding a bottle of whiskey in one hand and two glasses in the other. She vanished once again to slip into something comfortable, after suggestively running her fingers through my hair. While I could hear my racing heartbeat once again pounding my chest, my hands were steady pouring the stiff one. From behind the connecting door of the bedroom, I could hear her declaring that they were leaving Ahmednagar the next day, to return to their unit. I never got a chance to meet her ever again but I believe my decision to beat a hasty retreat after pouring a stiff one into her glass was in keeping with the highest tradition of chivalry.

Besides the humdrum of life and work with the Russians, nothing of major importance happened during this period. The refugee problem still loomed large, as no solution appeared workable. Somehow in the happier environs of Nagar, the refugee problems sounded like a cry in the wilderness. Each one who had heard the cry carried the conviction that many others also would have heard it, hoping that this in itself would bring relief and help to the unfortunate. Human memory has a strange way of forgetting all that is unpleasant and painful. I found myself sliding into what life had to offer under the wide umbrella of Nagar.

The ACC&S received the task of making contingency plans in case a general mobilization was ordered. This, however, was nothing new and we were all convinced that even though this meant earmarking of reinforcements and the possible move of officers to other regiments, it would not amount to much. The necessary precautionary steps had to be taken, in case there was an outbreak of hostilities. Then, one day, posting orders announced that a certain number of officers would be reverted to their parent regiments. This news spread like wildfire. It included a large number of officers who had completed their tenures of two years, besides a few others. For the moment, the recall of some officers back to regimental duty was the first note on the war drum, registered by all those looking for armed action. News that the Raksha Mantri (RM) Shri Jagjivan Ram would visit ACC&S electrified the town and set all rumours and speculation to rest. Nagar was completely spruced up, keeping alive the old military dictum, 'everything stationary had been painted and everything moving repaired'. Lists of shortages in manpower, equipment, spare parts, and vehicles to cater for the needs of mobilisation were prepared. This followed a spate of conferences, coordination meetings, rehearsals, et al. On the appointed day, the RM arrived with a battery of officials from the Ministry of Defence as also key officers from Army Headquarters and HQ Southern Command. Unlike routine VIP visits, this one listed a combined lunch for all officers and visiting dignitaries. While we were not privy to what transpired at official meetings or discussions, we welcomed a very cheerful and beaming Defence Minister into the Officers' Mess, looking quite resplendent in his sparkling white *dhoti–kurta* and Gandhi *topi*, followed by a large retinue of grim looking senior military and civilian officials. The captivating speech was heard in pin-drop silence. To a question raised by the commandant about the problems relating to equipment and manpower, he replied: 'That is why we have a Commandant and a Defence Minister. This war would be fought without shortages. The deficiencies would be made good and commanders at levels must assume responsibility for the same.' His awe-inspiring speech mesmerized the young audience, and the thunderous applause he received brought the roof crashing down.

October is balmy weather in Nagar. Kutub Hai (3 Cavalry) and I were finishing a round of golf when V.K. Malhotra, 17 Horse, came up, waving the Military Secretary Branch signal announcing the posting of all three: Mallu, a friend and course mate, was to revert to his regiment, 17 Horse. Kutub Hai, my golfing companion, and I were directed to report to 80 Armoured Delivery Regiment located at Delhi Cantonment. All three were placed on seven days' notice to report to our new duty stations. Considerably deflated and demoralized at the prospect of serving in this new assignment, we contacted senior regimental officers posted at Nagar to suggest some way out of this predicament but to no avail. Deep in their heart, they all knew that even though a few officers were required to organize and ensure replenishments of tanks and personnel, it was far from satisfactory for a regimental officer from the elite corps of the cavalry, the teeth arm of combat soldiering, to squander a lifetime opportunity away from his regiment. Though happy for Mallu, Kutub and I were clear, determined, and resolved to find our way back to our regiments.

Posting orders, unfortunately, do not take into consideration the sentiments or private feelings of soldiers. These are official orders, which command legitimacy and demand unquestioned compliance. With the notice period ending, I found myself amongst the 'farewell wallahs' in the Annexe. While others stood and cheered the officers rejoining the parent regiment, I found myself braving the indignity of posting to an armoured delivery regiment. The farewell being a public ritual had to be borne with poise and dignity. Watching Kutub enjoying his drink in a nonchalant manner made one aware that any show of disappointment was open to ridicule. No one wants to hear your tale of woe or bad luck. Better to put on a brave front and quietly enjoy your drink. Kutub confirmed our travel arrangements, adding that his father, a senior doctor in the railways, would have his official saloon attached to the same train at Manmad Junction. Everybody in the Annexe sounded high and cheerful, as another evening of merry-making was underway. The officiating commandant announced the names of the 'farewell wallahs', adding that Kutub and I were going to the 80 Armoured Delivery Regiment. Friends turned up to shake hands and bid farewell. Each one had to make a short farewell speech. What was there to say except that while posted at Delhi, I would do my best to help the war effort from the rear. I was annoyed at the prospect, and as such, spoke only a single sentence: 'I have only one word to say for the glorious evening— thank you'. Soon after leaving the mike, I heard somebody say jokingly, 'Oh, that is more like a soldier!'

We left the following afternoon—Mallu, Kutub, and I. We had all been in the NDA together and, as such, were good friends. Mallu was a course mate and a friend with whom I had shared many happy moments during the initial phase of the Young Officers' Course, prior to breaking a bone in my right hand playing basketball. Kutub was a popular officer from the next batch, with whom I had completed the Young Officers' course. Kutub was a highly cultured and suave officer, and a regular golfing companion while in Nagar. Mallu would accompany us until Delhi and then catch a connecting train moving further north. While Kutub and I had taken due precautions of ensuring that no subordinate staff came to the Ahmednagar railway station to bid adieu, as was the military custom, we were pleasantly surprised to find a large 17 Horse gathering. Mallu, in the midst of this fraternity, appeared more like a CO taking leave of his command. He was a very fine, spirited, and popular officer, and an extrovert to boot, who felt a great need for reaffirmation. The farewell ritual of saying goodbye with flowers had to be gone through at the railway station. This is a standing practice in the Army. It is customary for a sizeable number to turn up with flowers and garlands (more with an attempt to suffocate you) to make your departure become a memorable one, giving you the feeling that your absence will be felt (with smiles or tears), little realizing that the Army routine leaves you little time for either. As the train chugged out of the station, Mallu's eyes became moist, for unknown to many, under his carefree exterior, hid a very soft and sensitive human being. While we were in the process of settling down for the long journey ahead, the train made an unscheduled halt at Vilad. No sooner had the train stopped that a JCO from the range wing came into our compartment with a garland in his hand.

JCO: 'Jai Hind. Staff members are waiting outside to say farewell.'

Me: 'Orders were issued that there will be no farewell at the railway station.'

JCO: 'Yes. Your orders were no one would come to Ahmednagar railway station. We obeyed your orders, Sir.'

Me: 'What station is this?'

JCO: 'The train is now at Vilad railway station.'

Me: 'This is not a regular halt. How has the train stopped here?'

JCO: 'Emergency stop, Sir, please ask the station master, he too is waiting outside.'

Frankly, I was perplexed because that is exactly what I had mentioned. Soon after stepping out of the compartment, I was greeted with loud cheers and profusely garlanded by the unit personnel. I shook hands with all and thanked them for their deep affection and memorable farewell. The honesty and straightforward attitude of the soldiers touched the inner chords of my heart. These soldiers had come a considerable distance and spent money from their tight purses for the flowers and farewell, all on their own initiative. The goodwill that they had displayed would be difficult to forget as a majority came from regiments other than 45 Cavalry and it could be years before we met again, if ever we did.

The station master was now waving his green flag to set the train in motion once again after the unscheduled halt. Waving back at the assembled group, I continued to view the now diminishing Vilad station while still standing at the door of the train compartment. The intensity of emotion within was overwhelming, resulting in two droplets breaking through many barriers to roll down an unaccustomed cheek, and evaporate as vapour into the head-on gentle breeze caressing the face. Living such an experience brought a strange sense of peace to the soul. The quick effort to compose and wipe away any tell-tale traces of tears was unnecessary, as the two comrades in arms had undergone a similar surge of emotion. They thoughtfully averted any dialogue of the unscheduled stop by thrusting a glass of beer in my hands. Much later, in time and distance, sitting amidst empty beer bottles staring at us, I was to recite to them a couplet by Omar Khayyam, 'Drinking when dawn's left hand was in the sky, I heard a voice within the tavern cry, awake my little ones and fill thy cup, before life's liquor in the cup runs dry.'

The luxury of travelling by a saloon car was a new experience. Kutub Hai's father was a senior doctor in the Indian Railways and had his saloon car attached to our train at Manmad Junction en route so that he and his wife could spend time with their son before he rejoined his regiment. Kutub's mother had invited us to a lavish Hyderabadi lunch in the saloon. She had specially cooked the family delicacy of mutton with chana dal, chicken biryani, along with a number of other mouth-watering dishes. The grace, charm, and warmth with which we were treated gave no indication of the private fear, worry, and concern that as parents they must have felt knowing that it would be a long time before they would meet their son again. On hearing that I had seen the plight of the refugees around Calcutta, Mrs Hai surprised me by her keen observation that India was a great country as, in spite of financial burdens, it never closed its borders to refugees on humanitarian grounds.

On learning that three of my brothers were already deployed with their units on the border, she expressed deep concern for my mother and her well-being. When I mentioned to her that the youngest had deferred his call from the Services Selection Board so that he could look after Mother, it left her deep in admiration for the family. She spoke about Kutub in glowing terms, saying she was proud that as a son he understood his duty towards the country and his regiment. That she would pray for the well-being of all and hoped and that we would all meet again in happier times. Her elegance and charming face and soft gentle voice, full of warmth, did not permit her personal fears and turmoil within to show up. I have often remembered it as an outstanding example of grace under pressure. Through her I could fathom the anxiety and deep concern my own mother would be going through and the maturity of my youngest brother, declaring that when 'four are on the frontier, one must stay in the rear to protect home, hearth, and mother'!

6

VOLUNTEER FOR COMBAT

Amongst the first things Kutub and I did on reaching Delhi was to make a beeline for the Army Golf Course. It was a Sunday and what better place than a golf course on a Sunday afternoon. The mission included meeting Col A.P. Singh, Commandant 80 Armoured Delivery Regiment (ADR), under whom we were to serve. He was a renowned Services level golfer and we had no difficulty in introducing ourselves, being members of the black beret fraternity. He knew about our posting but not our plans, when he welcomed us wholeheartedly. The greying old cavalier must have read our thoughts and directed us to meet him in the office Monday morning at 0900 hrs. Mission successful, we moved on to finish our round of golf and lunch before returning to the 80 ADR mess to unpack and prepare for what we hoped would be a very brief tenure of duty. Our resolve to return to our parent regiments had become a single-point agenda.

Col A.P. Singh stood out as a fine soldier and a man of few words. He appreciated honesty and frankness, and was not surprised that I wanted to return to the regiment. He went a step further to say that had he been in my place, he would have done the same. Speaking as Commandant 80 ADR, he made it clear that he was in need of good officers to run the unit. He was, therefore, prepared to give us 72 hours within which we should arrange a posting, failing which, we should join his team. He further added that I should have no difficulty as Gen Virendra Singh, an influential retired 16 Cavalry officer, had been recently appointed as the Colonel of the Regiment of 45 Cavalry.

The first meeting with Gen Virendra Singh turned out to be no great joy. I had made a few enquiries to learn about his professional graph while in service. He was chairperson of the Indian chapter of the Cheshire trust and managed the family run Modern School in Delhi, besides playing the share markets with proficiency—a generally popular figure with Delhi-based officers as also with the larger cavalry fraternity. Reports had warned that he was brusque in speech and capable of giving vent to anger without a cause. This was the sum total of information provided by friends and colleagues who knew him. As Colonel of the Regiment, why would he say no for meeting an officer of 45 Cavalry? Without further delay, I found myself dialling his number, conscious of a little lump in my throat.

Gen: 'Yes!'

Me: 'Sir, I am 45 Cav . . .'.

Gen: 'Yes, yes, speak up.'

Me: 'Sir, I am posted to 80 ADR.'

Gen: 'Yes I know, what do you want?'

Me: 'I want to meet you, Sir.'

Gen: 'So why are you ringing up? Come to my office and meet me.'

With that, the line went dead. No sooner had I walked into his Modern School office, the General, after a gruff 'hello', started firing a battery of questions about ACC&S. He wanted information about officers, regiments, visitors, social life. Somewhere in between this flow of data, I recalled the purpose of my visit. I did not have to repeat or explain my request. He picked up the telephone receiver and growled some instructions to his PA, adding that the call was urgent. Without a change in speech or manner, he spoke to someone, who, in turn, must have transferred the call to some officer handling the posting of officers. While he was still returning the receiver to its cradle, he said that he would confirm after two days. As far as he was concerned, the meeting was over. Perhaps a little stupefied at the speed at which the meeting closed, I sat motionless, still in doubt about whether my request had been addressed, as I had not heard my name being mentioned. On raising his eyebrows and finding me still there, he enquired if there was anything else I needed. While I was still gathering my wits, he got out from his chair to shake my hand and bid me good-bye. Still in a stupor, I began looking for the door through which I had come, when his telephone rang again, to be answered with a loud 'Yes'.

I beat a hasty retreat, cursing my luck at having stumbled on this human volcano. I soon found myself standing outside his office, nursing doubts in my mind on the suicidal course I had adopted. I did not know whether to be happy, grateful, or just plain angry with myself. The General had gained a reputation as a wonderful person, not without reason. True to his word, he rang up two days later to inform me that posting orders for forthwith return to the regiment had been issued. More than elated, I thanked him profusely. He appreciated my determination to revert to the regiment when war was imminent. He wished the regiment good hunting and good luck.

The next day, accompanied by Kutub, we visited the MS Branch in South Block to collect the posting order. Major Chengappa informed us that the Colonel of 3 Cavalry had asked for Kutub to be reverted for which orders would soon be issued. He invited us for drinks the same evening where we learnt that Chengappa had also volunteered for reversion to 70 AR and would be joining within a week. Chengappa, once empanelled for posting to 45 Cavalry, on completion of Staff College, had proceeded to France for training on missiles and, on his return, transferred to 70 Armoured, a missile regiment. An intelligent, soft-spoken officer, he stood out as a role model, possessing all the good qualities of a cavalry officer. His invitation for dinner remains a cherished memory as a celebration of the armoured corps spirit to volunteer for service when the regiment is mobilized for war.

Kutub, ever thoughtful and considerate, arranged a grand evening, recalled with warmth even today. We first went to the Defence Colony house of his family friend Their two lovely daughters joined us over coffee and cakes while the father explained the technical problems they had to overcome to make the Rajdhani a reality. This culminated with a visit to the recently opened discotheque, the Den, near Rivoli Cinema in Connaught Place. The mind-blowing music, psychedelic lights, alcoholic drinks, and wild dancing into the wee hours of the morning made it an evening to remember.

In the excitement of leaving Delhi, I had ignored sending my ETA (Estimated Time of Arrival) to the regiment. Detraining at Kanchrapara and finding that the local military exchange was out of order, left limited options of choosing a rickshaw, pulled by some undernourished local or waiting for any passing Army vehicle, in this small one-street town. I chose the latter course.

I was astonished when the driver I accosted asked me to name my unit, 'I am from the cavalry, tank regiment, dammit.' The young driver feigned ignorance. Raising my voice, I burst upon him, 'Which unit are you from?' 'Sorry, I can't tell you.' His nervousness betrayed his reluctant reply. 'Then call for your vehicle commander,' I said in a forceful voice, leaving him in no doubt that this was serious. He disappeared quickly to return double quick time with a Havildar wearing the three stripes of his rank. 'Jai Hind, Saab. Welcome Saab. *Apna* identity card *dikha dijiyeh*' (Please show your Identity Card).' I was dressed in civvies, and my I-Card was not on my person but lying locked in my suitcase. Security instructions clearly stated that while travelling in civvies, you had to carry your I-Card on your person. To seek exemption appeared undignified. I chose the long walk back to the railway station to prove my identity. He scrutinized the card thoroughly before placing my suitcase onto the vehicle to undertake a bumpy ride to the artillery regiment.

The security conscious Havildar was now singing like a canary while en route to the duty officer at his Regimental Headquarters (RHQ). A smart young officer, after a quick word with his adjutant, escorted me to their Officers' Mess. Drinks followed introductions and everyone agreed that the information our soldiers would willingly give away to strangers a few months ago, was now a carefully guarded secret. The refusal to divulge the presence of the tank regiment, knowing that their unit was 'in a direct support' role, was not due to ignorance.

'Good to have you back in the squadron! Welcome!' The joyful response of the squadron commander was heartening. Major Daljit Singh Narag was a very colourful personality. I had earlier worked as his squadron second-in-command and I knew him very well. He was a short-statured Sikh, with broad shoulders, heavyset and strong, with a round face displaying a keen set of eyes and a well-nourished, trimmed beard, and moustache. He had a slight limp and needed to wear a kneecap to support his robust frame. He was straightforward and forthright in his attitude to life and work, and displayed a remarkable sense of fair play and justice in all his dealings. He had a keen practical sense and was immensely proud of both his heritage and his profession. He had the uncanny ability to learn different languages, and spoke with some fluency, such diverse languages as Punjabi, Pushto, Tamil, Telugu, Bengali, Marathi, and even Gorkhali. Though he did not attempt to gain proficiency in these languages, he could converse with ease to befriend strangers and entice desperate women in distress. Chiefy, as he was popularly called for the gastronomical delights he could produce, was necessary at all social gatherings and parties.

No mess gathering was complete without Chiefy being present. The normally lively mess dinner night once became unbearable as the evening dragged on. While trooping in for dinner, the Colonel observed the absence of Chiefy. His query, however, went unanswered as each one feigned ignorance. It was no secret that Chiefy had collected a bottle of rum from the squadron and ordered a chicken from the adjoining village to spend an evening of pleasure with his companion of the evening. Next day, during the lunch break, we overheard his narration of what had transpired in the orderly room:

Comdt: 'Major Narag, where were you during dinner night?'

Chiefy: 'I had gone to meet a friend, Sir.'

Comdt: 'You were missing from dinner night which is a parade.'

Chiefy: 'I had to honour a previous commitment, so I missed the dinner, having informed the Adjutant'.

Comdt: 'So you walked to your friend's house, is that true?'

Chiefy: 'No, Sir, I could not have walked that far.'

Comdt: 'So how the hell did you go?'

Chiefy: 'I took lift in a military vehicle, Sir.'

Comdt: 'Exactly, you disobeyed my orders by using a unit jeep.'

Chiefy: 'No, Sir, I travelled in the squadron water truck!'

After I reported to Chiefy for duty, he briefed me on all that had transpired in C Squadron and the regiment during my absence. We then went around the squadron training area where I had the opportunity of meeting others I knew so well; tank commanders, drivers, gunners, radiomen. Everyone was busy completing the tasks assigned. The morale of all ranks seemed considerably high. The 'teeth arm' of the Army was prepared for every eventuality and I for one was happy to be a part of this war-machine: the home, the heart, and the love of every regimental soldier—his regiment.

One of the major changes that had taken place was that the War Establishment (WE) of the regiment had been changed from a Light Armoured Regiment to a Standard Armoured Regiment. This implied that each of the three squadrons would now be authorized four tank troops instead of three, after sacrificing the two rifle troops. With each squadron entitled 14 tanks, the regiment authorization was raised to 45 tanks.

Another noteworthy change introduced by Digby, the commandant, was to impose a four-man crew in the PT-76 tank even though it was designed to carry a crew of three only. Most tanks of the Western block had separate crew members to perform the duties of driver, gunner, operator, and commander. Each function was of a specialist nature and training of the tradesmen at ACC&S was designed accordingly. For PT-76 crews, the duties of commander and gunner stood combined. The other two members would perform the traditional duties, without change. The merit / demerit of the three vs four crew is not the discussion, as it stood accepted within the regiment. To accommodate the fourth crew member, the backrest of the original tank gunner's seat was modified such that the commander could now stand on a slightly elevated platform, rising above the gunner's seat. The elevated platform would leave the commander constantly in the standing position with his hip, shoulder, neck, and head above the turret, with the commander's cupola open. In case the commander's cupola needed to be closed, the commander would stand between the gunner and operator within the restricted space behind the gun recoil mechanism, making the commander virtually persona non grata and the tank gun non-operational. Being an amphibious tank, it was evident that additional crew inside the tank would restrict operational employment during river crossing.

Training continued at a hectic pace. Special emphasis was on battle drills which were practised so often that we could perform them virtually blindfolded. The other important aspect of our daily schedule was the Field Miniature Range (FMR) to practise and hone the gun and crew drills. Though great emphasis was laid on training, it never became a question of all work and no play. Each one of us played equally hard. The lucky one would even accompany Digby to the nearby golf course. More often, we would sweat it out on the basketball court in the Officers vs JCOs matches or participate in inter-troop or inter-squadron tournaments. The close bonds of affinity and friendship that developed on the playfields cut across all barriers of rank, service, seniority. Group activity helped shed angularities in individual personalities and moulded each one to develop into strong, cohesive, well-knit members of the regiment. In the evenings, we would all assemble in the Officers' Mess, where, after being briefed on the border situation and the activities of the Mukti Bahini, we recharged and fortified ourselves with 'whiskey pani'. The weekend usually found us in Calcutta, looking up old friends, attending dance/dinner sessions or busting up our otherwise meagre resources on the turf club betting on horses, and also the nightlife that this city of joy could provide.

While India was swamped by the influx of refugees, the military and political leaders had put their heads together to protect its sovereignty. The military had made a realistic assessment of Pakistan's capability and our response. The Border Security Force (BSF) under Director General Rustamji and the Research and Analysis Wing (RAW) under R.N. Kao were complying with directions issued by P.N. Haksar on behalf of the government. As per the grapevine, camps had been set up along the border to train the Mukti Bahini. In addition, the Army had targeted raising of three brigades worth from erstwhile soldiers of the East Pakistan Rifles to train them to fight alongside the Army, as also to provide training to up to 75,000 guerrillas. It hoped that these guerrillas, trained in elementary techniques involving ambush, demolition, and disruption of communications would slowly bleed the Pakistan Army. If the Mukti Bahini could sustain the struggle for a period of six months or more, it would blunt and demoralize the Pakistani soldiers' will to fight.

The Mukti Bahini had trained and organized itself during the monsoons into a formidable force. It consisted of a nucleus of the erstwhile East Pakistan Rifles and other Bengali military units and paramilitary organizations, including Bengali soldiers serving in the defence forces of Pakistan. The senior most officer who had defected, Col MAG Osmani, had been designated as their Commander-in-Chief by the Bangladesh government-in-exile. The call for freedom and independence given by Sheikh Mujibur Rehman had stirred the right patriotic chords amongst the youth who came forward in large numbers to enrol and receive military training. That moral, material, monetary, and military help was provided by India was no secret, then or now. The training had inflamed their patriotism and confidence, and they were now fully determined to settle for nothing less than total independence. With this aim in view, they conducted a large number of guerrilla type attacks on the Pakistanis and inflicted heavy casualties. These attacks, which started as mere hit-and-run attacks, gained in strength and offensive capability, such that by mid-October 1971, pitched battles supported by mortar fire had become routine and started posing a definite threat to the Pakistani ground forces. The high casualties had become a source of constant embarrassment and soon the Pakistanis started withdrawing isolated troops closer to their prepared defences and cantonments, leaving behind large tracts of border unprotected which the Mukti Bahini quickly occupied and converted into regular bases to launch fresh attacks, with the support of Indian artillery.

By the first week of November, the press was reporting blackouts and border skirmishes regularly. In New Delhi and Calcutta, two blackouts had prepared the residents for the possible outbreak of open warfare. In Dhaka (erstwhile Dacca), the East Pakistanis were encouraged to dig trenches in the compounds of their buildings 'to face any eventuality'. With regular troops deployed on both sides of the border, 'minor' border and air-space violations and shelling had become commonplace. During the three-week journey to rally sympathy for India, Prime Minister Indira Gandhi conferred with French President Georges Pompidou and West German Chancellor Willy Brandt to extract contributions for refugee relief and also to win diplomatic support. The USA had earlier announced that it was revoking licences for US$ 3.6 million worth of arms for Pakistan besides laying down an embargo on arms sales to Pakistan. The Pakistani delegation to China headed by Zulfiqar Ali Bhutto had attempted to counter India's recently signed Friendship treaty with Moscow. While Peking vaguely pledged help, 'should Pakistan be subjected to foreign aggression', it also urged the Pakistanis to seek a 'reasonable settlement' in East Pakistan. The stage was being set for the birth of a new nation.

The Mukti Bahini gave us invaluable insights into the designs and deployments of the Pakistani units. Substantial ground support was not expected, as they were ill equipped to meet any full-scale attack by the Pakistani troops. The Mukti Bahini was later to play a significant role by becoming the eyes and ears of the advancing Indian troops once war was underway. Yahya Khan and his coterie of Generals continued to threaten India with imminent war if it did not stop its support to the Mukti Bahini. It was their firm belief that India was providing arms, ammunition, food, and shelter to the Mukti Bahini. Press reports of 'Hate India', 'Crush India' posters appearing in all the major cities of Pakistan became commonplace. Everybody felt convinced that Pakistan had given up all attempts to find a peaceful solution and was hell bent on a war, which even at that stage, appeared avoidable. India, on the other hand, continued to appease the comity of nations. Various diplomatic moves, to curb what Pakistan considered inevitable, were undertaken. Fresh appeals were made to the big powers to understand the refugee problem and to assist India in finding a suitable solution. At the same time, India warned Pakistan that war would settle nothing, and would only further aggravate the economy of the developing countries besides the unnecessary bloodshed and loss of human lives, making the relationship between them only more bitter. A word of caution was added by the then defence minister that India was all for a peaceful solution and that if war had to be fought, it would be fought on Pakistani soil.

By mid-November, the number of refugees had gone up to 9.7 million, requiring US$ 830 million for their upkeep. Beyond the financial cost, the presence of so many refugees was threatening social turmoil and increased communal tension, especially in West Bengal. The harsh reality was that many felt that free food, clothing, and medical care made the locals envious, as similar facilities were unavailable to them. Similarly, in the job market, the refugees were in greater demand as they were prepared to work at 1/3rd of the pay demanded by the local residents. The memory of the communal divide in 1947 when four lakh Hindus were pushed into West Bengal was still fresh in the minds of Indians. Praying for peace was only one side of the coin. It was evident to the hard realists that military preparations would not be put on hold.

The fundamental task of the defence forces remains preparation for war, notwithstanding the multiple efforts of the government to work out political, diplomatic, or other initiatives. The number of times the commanding officer and squadron commanders were summoned to Division and Brigade Headquarters and the number of times ground reconnaissance was carried out was not lost on the junior officers or the troops. At the regimental level, this meant long, dreary hours, conducting back-breaking reconnaissance repeatedly.

Commanders, down till troop level, were made to go over concentration and assembly areas and memorize routes leading to every important landmark—be it road, track, bridge, junction; anything and everything. It was an old belief of our senior officers that 'time spent in reconnaissance is never wasted' and they made us live by it in the days to come. Amongst the innumerable reconnaissance missions that I carried out, special emphasis was laid on the concentration and forward concentration areas for the regiment. The areas selected were close to the border from where units launched into battle. Affiliated units and units placed under command carry out what in military parlance is called 'marrying up operations', virtually getting to know each other better as also coordinating their battle plans as a battle group before moving into attack. The secrecy and security of these areas is of paramount importance as enemy interference or artillery shelling can jeopardize battle plans or delay operations.

Then, one day, when we were least expecting it, word came from higher headquarters ordering us to move into the concentration area. The order implied that, A Squadron of the regiment would operate under command HQ 4 Infantry Division and be deployed accordingly. 45 Cavalry less A Squadron was on the ORBAT (Order of Battle) of 9 Infantry Division and would move to a separate designated concentration area. A spate of briefings, verbal and written orders, radio instructions, administrative and logistics details came pouring in to make us realize the benefits of SOPs prepared for such contingencies. On the appointed day, having briefed the harbour party of the regiment, we set forth to the concentration area by road. The party consisted of the harbour truck of each squadron and an assortment of other essentials vehicles, including langar and POL (Petrol, Oil, Lubricants) lorries, and mess shelters. The harbour trucks were equipped to carry the required number of signposts displaying the unit's tactical number along with rectangular and conical shaped tin containers within which lanterns (hurricane lamps) could be placed for use as night signs. The perforations on the containers helped diffuse the light of the lantern to illuminate the geometrical design of the sub-unit to guide their tanks and B vehicles along specified lanes in complete darkness. A separate colour code for each sub-unit was displayed on each night sign. The concentration area, spread over 4–6 sq km, was holding approximately 150 vehicles of all classes. Security was a cardinal prerequisite as any enemy observer overlooking the concentration area could cause grave damage and disruption by directing enemy artillery fire. Chiefy had accompanied the harbour party to mark diversions over suspect culverts which may not take the weight of tanks on this Class 9 axis. He was to return after midday and lead the regimental tank column to this area.

An armoured regiment's efficiency and operational preparedness are reflected in its ability to glide into harbour blindfolded in complete darkness, while under radio silence. A mini-conference was held with the squadron representatives to finetune preparations for receiving the regimental tank column. The tanks would cover a total distance of 90 km on tracks. It was estimated that six hours of travelling time would be the minimum, as detours around three weak culverts en route had also to be negotiated. The harbour party briefing and posting of sentries as per SOP had been coordinated and instructions issued. The leading tank would roll in around midnight. The luxury of a few hours of rest after hyperactive activity now appeared justified.

'The tanks are coming,' the jeep driver passed on the message to me. Stretching out from the makeshift hammock, I sauntered out to prepare for the night ahead. The senior JCO was waiting at the vantage point. Raghubir Chandra, holding a hooded torch, reported, '*Sab sentry upni post per hazir hain. Check kar liya saab*'. (All sentries are on the appointed posts, physically checked, Sir).

'So what is your estimate, when will the first tank roll in?' 'It will take at least another twenty minutes, Sir,' the JCO said. 'Are they behind time—must be a delayed start.'

'Possible, Sir, it may be also because of the diversions on the culverts.'

'Not possible, those culverts where diversions were ordered, are smaller,' I said.

'Yes, Sir, I agree. May be a visibility factor.'

A couple of minutes ticked away in expectation.

'I hope they are still moving, the sound is hardly audible now,' I wondered.

Another trooper, the Regimental Dafadar Major Toppo chipped in with his analysis.

'Sir, the wind direction has changed,' Toppo sounded confident.

'Maybe they are now at the wide road bend,' Raghubir Chander interjected.

'Tank noise can be deceptive; we have experienced that during exercises also.'

A couple of minutes later, the tank decibels become distinctly clear and closer.

'Better to light up the lamps instead of waiting.'

'Yes, you are right, Sir; I will send runners to the squadrons.'

'Did the squadron commander give you the order of march? Which squadron is leading the column?'

'Not known, Sir. Must be C Squadron in the lead, like always, Sir.'

No way of checking as radio silence was imposed.

Minutes ticked by and the engine noise of the tank increased appreciably, assuring us that soon they would arrive at the concentration area. From the rate at which the noise was increasing, it was evident that the tanks were coming 'full speed ahead'. Another couple of minutes and the first tank would turn near the prominent school building on to the desired track. The noise increased in intensity, louder, still louder, until finally it reached a crescendo. The sound of tank tracks and roaring engines was all around us. As the road was some distance from our location, we waited for the appearance of the lead tank. Seconds ticked away into a minute and more. Suddenly, above the din and noise of tank engines, I could hear the cry of alarm in the voice of Toppo, '*Turn nahi kiya main road say, tank aage nikal gaye.*' (They haven't taken the turn off the main road, the tanks have gone ahead.) His voice, expressing concern, disappointment, and distress, also sounded an alarm. '*Aage nikal gaye tanks*', piped in Ramesh Chandra. Toppo, an Adivasi from Jharkhand and an experienced driver, was the first to sense that the sound of tank tracks churning the metalled road had not reached his ears. The tank driver, while slowing down, pulls on the driving stick, arresting power transmission to one track, while the tank completes the turning movement. The powered movement of the other track bites into the black top of the road and creates a distinctive screeching sound. Though deafened by the upsurge of engine noise, Toppo's sharp ears had missed the sound he was waiting to hear when he gave vent to his anguish. The gradual drop in the noise decibel further confirmed the fact that the tanks were driving past our location, with the wind carrying the sound further away from us. The thrill of listening to the roar of fast approaching tanks of the regiment, the excitement of waving them into the harbour suddenly evaporated. A sense of alarm and anxiety engulfed everyone watching this high drama—helpless and stupefied. It was like a marriage party waiting expectantly on a railway platform for their train to arrive. The metallic clatter and sound of the approaching train and the hoot of the engine brings to life the bridal party along with the *band, baja, and baraat,* with all the pomp and show. There is excitement and hectic activity for the well-rehearsed grand welcome when suddenly the realization dawns that the truant runaway train has shrieked past the excited marriage party without making a stop, leaving in its wake despair, despondency, and desperation.

Whoever was leading the tank column had missed the turn at the road track junction. Chiefy had summarily rejected the suggestion of posting a sentry at the road track junction as he would be personally leading the tank column. 'Such a prominent school building at this junction, how can you miss it?' is what he had said, twittering with confidence. Surely, some other officer would be leading the tank column. A few kilometres away, the Divisional tactical Headquarters had established itself. God save us merry cavaliers in case the tank column trespassed that location. The prospect of a major calamity uppermost in mind, I yelled across to Raghubir Chandra, 'Get the Rover, quick, double time.' The tenor and language demanded immediate compliance. Those standing around were stunned. 'Hop in, Toppo,' I called out while quickly occupying the now vacant driver's seat as Raghubir slid across to the co-driver's seat. *'Kya tamasha kar diya hai tankon ne.'* (What a spectacle this tank column has made.) We virtually flew over the track leading to the road track junction. At the main road, we signalled the first tank sighted to stop. 'How many tanks ahead of you'?

The alert commander responded: 'C Squadron and B Squadron one troop.'

'Stop all tanks and switch off the engines', was the forceful command delivered. Toppo dismounted to leap onto the tank, having understood what was expected of him.

The tank column, heading toward the Divisional Headquarters, must have traversed a few hundred yards by now. *Saab aap dipper per dhyan rakho, overtake karna hai. Thik hai, Saab. Jo bhi lead mein hai uski khair nahi'* (God save the guy who is leading the tank column). Raghubir was a wise one and knew instinctively when not to respond. By now, we were attempting to overtake the rearmost tank. Raghubir was aghast, 'Slow down, slow down, Sir', were the only words left in his vocabulary. 'Shut up and use your torch to grab the attention of the tank commander,' I said. The tank speed was nearly 25 kmph, leaving no choice but to press on the accelerator. Raghubir was back to his loudest best, 'Slow down, slow down', of course, this time looking more directly at me. His mature advice went unheeded. I countered him with, *'Aage 5 km par division headquarter hai; Tamasha ho jaye ga'* (5 km ahead is the Divisional Headquarters; calamity awaits us, if they cross). Closing in with the tank ahead, we found the entire road surface covered. The repeated flashing of a torch or the frenzied dipping of the Jonga's dancing headlights was not effective. The dust storm raised by the tank column, racing at top speed, the gradually descending smog, combined with the smoke of the diesel engine, had created a haze. Our antics had made no impression on the tired tank driver who had been driving for over six hours. The tank commander, expected to be standing upright, with his head popping out of the commander's cupola, was nowhere in sight. The long journey, evening chill, dust, and diesel fumes must have broken his resolve and led him to nestle into some cosy corner inside the tank. 'Make a note of this tank: must teach the bastard to remain alert on duty,' I said angrily. 'Yes Sir, it is from B Squadron.' An open patch ahead helped us overtake the tank, after a narrow miss with the hull plate. Fortunately, the driver responded and pulled his tank to the right just in time. The horn served no purpose except to give us the satisfaction that we had utilized all available means in this dangerous chase. The gap between the following tanks permitted putting the Jonga into top gear. Spotting an alert commander responding, we whizzed past the tank from the left. I could hear the suppressed hiss from my co-traveller. The situation demanded bravado and driving skill in equal measure. At the speed we were now travelling, a small error of judgement could have ripped the Jonga into two if the tank in front took a sharp turn. The likelihood of being driven off the road into a ditch was not a probability but a distinct possibility.

'*Kitne tank cross ho gaye Saab?*' (How many tanks have crossed?) A not-too-cheerful response announced 'Six only, Sir.' Never before had I tried overtaking speeding tanks on a narrow Class 9 road, and unless you have experienced this yourself, you cannot imagine what a nightmarish experience it can be. Fortunately, I did not have to overtake the complete column. Half way through, the tank column was beginning to slow down. One could see the tank in front pulling towards the left of the road, virtually crawling to a halt. I steered to overtake from the right and stopped abreast, with the tank driver now loosening his headgear, to emerge out of the driver's cupola. Raghubir, who was within hearing distance, called out the driver's name to ask in Haryanvi dialect 'Who is this son of a bitch leading the tank column?' the question needed no answer. Emerging from behind

the row of stationary tanks, from the direction of the Divisional
Headquarters was a Jonga flying the pennants of the C Squadron
commander. A carefree, none too perturbed Chiefy emerged
with a mischievous wink and sheepish grin, saying, 'Sorry Balli,
I dozed off before the road track junction.' He continued, 'One
for the road did the trick! Must be one too many for the long
road.' He smiled, putting his arm around me. He appeared tired
and understandably embarrassed. His frank admission left no
scope for a showdown or display of anger. A sense of relief that
the tanks had stopped was paramount. No further discussion
was necessary. I asked Raghubir to hop on to the nearest tank
and lead them into the concentration area as deployment had to
be completed before sunrise. Tomorrow would be another day
to resolve pending issues. On the journey back, in Chiefy's well-
padded, comfortable Jonga, I could not help but ask what made
him stop. His answer revealed his true personality: his driver had
stopped the Jonga on seeing a signboard on the road: TCP 500
metre ahead. Scrawled below that was the tactical Number of
that Divisional HQ. There would be no more questions to ask.
The secret of 'a small navigational error' was locked and sealed.

Someone from the Divisional Headquarters had asked the
Adjutant, Inder, about the churned tarmac, near the Division
TCP (Traffic Check Post). The visible tank tracks were a clear
giveaway. Chiefy had by then admitted to Digby about how
'the one for the road' led to a 'the slight navigational error'. We
later learnt that though infuriated at this snafu, Digby closed
the case with advice to the squadron commanders not to mix
drinks and duty in future. Chiefy had set a good example of
'taking it on the chin' and Digby by confirming that the spirit
of the cavalry was alive in the regiment and would flourish in
the years ahead.

An anecdote repeated often while undergoing the Young Officers (YO) course at Ahmednagar comes to mind. During certain manoeuvres, a tank regiment lost its way and could not reach the objective by the given time. At the summing up held after termination of the exercise, the General Officer Commanding (GOC) said: 'This was the fault of my staff officer.' The director of the exercise commented, 'The GOC has blamed his staff. This cannot, for a moment, be permitted. He, alone, is responsible.' At the same manoeuvres, one combat team, detached from the brigade to carry out a certain task, went utterly wrong. At the summing up, the brigade commander was asked, 'And did the combat team leader carry out your orders?' The brigade commander knew that they had not but although he may have fucked them in private, he would not 'give them away' in public, and he replied: 'To the letter, yes, to the letter.' That is the cavalry way of doing things.

At first light, the tanks had readjusted their positions within the concentration area to carry out camouflage and concealment as we were sitting closer to the border. Fatigue was written all over the faces of the tank crews but there were no signs of tension. Having covered a considerable distance in one night, it was important to complete all periodic maintenance tasks and also check out the serviceability of all systems as well as replenish fuel and top-up lubricants. Checking of the 'nuts and bolts', greasing nipples or otherwise checking the serviceability of bogie wheels and tracks which must have taken a considerable beating, was already under way. Preventive maintenance tasks on a few tanks were due and these were completed with the help of the Light Repair Workshop (LRW) personnel. Rumours were afloat that India would launch an attack on Eid, a Muslim festival, the next day. It was difficult discounting this rumour for our move into the concentration area was a reality. Somehow, the feeling persisted that India would never attack and that this move was at best a stratagem. The overall atmosphere was one of participation in some large-scale military exercise. Digby, on his return from Divisional HQ, brought word that the Corps Commander, Gen Tappy Raina would visit us the next day and that virtually confirmed our belief.

The adjutant had informed all the officers to assemble in the Operation Room for the commandants' conference. As young officers, we would often keep score of the number of times Digby would repeat his pet phrases, 'spit and polish', 'buttoning up', and 'pull up your socks' during his conferences. Side bets amounted to free drinks for the one who was nearest to the number counted. These conferences would start with the Intelligence Officer (IO), Ravi Bains, giving us the intelligence summary and topographical information, followed by Inder, covering own and enemy activity during the last 24 hours in the divisional area of our interest. While waiting for Digby to descend, the squadron commanders and staff officers utilized the time gap to share data of a routine nature relating to manpower, equipment, or points of coordination. Inder as adjutant had established a reputation for being meticulous and sincere in the discharge of his responsibilities. Chakraborty, his close friend and confidant, was an experienced technical officer who kept an eagle eye on the entire fleet of tanks and vehicles. He could rattle off numbers of tanks/vehicles undergoing overhaul in the repair bay. Digby then descended, nursing a glass of whiskey in one hand and a notebook in the other, to brief us on the tactical picture and discussed plans. One could sense a note of seriousness while he went through his list of points jotted in his diary. The corps commander's visit was the first to the regiment and, therefore, the importance of 'pulling up your socks'—the countdown had begun.

During the night, the Regimental Headquarters (RHQ) shelters were pitched alongside the Operation Room (Ops Room) where battle maps, distance charts, situation reports, and telephone logs would be displayed. A small detachment from the corps of signal, attached to the regiment, would operate the forward and rear radio links to the squadrons and the Brigade, Divisional and tac HQ. The landlines to the network were to be laid out and made functional in keeping with the signallers' motto of 'Teevr Gati'. The signals personnel attached to armoured regiments always had a harrowing time, as hurriedly laid landlines, spread over the ground, would snap due to frequent tank movement. Track marking, signposting, camouflage and concealment of tanks, air-alert shelters, weapon pits, and other mundane activities were completed before midday. The SOPs were well rehearsed and understood, and ensured that all preparations were complete to receive the VIP.

The corps commander arrived at 1500 hrs with a large entourage of commanders and staff officers to the 'buttoned up' regiment. Digby's operational briefing was limited to squadron commanders and above. Soon after the briefing commenced, Ravi Bains and Bhandari, a troop leader with B Squadron, were spotted walking towards the field mess where I joined them. Ravi was privy to situation reports received from higher headquarters as also enemy movements opposite our sector. 'Fuck all is happening,' he said. 'All show and no go,' observed Bhandari. 'We will just hang on in these forward locations, buggering ourselves.' While the banter continued along these lines over a cup of tea, suddenly, the air alert siren sounded. 'OMG another air alert practice,' snapped Bhandari, as we stepped out of the mess shelter reluctantly, leaving behind our steaming cups of tea. The scene that unfolded in front of our eyes astounded us and left us flabbergasted. The military brass, assembled in the Ops Room, were rushing around as if their tails were on fire and bedlam had broken loose. The realization that the Army brass was all in a frenzy was sufficient evidence that the Pakistan Air Force (PAF) air attack was for real. While we were still fumbling, a squadron commander yelled, 'Get into the nearby bunker.' He was leading the charge of half a dozen senior officers, now wearing helmets, quickly snatched from a stack placed outside the Ops Room, charging in our direction. Two rolled over into the trench now occupied by us. This was no time for introductions, as physical safety had superseded rank. With shoulders rubbing against a harassed Brigadier, we had our eyes transfixed on four small dots on the eastern sky. Someone appeared more knowledgeable, and identified the aircraft as the 'F-86 Sabres'. 'Look out', he said. Before we could say 'Jai Guru Dev', the four Sabres had crossed into Indian air space to fly over our location, displaying their naked underbellies. It was an awesome sight, soon broken by the shattering noise of the anti-aircraft guns, and the staccato of machine-gun fire. A little while later, two Sabres, after circling over us once, could be seen dropping height and diving towards us. A puff of smoke sighted from the underslung gun of the fast approaching aircraft sent a shiver up the spine. The fire appeared directed straight onto us. The 'ack ack' guns were active again and the smell of cordite reached our nostrils. We heard the clump, thump of something dropped close by, before two huge explosions shook the earth below us. The target selected for the air attack by the Sabres was further from our location, but it was, nonetheless, a nerve-shattering experience.

Those four Sabre pilots were having a ball, unconcerned about the havoc they were creating.

That the Indian Air Force (IAF) was not responding, meant that the bastards would live, to come back another day. Soon after, the visiting brass regained their composure, having dusted themselves and discarded the unwieldy heavy metal helmets. Berets and hats of different denominations reappeared, displaying the red bands of military authority. The air attack had the senior tongues wagging and the radio sets buzzing all around. General Raina walked briskly into the Ops Room for an urgent message from Fort William. Most senior officers were veterans of the 1965 War and could be heard saying that war was inevitable now. Nothing To Report (NTR) had come from the squadrons. It appeared that a gun position in the vicinity of our location was the PAF's target. For us, this was the first experience of real danger. We were lucky not to have been under the direct attack of the Sabres.

The deafening sound of the flying machines and the helplessness of the ground troops against aircraft would stay embedded in the memory. Digby saw off the corps commander and divisional commander but soon returned to the Ops Room. A peep inside revealed that he was in a serious discussion with a Brigadier who had appeared as my trenchmate while the Sabres were strafing us.

'Ravi, who is that Brigadier sitting with Digby?'

'He is the one I was telling you about when the alert was sounded, Brig Gharaya, Commander 42 Infantry Brigade.'

Bhandari rejoined us after his usual information-gathering chukker around the RHQ. He wanted confirmation of a rumour now doing the rounds that the ongoing discussions had something to do with the call from Command Headquarters,

Fort William. 'Why did the corps commander rush away without the usual handshakes?' He capped this response with yet another question to prove his point. 'Even the demonstration of night vision devices got cancelled. Why?' Someone had contacted the radio operator of the Corps C1 link and started the rumour that Pakistan had declared war. An air of excitement and expectation permeated the environment as the rumour circulated. Not long after, Inder stepped out from the Ops Room to instruct Ravi that the 'O' group would assemble after 20 minutes. While returning, he winked at me and announced, 'It will be a busy night, better button up your squadron.' Much later, we were to learn that due to the shelling of our border posts, Army HQ had decided to allow our troops to go into East Pakistan. The Fort William call was the green signal to secure specific areas to improve our offensive posture. Brigadier J.S. Gharaya received orders to secure Garibpur and cut the Chaugacha–Afra road axis, if required.

As per orders given by the RHQ C Squadron was to be split into halves. Chiefy was to command a squadron less two troops. The remaining two tank troops under my command were ordered to move to the forward concentration area during the same night and 'marry up' with 14 Punjab, a unit of HQ 42 Infantry Brigade. Teji (Speedy) Sidhu was one of the troop leaders while Chakraborty, a JCO, commanded the second troop. The forward concentration area was about 20 km from the current location, which tanks could cover in two hours. The routes earlier reconnoitred by a section of the recce troop under Mahato would guide the tanks. This was an effortless move carried out smoothly, the tanks deployed within the defended area occupied by 14 Punjab.

With the tank troops in position, Speedy joined in for 'marrying up' with the Company Headquarters of this new sub-unit. A young subaltern, Amar Jeet, whom I had come to know during our pleasure trips to Ranchi, greeted us. We were meeting after a long break, under war-like conditions. With the drop in mercury, the weather demanded warmth and nourishment for both body and soul. We were with the Nabha Akal battalion where the elixir of life appeared in the form of a bottle of rum along with some hastily prepared snacks. The talk centred around our various exploits in Ranchi, with much leg pulling. The nice warm feeling of being with good friends was all that mattered. 'Why worry about tomorrow if today be sweet?' carried a ring of truth. Deep down in the inner recesses of the heart, the stark, naked reality that we were all sitting on the threshold of a shooting war was accepted. Gradually, with the diminishing contents of the now near empty bottle, the talk veered to what was uppermost on our minds. A shooting war would soon start and who knew what was in store for us! In a sudden fit of inspiration, I told them that our first encounter with the enemy would be a big success. Speedy, Amar Jeet, and myself would be in the thick of it together, but would remain unharmed. Both agreed that we must teach these bloody Pakistanis a lesson. We drank a toast to victory and bade each other good luck. Before sunrise, the tank crews got busy with camouflage and concealment, which included erasing tank tracks, a sure giveaway of our location to aircraft. Movement of tanks and crews was restricted to avoid undue attention. Daybreak provided an expansive view of what lay across the international border. Earlier recce to these locations was of a perfunctory nature. Binoculars in hand, from a vantage point of view, every small detail of the landscape, obstacle, and route was analysed. From the forward concentration area, we could see the Kabodak river demarcating the international border. The civilian population had deserted the village due to the intermittent shelling by the Pakistanis. It had suffered considerable damage and only a few huts remained. A large number of bamboo clusters and thick foliage that provided excellent cover surrounded Boyra village. The area just across the river was a flat open stretch for approximately 3 km beyond which there were various bamboo thickets and hutments. The meandering river Kabodak is a natural barrier. The PT-76 tanks were amphibious and could swim across such obstacles. Common military knowledge suggested that attacking troops never spent more than 24 hours in the forward concentration area. No further evidence of the corps commander's discussions during his meeting with Digby was now necessary. No formal declaration of war had, however, taken place.

The date: 20 November 1971.

7

TANK BATTLE

The adjutant of an armoured regiment is a key staff officer of the commandant. The Regimental Signal Officer (RSO) and the IO assist him in maintenance of the Ops Room, and communication with units affiliated, attached or placed under command for different operations. A telephone call or radio message to the Ops Room rarely goes unanswered, as it is staffed round the clock during active operations. Around midday, I received a call from Ravi Bains that Digby had sent word from the Infantry Brigade HQ that I should stand by for fresh orders shortly. On further probing, he revealed that, as per intelligence reports, the Pakistanis had been building up a massive force just across the border, with the likely aim of capturing Boyra. The danger was imminent and an attack expected within 24 hours. Things were getting exciting after all. I visited the RHQ on 20 November in the afternoon to clarify the change in orders. I had warned Speedy that he should be prepared to cross the IB around 1600 hrs. Inder informed me that two of my troops were to revert under command of Chiefy. As the distances involved were small, we would cross the order and establish a quick link-up with the squadron. There was no jubilation or sense of excitement at the prospect of crossing the international border. It was just another job at hand, which needed execution—promptly and efficiently. The crossing would take place during the hours of daylight and would present no problem. The enemy aircraft that had recently become very active, would not interfere as they had just completed a sortie over our area. I adjusted my headgear and depressed the presser switch to put the radio on the send mode to pass my first message, heard by all commanders, on the regimental radio net:

'Delta 40 for Delta 1 and Delta 3 Orders: Advance. Order of march, Delta 3 leading. Over.'

Delta 1: 'Wilco. Over.' Delta 3: 'Wilco. Over.' Delta 40: 'Follow me. Out.'

Great emphasis was laid on the cross-country mobility of PT-76, rechristened Pippa, to compensate for its poor firepower and lack of armour. Due to its low weight to ground ratio and ability to float in water, it becomes an ideal tank for riverine terrain. The Pippa had now been unleashed to move across the international border into East Pakistan carrying the flag of 45 Cavalry, shedding forever the many centuries old defensive mindset of India.

Before reaching the home bank of the river, the tank troop was deployed to provide mutual fire support during the crossing. The river was over 300 feet wide, however, the waterway was not more than 100 feet over which the bridging effort was required. The engineers had calculated that the riverbed would be about 40 feet deep and the current not more than 3 knots. Downstream from the bridge site, approximately 70 metres, the Punjab battalion had marshalled a few boats after securing the

area across on the far bank. An air alert whistle had sounded the all-clear a few minutes earlier. Speedy moved his tank towards the site selected for entry into the water.

He reported: 'Shallow water, gradual slope: perfect crossing site', followed by 'afloat now'. Speedy traversed another 200 metres to position his tank within the earmarked bridgehead. This was the signal for the second tank of his troop to move forward and enter the river.

'Delta 3 for Delta 40, In location. Over.'

'Delta 40 for Delta 3: Congratulations on leading historic Indian armour advance into East Pakistan.'

'Delta 3 for Delta 40: Congratulations to you and celebrations . . .'

Unknown to many, this was a historic moment in the military history of India and its mechanized forces. India's political leadership had accepted the military dictum: 'Attack is the best form of defence.' The unheralded silent invasion by India would soon send shock waves across world capitals. A fragmented Pakistan, split into two, would be humiliated and its Army disgraced into surrender before a triumphant India.

My tank had crossed the river while the fifth was now negotiating the river when unusual loud cries of *bachao, bachao* (save me) filled the air. Instinctively, I looked towards the ferry site of 14 Punjab. Bedlam had broken out. Loud screams, cries, swear words, appeals for help broke out in unison, as somewhere in the middle of the river an overturned boat was partly visible. Around it two or three figures, in full battle dress, were struggling for life. Closer to the ferry site, men were jumping off the boat into chest deep water so that rescue parties could reach out to those in distress. Along the waterfront, comrades could be seen praying for deliverance. The brigade, battalion, and field

regiment commanders were witness to this tragic event. Each
one must have felt devastated as they impotently watched the
pandemonium and mayhem that cruel fate had imposed on this
brave unit. The move across the river stood suspended while
engineer divers began the search for the bodies of the drowned
soldiers. With recovery delayed due to the water depth and the
underwater seaweed, the battalion set in motion to complete
its assigned military mission in spite of the gloom, sorrow,
and heavy hearts. The arrival of the Regiment Medical Officer
(RMO) and ambulances brought no hope or cheer. The brave-
hearts, dressed in full combat with Field Service Marching Order
(FSMO) packs on their backs, carrying their weapons and battle
loads, had descended into their watery graves with no chance of
survival. The body count was of 9 soldiers and a young artillery
officer, the Forward Observation Officer (FOO), travelling
on the same boat who had been snatched by the cruel hand
of destiny. The pause in the operational task was painful and
inescapable, but the battalion overcame it to complete the task.

Six tanks were now in the bridgehead across the river. The
seventh tank was close to the far bank when the commander
reported that his tank was unable to take the gradient of the
bank. We could see the tank climbing halfway up the slope only
to roll back while the engine rpm dropped sharply. The entire
crew dismounted and took turns to heave the heavy hammer and
cutting pliers to free the mangled concertina enmeshed around
the sprocket. Contact between the barbed wire and sprocket was
attributed to the negligence of the driver who had to hear taunts
from the harassed crew. When he could not bear the verbal
assault any longer, he jumped into the driver's seat, engaged
the reverse gear instead of the forward gear, and pressed on the
accelerator. The gamble paid off as the hammering had loosened

the concertina grip. A relieved driver and a beaming crew soon joined us in the dash forward to the chosen rendezvous.

Briefing is an informal method adopted by the commander of mechanized forces to convey his battle plans for execution by the sub-units. Speedy and Chakraborty attended the 'O' group for the final briefing. Chiefy looked impressive in his black dungarees and well-trimmed moustache. The dust goggles mounted on his turban, swagger stick in hand, he had a battle map hung on one side of the tank hull to brief the combat team. The manner in which Chiefy addressed the 'O' Group gave us the feeling that this was like any routine peace-time tactical exercise with troops, being conducted in own territory. Two companies of 14 Punjab were to travel piggyback on the tanks of C Squadron covering a distance of 10 km. The balance elements of the battalion would march on foot. Intelligence reports had indicated that the enemy had deployed near Chaugacha.

The report lines selected are based on identifiable landmarks or prominent places marked on the map, which the leading troop leader must report on crossing. Speedy had a genuine doubt on the report lines selected.

Speedy: 'Can I have the report lines again, I have noted only two.'

Chiefy: 'Of course.' He pointed towards his map, recounting all three.

Speedy: 'But the second one is not on the route given by you.'

Chakraborty: 'That is true, Sir. Some mistake.'

Chiefy: 'So what. We may have to change route due to enemy action.'

Speedy: 'So I have to report crossing only two, if the route remains unchanged.'

Chiefy, a little perplexed: 'I will simplify it for you.' He got closer to the map and after a brief interlude said, 'Forget report lines, I will give you code names for important villages en route. All of you make a note.'

He picked up the names of four prominent villages and off the cuff gave them names of Pakistani towns at random— Lahore, Rawalpindi, Karachi, Islamabad. With a little chuckle, he added: 'This will scare the hell out of the Pakis. Bugger them.'

While some in O group chuckled, Speedy let go, as it was easier remembering Paki town names than fancy codes for report lines.

Ramparikshan (another troop leader): 'Will we advance one up or two up?'

Chiefy: 'I leave that up to the leading troop leader.'

Company Commander: 'We have a local Mukti Bahini guide. Can we take him along.'

Chiefy: 'Good, put him on leading tank troop.'

Chakraborty: 'I will despatch a Bengali-speaking crew member of my troop.'

Company Commander: 'Should I travel with the leading troop leader?'

Chiefy: 'No, you travel with Pandey's troop.'

FOO Operator: 'My radio sets have been fitted on 2IC tank, as ordered.'

Chiefy: 'Fine. OK. Where is the FOO?'

FOO Operator: 'He is at the bridge site and will induct shortly.'

Chiefy: 'He should report to 2IC for briefing.'

Pandey: 'On whose order can we open fire?'

This stumped all present. We had come 3 km inside East Pakistan without firing a single shot. Having crossed the IB, no one had raised such a basic but relevant issue. Mentally conditioned to the battle procedures practised during the annual training, the subconscious was tuned in for an exercise enemy to fire his blank rounds or the red, very light pistol flare to signify the presence of enemy troops. The question–answer session was a true barometer of the mental refusal to accept the reality that crossing the IB meant a shooting war, with no holds barred. When bullets start flying, true learning begins.

With no further queries, 'O' group dispersed. Radio sets switched on to 'listening watch' to await the executive order for the advance to commence. I was sitting with my back resting against the tank turret having informed Inder about the briefing as also the order of march. Just then, somebody tapped me on my leg that was dangling over the tank deck. Looking down, I saw it was none other than Lt Col R.K. Singh, commanding 14 Punjab Battalion. I had met him many months earlier when I was writing my part 'B' examination where he was an invigilator. The warmth and ardour with which I responded, left him taken aback a bit, as we were mere acquaintances.

Sensing that I still had a couple of minutes of free time before advance commenced, I went around meeting the crew. They were all in fine fettle and devoid of undue signs of tension of being in enemy territory. Confidence reflected on their faces but deep down, apprehension of the danger that enveloped their present environment could be read in their eyes. My own reaction was similar to that of a boxer about to enter the ring. That slight empty feeling in the pit of the stomach, coupled with anxiety, before the first blow. The memory of the blow then drives away anxiety and propels you into heightened activity.

The radio message 'Delta for all stations, Delta One report my signals over' served to relieve us of all other anxieties.

D1: 'OK. Over.'

D2: 'OK. Over.'

D3: 'OK. Over.'

D4: 'OK. Over.'

D40: 'OK. Over.'

D for all stations. D1: 'Advance now. Out.'

The countryside was similar to that in West Bengal. Looking through the binoculars along the route of the advance, all that met the eye was open patches of flat land and paddy fields, interspersed with dense clumps of bamboo, date palms, and other thick foliage around small hamlets. While each hamlet had fish breeding ponds, the villages were based on a large community pond used by the population and the domestic animals as a central amenity. The open patches represented farming land and grazing areas. From the tank commander's point of view, concerned about security and speedy movement, foliage obscured observation beyond the hamlet, imposing tactical caution on the leading troop leader. This was overcome by practising the 'one leg on the ground' manoeuvre in which movement around the hamlet had to be supported by one or more static tanks providing fire support.

A cloud of dust and smoke spread across the horizon. It was a grand site as the tank column stretched out against the backdrop of *khaji* trees (date palms) and clumps of bamboo groves, cutting across patches of flaming mustard seed flowers in the late afternoon November sun. The dull cherry and beige pennants fluttered over the radio antennae as the odd bird flew out of its nest, distressed by the unusual sound and roar of the engines. The mounted infantry, unaccustomed to the high decibels of tank engines, combined with the spray of diesel vapour and smoke emanating from the engine exhaust, could not be enjoying the pitch and toss of the tank movement across water channels and undulating ground. I remember a Havildar with grey hair, struggling to hold on to his place on the tank deck, telling his comrades, 'This is worse than getting buggered,' in straight Punjabi. His companion, hanging on to his humour, even under adverse conditions, added in jest, 'Oh, you have been buggered before,' spreading laughter all around.

Speedy was justifiably under greater pressure being the 'eyes and ears' of the squadron. My own position in the order of march was directly behind Chiefy, as per the book. Having advanced deeper into enemy territory, Speedy stopped on observing the movement of civilians in a hamlet, approximately 1000 metres from his position.

'Delta1 for Delta: Observed movement of personnel ahead. Over.'

'Delta for Delta 1: Did you draw any fire? Over.'

'Delta 1 for Delta: No. Could be Razakars. Over.'

'Delta for Delta 1: Outflank from right. Out.'

Chiefy asked him to outflank the position and resume advance. What was not correctly appreciated was that the outflank was time-consuming and was affecting the speed of advance. When my tank went past the hamlet, I realized that a large number of civilians had emerged from their huts out of curiosity to watch the tanks but also to greet us as liberators, as was evident by their smiles, and their hands raised in welcome. Chiefy and Speedy agreed that the presence of civilians confirmed the absence of enemy troops and made outflank of such hamlets superfluous. The need for caution remained paramount but this shift in the thought process speeded up our advance. It also revealed that trained soldiers are not trigger-happy mavericks and need time and the trajectory of events before being provoked into killing.

Speedy was living up to his name and making good progress. Having covered nearly half the distance, Chiefy directed him to change the axis of the advance and proceed towards 'Lahore'!

'D for D1: Proceed toward Lahore, repeat, Lahore. Over.'

'D1 for D: Lahore, wilco. Out.'

'D1 for D1A and D1B: Advance for Lahore.'

There was a brief pause in the advance while the leading two tank commanders orientated their tanks and semi-gyros towards the direction indicated. Confusion broke out on the squadron radio net as soon as the advance resumed. The direction in which Speedy was heading was not the one that Chiefy intended. Chiefy came up on the air and clarified the confusing code words saying, 'Delta for Delta 1: Speedy go for Lahore, not Rawalpindi.' As the subordinate tank commanders recognised the voice of their squadron commander, they slowed down, expecting fresh orders from Speedy. Frustrated, Speedy got into the lead himself to cut out the misunderstanding. No sooner had Speedy started, that Chiefy was on the blower again. 'Delta for Delta 1: you are heading towards Karachi, no go for Lahore, I repeat Lahore. Over.' A spate of radio messages between the two continued till finally Speedy stopped all movement, for whichever direction Speedy attempted to advance in, it appeared to be wrong. Somebody who was carefully listening to all the transmissions finally suggested the use of cardinal points to indicate the axis of advance. The confusion soon came to an end and the advance resumed. I was present at the 'O' group as also on the squadron net to confirm that this actually happened. The code words used are actual. We could not have confused the enemy if they were listening to this conversation on the radio, but it became a standard joke amongst the tank commanders. The tank commanders had jotted down the code words given during the briefing and sympathized with Speedy. Chiefy had consigned it to memory. As tension mounts, memory fades. Such is human nature.

The sun had already set by the time we came within the vicinity of our objective. On orders from the Brigade HQ, further advance was stopped and R.K. Singh directed to deploy in the same area. The two infantry companies dismounted and soon dispersed to occupy a hasty battalion defended area after a preliminary recce. The tanks firmed in the same location for the night. Our short advance into enemy territory had helped us graduate from the annual exercise syndrome to the trepidation that we were on the threshold of a shooting war.

With descending darkness came the apprehensions about being in enemy country. This made us doubly conscious of duties and responsibilities. A strict night watch was kept of enemy movement for we could not have moved in unobserved. This meant detailing men to patrol certain areas, also establish listening posts. All such movement had to be coordinated with the Battalion and Company HQ. The fact that we were in open harbour increased the need for security. The tank crews were directed about the rationale for the current deployment and overall plan. The troop leaders arrived at the appointed time to report on the state of manpower and equipment. This was a standard drill and provided an opportunity to take stock of problems faced during the advance and resolve the issues raised. Coordination of operational, logistics, and security orders in keeping with the changed state of affairs were completed. Radio contact was critical, as directives received from the Regimental HQ could then be shared. One tank per troop, assigned as 'guard tank', would keep the radio set on listening watch throughout. After I had finished, Chiefy addressed them, laying special emphasis on vigilance and realigning of tanks before first light.

While this briefing was in progress, some elements of the remaining two companies of the Punjab Battalion, who had foot-slogged, started arriving. These columns arrived as stragglers of a large-scale training exercise. Whatever training they may have received in the occupation of a defended locality was currently irrelevant. The harsh reality was that unless their subordinate commanders briefed the troops, they had no way of knowing what the tactical situation demanded. In my view, this was a special difficulty with the infantry, which tended to work on the principle of minimum information sharing with soldiers. The more practical reason was that neither side had fired a single bullet.

The infantry soon got busy digging up their foxholes and trenches, roughly aligning them to the deployment of the tanks for, on a pitch-dark night, no better landmark was visible. Sitting atop my tank, I could hear the detachment closest to me speaking amongst themselves in Punjabi in low tones. Evidently, the boat that capsized had claimed a friend from his village as a victim. They appeared surprised at the drowning of one of their comrades who was an outstanding athlete and a command-level swimmer. Further away, a pickaxe handle being hammered into position or pakhals (water containers) being unloaded from a vehicle were the sounds one heard in the cold winter night. Apparently, the 'F' (Fighting) echelon of the battalion carrying ammunition, mines, and field stores had arrived. Occasionally, somebody, a smoker, would strike a match and quickly cup the flame to light a cigarette.

It was a bitterly cold night, so I wrapped the great coat and a blanket (all that I was carrying) closer, hoping it would relieve me from the biting cold. Finding little relief, I too lit a cigarette, carefully covering the glow while inhaling between the folds of my overcoat. Not more than an hour and a half must have elapsed when an urgent message came up through the receiver that I had slung over my shoulder. It was the troop leader, a JCO, Risaldar Ramparikshan (RP) Singh. In hushed tones, suppressing excitement and concern, he whispered into the radio:

'D1 for D40: Movement of enemy vehicles observed. Over.'

'D40 for D1: Tanks or vehicles, clarify.'

'Nor sure. Over.'

'Report what you observed. Over.'

'Seven headlights of vehicles were seen moving on road Jessore–Chaugacha.'

'Can you still see them moving?'

'No, cannot see them moving; may be headlights switched off.'

'Indicate area where you saw them. What made you think they were tanks?'

'The speed of movement and possibly the sound of engines.'

'For how long did you observe these lights?'

'About one minute, near road bend on main road.'

'Keep area under watch. Out.'

It was difficult to contain the excitement after receipt of this information. Confirmation of the type of vehicles was necessary. R.P. Singh mentioned that he had spotted these lights at a distance, probably when they were negotiating a turn on the road, more than two miles away. From the engine noise, it was difficult to discern the type of vehicles they were. They could be 3-ton lorries or maybe even tanks.

I ordered him to move forward, along with his radio set, keep them under constant surveillance, and share this information with his company. I then informed Chiefy:

'Delta 40 for Delta: Important message. Over.'

'Delta: OK. Over.'

'Delta 40 for Delta: Vehicle movement sighted opposite our location on main road axis, suspected tanks.'

'Delta 40 for Delta: Two patrols keeping the area under observation. RHQ informed. Over.'

Besides informing the squadron commander and the Regimental Headquarters, I alerted the tank troops to keep a strict vigil on the area directly ahead. Another anxious 20 minutes passed by before R.P. Singh again came on the air. He corrected his earlier transmission and said that the total number of lights was eight, and not seven. It was difficult for him to say with any degree of certainty that the engine noise was that of tanks; however, it was distinctly different from that of 3-ton lorries. All these vehicles had slowed down directly in front of our position soon after which the headlights and engines were switched off. I stepped into my tank, closing the cupola behind me to study the map more closely.

A quick study of the map and the implication of RP Singh's message started to sink in. It suddenly emerged that these enemy vehicles or may be even tanks, were not more than 3 km away from our position. The physical presence of the enemy was a matter of crucial importance, and grave apprehension and uncertainty if these were tanks had to be dealt with. I had heard of the M-47 and M-48 tanks on the Pakistan inventory. These were medium tanks. Chances of their deployment in this terrain were doubtful but could not be ruled out altogether. They could be the Chaffee or the AMX tanks. I was still studying the map and scratching my head to arrive at some reasonable answer. It was getting a little uncomfortable sitting crouched inside the tank. Lifting myself out of the cupola, the cold winter breeze provided instant relief. While I searched my pockets for the Charminar lung buster, an old Army dictum flashed through my mind: 'All first reports of the enemy are exaggerated.' This bit of military wisdom, along with the first few puffs of nicotine inhaled would have led to a mood swing when the earphone crackled again:

'Delta 2 for Delta 40: Message. Over.' The excitement in his voice was indicative of what followed.

'Delta 40: OK. Over.'

'Personally observed five headlights coming down the road.'

'Indicate direction of movement. Over.'

'Yes, I repeat, from my left to right.'

'You mean from Chaugacha towards Jessore. Over.'

'Yes, repeat, yes. Over.'

'Confirm figure, 5 or 7 lights. Over.'

'Confirmed 5 only. Over.'

'Where are they now? Can you see them?'

'Not now, must have switched off.'

'Could these be the same reported by RPS earlier?'

'No, repeat, no. They came from opposite direction.'

'Your assessment: tanks or lorries?'

'Must be tanks. Over.'

'Delta 40 for Delta 2: Standby.'

'Delta 40 for Delta 1: Did you receive? Over.' (No response) 'I repeat, Delta 1, did you receive? Over.'

The timid voice of a radio operator, 'Delta 1 abhi recce par hain. Over.'

'Delta 40 for Delta 1: Out to you.'

'Delta 40 for Delta 2: Meet in fig 5. Over.'

'Delta 2 for Delta 40: Wilco. Out.'

Before Chakraborty arrived, I had a little time to recap the recent events reported. The tanks were deployed in a semi-circle, with the Squadron Headquarters (SHQ) in the middle. The left half segment had tank troops 1 and 3, and the right segment had troops 2 and 4. The layout of the ground dictated the gap between the two segments. Chiefy had split responsibility by assigning the left half to me. Sequentially, therefore, the semi-circular defensive perimeter had R.P. Singh on the extreme left, then Speedy. The right half had Chakraborty, with Pandey further on his right. To use a cricketing analogy, Pandey was at the Jessore end while R.P. Singh was at the Chaugacha end. Overlooking the gap and to the rear was the SHQ. Movement was spotted by R.P. Singh from the Jessore end, towards Chaugacha (right to left) whereas Chakraborty had reported movement in the opposite direction (left to right). Neither could see the movement reported by the other, however, both had reported lights being switched off or disappearing somewhere in the centre. Pandey and Speedy had not reported or spotted the movement. This could be attributed to the layout of the ground, cover from view, and many other intangible factors. They had conveyed their individual assessment as experienced JCOs. Neither was in a position to give a definitive yes/no answer. The description of the headlights observed by both was identical. Night conditions, inter-se distance, visibility, nature of sound heard, the duration for which the activity was under observation, and individual predilections were relevant factors in influencing judgement. It was imperative to debrief both to extract additional hard evidence to authenticate the presence of enemy tanks before any serious reporting to the higher HQ.

What was the distance between the successive headlights? Tank columns tend to bunch in closer, unlike B vehicles, which have a lower 'vehicles to a kilometre' (VTKM) imprint. Any unusual feature observed—light/fitment item/shape/height—would be a clear giveaway. We drew a blank. Both were interrogated on the time lag between headlights becoming stationery and engines switching off. On this point, there was a divergence of views. Chakraborty's explanation revealed that he had 'instinctively' concluded that the vehicles under his observation were tanks. R.P. Singh admitted that his assessment was influenced by the intensity of the engine clamour and the sound decibels. My mind was racing ahead, searching for that one convincing clue which would solve this jigsaw. I reasoned that Chakraborty was a driver by trade. His 'instinctive' response to what he had observed was reflecting his mental conditioning, developed over years of practical experience as a tank driver. Why did he not 'instinctively' assume them to be B vehicles? I felt that Chakraborty would have reached the same conclusion even blindfolded. The five vehicles spotted by him were probably tanks. R.P. Singh's basic trade was gunnery. His mental conditioning, training and experience directed towards acquisition of target, range estimation, speed, and movement. 'Instinct' represented the coming together of all senses and experience, and appealed as a reliable means for assessment. In R.P. Singh's initial statement, he had made mention of the speed of the vehicles at road bends and the distance of the headlights from his vantage point. In case both had observed tanks, the figure was adding up to 13 tanks, approximately the number authorized to a squadron.

In case both were right, it would become a tank vs tank battle between two equals. It was closer to 0230 hrs on 21

November 1971. In an effort to display supreme confidence, I bragged, making a prediction, 'Alert tank crews and tell them about a big victory tomorrow.' I was convinced that the time had come to inform RHQ about the enemy tanks deployed in our area.

Chiefy had signed off for the night into his makeshift shelter attached to the tank soon after receiving information about the headlights counted. His operator had switched over to the squadron commander's Rover and turned the radio set to listening watch, on the squadron radio net. Chiefy was to be disturbed only if there was an emergency. This was a normal order, as the Squadron 2IC operates the squadron rear link with the regiment. At the RHQ also it would be the adjutant and IO operating the rear link with the Divisional HQ. I got in touch with Inder and informed him of the development during the last hour. We agreed that the situation was serious and demanded a high state of alert. He added that the infantry battalion commander had received a directive from the Brigade HQ to send an officer led patrol with the specific task of establishing the strength and location of the enemy, and to confirm the presence of tanks.

There was nothing to do but wait for the enemy to show his hand. Our perimeter patrols and listening posts were on alert. The moon had just come out from behind the clouds, spraying the area around with soft light. One could spot movement of soldiers within the company locality, up to about 50 yards beyond which the figures would blend into darkness. The sound of digging of shallow trenches and some weapon pits surfaced intermittently. I looked at the faces of my crew and felt a pang of sympathy. To sleep so soundly on a cold night like this, the poor blokes must be dog-tired. A sudden calm descended all around, interrupted only by the continuous mush, which came over the radio set. Transfixed in this mood, I began mentally floating through my childhood days and early life. News of the death of my father received that dreadful, cold December night, during a heavy rainstorm, accompanied by an unusually strong spell of lightning, as if expressing my angst. The sorrow and suffering that would engulf the family, struggling for years. The dilemma, grief and mental anguish of Mother when she learnt that four of her sons stood as sentinels, deployed for war, and that all four may not come back. My youngest brother and sister caught in the vortex of war, dreading the suspense and fear that only a postman could inject by announcing delivery of a telegram during war-time. Postponement of her marriage again, bringing disappointment to both families. A sudden realization dawned that I was a very, very lonely man. I needed somebody I could speak to, somebody to whom I could unburden myself.

I looked around, half hoping that somebody would appear. A strange awareness engulfed me like a shroud. The unbroken chain of thought suddenly snapped as I became aware of the mush sound coming from the radio receiver. I involuntarily searched for the presser switch and through sheer force of habit called for Delta 25. I was greeted by the reassuring voice of Bains, loud and clear over the radio.

'Delta 25 for Delta 40: OK. Over.'

'Delta 40 for Delta 25: How are you? Over.'

'Delta 25 for 40: Fine. How are you? Over.'

'Delta 40 for 25: Feeling cold and awfully hungry. Over.'

'Delta 25 for 40: Hungry or horny or both? Over.'

'Delta 40 for 25: Plenty of crunch for breakfast tomorrow. Over.'

'Delta 25 for 40: What is the count? Over.'

'Delta 40 for 25: 13 and still counting. Over.'

'Delta 25 for 40: Hearty breakfast, Happy Hunting. Out.'

Around 0500 hrs, the tank operator Shibe Lal woke me up to respond to Inder waiting on the radio link. A short nap had not done much good for I moved away from the warmth of my blanket rather reluctantly. He said that reports regarding the build-up appeared confirmed through other sources about the enemy and we should take all precautions against a possible attack. This was enough to shake off all lethargy and return into the world of reality. I was grateful to Inder, for his transmission afforded a little extra time to think more clearly about the course of action to be adopted and plan the necessary steps for speedy implementation. With 'morning prayers' completed, all the troop leaders were briefed on the arcs of fire and responsibility, reminding them once again to realign their tanks in the direction where the enemy vehicles had switched off last night. With no suitable hull down position available, wherein the tank is protected from enemy observation and fire, each tank commander would have to position the tanks where cover from view at least was available. After aligning the tanks, the troop leaders were to switch off the engines.

The tank troops started adjusting at about 0500 hrs. During this period, I also moved up my tank and came in line with the left half of the semicircle. As and when the tanks realigned, they switched off their engines and got busy with camouflage. By about 0545 hrs the tank troops had got into good shape and had started 'brewing up' tea behind well concealed positions. Speedy, who had seen me coming in close to his position, walked over to my tank to inform me that his troop was ready for action. We soon got chatting about the night we had spent and the mysterious lights we had noticed. Speedy waved aside any chances of an attack by the enemy saying that very soon it was going to be first light and not a sound or trace of activity was visible. Our conversation was broken by a strong sturdy infantryman who came up with a written message from the battalion commander scrawled on a piece of paper that I should move with two troops to a fresh location as also contact Brigade Headquarters on the telephone at the earliest. I pocketed this piece of paper after showing it to Speedy. Speedy grinned from ear to ear as this confirmed his assessment that no attack was imminent. We decided it would be best to inform Chiefy and started walking towards his tank.

It was a cold, bitter morning with heavy winter fog. Due to poor visibility, we could barely see the outline of the bamboo grove fifty metres ahead. The tip of one's nose, the ear lobes and hands acted as sensors to indicate the severity of the cold. One could battle the elements with confidence but deciphering the cold irrationality of the staff ordering the move of two troops was our immediate concern, as we strolled towards Chiefy's tank. The squadron commander's tank was at a considerable distance, as it had not redeployed in the morning. His crew, having folded the tank shelter, was busy tying it onto the turret. This was the third time that orders for deployment were changed in the last 24 hours. Chiefy read the message received, as also briefed about the reports by patrols during the night. He tried speaking with Digby on the radio but could not get a response. He was of the view that this message needed confirmation on the command channel and not left to be passed on by the staff. He was right in this assessment and we agreed wholeheartedly. He advised us to return to our troops and prepare to delink once he received confirmatory orders from the RHQ. We started our journey back but not before borrowing some cigarettes from Chiefy.

Our walk back was more leisurely as it would be quite some time before anybody would be able to clarify orders. The cold winter morning and poor visibility made it difficult to get a clear picture of where we were or the layout of the defences the ground troops had taken or even the deployment of the tank troops. A blinkered view of the battlefield made one apprehensive of the perfidy of nature. Inability to see the layout of own defences or deployment of tanks made us a little stressed. We found Risaldar Chakraborty shaving by the side of his tank. Behind the tank, his crew was busy brewing tea on a kerosene stove, standard equipment purchased by tank crews, as it was not part of the tote items issued by the ordnance depots. Tea keeps soldiers alert and positive through the day. Tank crews are adept and capable of producing the brew even in the midst of battle, while the infantryman can treat you to this elixir while in the line of march. From the nearby trench, a tall handsome Sikh of the infantry, carrying some more tea, appeared. The two units had 'married up' and were now functioning as part of the same combat force to share the benefits of hospitality. Some light-hearted banter followed when in response to a question, the infantry man claimed that he would never ask for a tank ride ever again as it was back-breaking. He appeared a little unhappy that the company commander had kept everybody digging weapon pits and trenches all through the night and now the CO had asked the company to change the location. The atmosphere was still peaceful and serene and there seemed no cause for undue alarm. Perhaps the mysterious lights that we had noticed did not amount to much.

I had pulled a few puffs of my cigarette and taken a couple of sips of piping hot tea when all of a sudden loud, ear-shattering explosion disturbed the silence, peace, and the friendly chatter. The source of this loud explosion was obviously close to our position. The first reaction was that some overzealous tank gunners had by mistake fired a round at some suspicious looking target, or possibly, it was a case of jaded nerves. While I was still swearing at this nameless busybody, I turned around to see Speedy Sidhu, who rightly had sprinted off towards his tank. With slow deliberate steps, I walked over to the side of my tank and placed the now, half-full glass of tea on the tank deck and, in the same motion, mounted the tank. I was still adjusting the neck strap of my headgear when I heard a snippet of a garbled message being passed. The first words that penetrated my ears were, 'Enemy tanks approaching', followed by the sound of tank shells being fired. I surveyed the area in front, and sure enough, at a distance of approximately 300 yards, some hazy movement of enemy tanks was discernible through the cloud of mist and fog. The enemy tanks continued to advance and were now coming out of the fog with their guns blazing; spelling death and disaster for everything that came across their way. The smell of cordite hung heavy in the air with red balls of fire flying all around. 'See that big one, there, that bastard, get him quickly,' I heard myself telling the gunner over the intercom. The crew had reacted with lightning speed and were now performing crew drills with robotic precision to fire off a salvo of three successive rounds. The terrible swoosh of the gun and the heavy recoil, along with the dust and fumes, made it impossible to see what was happening in front. Then, suddenly, the voice of gunner came up saying, 'I've got that bastard Sir, I've got him.' Sure enough, an enemy tank had stopped dead in its tracks. The crew was bailing out in a flurry of activity as the tank was on fire. For full effect, as also to signify that the tank was his kill, the gunner let go another shot blowing the dismounted crew sky high to smithereens.

Pandemonium and chaos on the radio made it difficult to understand the battle scene or make an estimate of the likely strength or attack plan of the enemy during the first few minutes of the battle. Every tank commander, having heard the first shot, would have reacted in the same manner and on spotting or suspecting tank movement, imagined that the attack was directed at him. This heightened and intense phase of uncontrolled and nervous activity petered out, giving way to a trained response under effective command and control, as practised during training. The transition time between these two determines the success or failure of the battle. Battle hardened veterans and well-trained troops are conditioned to quickly overcome 'the fog of battle' and perform as a well-coordinated and effective team under a responsive leadership.

The mayhem of tank commanders and crews issuing fire orders, and directions using phrases like 'change position', 'traverse', 'corrections', 'firing now', 'destroyed', were all coming up continuously on the air. It was difficult to establish what exactly was happening or even who was winning this fast-moving tank battle when suddenly I recognized Speedy's voice claiming, 'One enemy tank destroyed', and then another one too, a voice claiming 'Ek tank barbad kar diya saab.' While listening to all this on the squadron radio net, I was also directing Gunner Harish, 'Reference last kill, 2 o'clock, tank.' Even while I was giving the orders, I could see the gun barrel turning in the direction indicated. While giving the final elevation movement to the gun to ensure greater hit accuracy, I heard Harish announce, 'Firing now.' In the intense gripping excitement of the battlefield, Harish had fired off the armour piercing tracer shell even as I was yelling the final command, 'Fire', into the intercom. In spite of the obscuration and smoke, I could see the tracer flying off the tank barrel and homing onto the target. A puff of smoke followed by the tank being engulfed by orange flames leaping out towards the sky. The jubilant claim by Harish, '*Tank barbad kar diya*', deserved my full-throated '*Shabash*'. The radio net was simultaneously announcing claims of tank kills by two other tank commanders. Were these claims referring to the same tank kills or different ones was less important. Each could bask in the glory of tank kills and joint success. Shibe Lal was ready with the next round loaded in the gun chamber and the one to follow up in his lap, a broad smile on his face. The driver expressed his happiness in his native Haryanvi, laced with a few choice expletives. Ramphal, his foot on the clutch and gear engaged was ready to change positions before the enemy tanks could target their guns by placing us under the cross-wires, ready to take a shot. With a sudden jerk, the tank lurched forward. While en route to the new tank position, Shibe Lal and Harish had counted at least four tanks burning bright in the middle of the battlefield. While sporadic firing by the tanks continued, it was evident that the initial wave of the enemy tank assault had stopped dead in its tracks.

The initial chaos on the air was now over and a semblance of radio discipline and procedure returned. The squadron, having overcome the initial shock, had quickly recovered this intrinsic balance, as was evident from the radio discipline. Messages from the RHQ had also started pouring in. As per reports filed by me and count maintained by Inder, five tanks were confirmed as destroyed, based on radio messages picked up over the network by RHQ. Digby had been repeatedly trying to speak with Chiefy but there was no response from the tank. The Rover operator could not give Chiefy's location, as he did not have a map nor was he in a position to move forward and establish contact with Chiefy as the tank battle was in progress. It sometimes happens that a tank station cannot communicate because of the effect of screening or low antenna output. I asked Ramparikshan, who was closest to Chiefy's location, to contact him and ask him to communicate with RHQ at the earliest.

Observation of the battlefield directly in front of the area where the tank crews had destroyed the enemy tank had become impossible due to obscuration and smoke. Heavy artillery shelling resulted in clouds of the smoke and dust they left behind, taking with them sometimes a limb or a life. During gunnery training, we had learnt that the enemy would easily pick up a tank target which had opened fire. It was practical wisdom to change location after firing the second round so as not to become a sitting duck. As we had engaged another target, I directed the driver Ramphal to a small bump in the ground 100 yards ahead as our fresh hull down position. The driver released the clutch and the tank slid backwords, knocking down overhanging branches and foliage. There was a tall *khaji* tree directly behind which made further movement impossible. 'Advance, right stick, right, reverse now quickly, left stick, left, left, advance, full right, take position in grove 100 yards.' Ramphal did his best to follow the rapid chain of orders. Whether enemy tanks had picked up our location due to movement or fire will never be known but two rounds in quick succession burst right in front of our tank, forming two large craters, throwing up dust and splinters on the tank and crew. A third shell went directly over our heads and struck the tree directly behind, splitting it into neat halves. Whoever the bastard was, he had us zeroed! Surely, the next round would seal our fate. 'Gunner, traverse left, 600, steady, on. Fire!' I waited long enough for the gunner to press the electric trigger before repeating 'Fire, Fire'. Finding no response, I yelled again, 'Use mechanical trigger but for goodness sake, fire.' While I was still giving this command, I found the enemy tank stagger and suddenly stop. Dense smoke from the turret of the tank was a sure indicator that needed no confirmation that it had been hit. Three other tanks of the squadron, covering my movement to the new hull down position, had noticed the gun flash of the enemy tank which had fired and promptly pumped it with high explosive anti-tank ammunition. The cupola of the enemy tank did not open and one could safely assume that the bodies of enemy crews were by now roasting in the fire as the tank burst into flames. This had been a narrow escape for us!

I peeped into the fighting compartment to see my gunner Harish Chandra and the loader/operator Shibe Lal bent over trying to press the breach block hand lever down to eject position as the heat round had jammed inside the gun chamber. During training, an eventuality such as this was visualized and a misfire drill evolved. Our problems, however, were more complex for even with the repeated use of tool extracting, the round lay jammed inside the chamber. Who could imagine a situation worse than this for the tank crew? At that point of time, I could not imagine anything worse ever happening. The crew now redoubled their efforts to extricate the jammed round with renewed vigour, with some supporting help from Saighal, our artillery observation post officer, travelling on the tank.

The unrelenting jammed round was cranking my mind, searching for a possible solution. My own knowledge of the gun mechanism as also handling of defective Russian tank ammunition turned useless as the only answer lay in the practical extraction. The type of trauma and nervousness the crew were undergoing was difficult to comprehend, as it is easier firing a gun than repairing one in the face of the enemy. As the squadron 2IC also performs the duties of operating the rear link, I continued to communicate with RHQ whose queries came in torrents. One sometimes got the feeling that the bigger battle for survival was perhaps going on at the divisional and regimental levels. The thought that crossed my mind and which I shared with the crew was an anecdote from the book Defeat into Victory where, when questioned by retreating troops as to what could be worse than the defeat suffered in Burma, Gen Slim had replied, 'It could be raining.' Rain under the circumstances would have brought relief to our present despair. Could there be anything worse? It now dawned on me that the same defect in the initial phase of the tank vs tank battle would have left us facing the enemy with a disabled gun. Surely, nothing could be worse.

The will of the Almighty can throw up challenges to test your strength, fortitude, wisdom, sagacity, and courage. In spite of all this, you can falter unless the supernatural provides divine intervention. Providence had set the stage for living through one such experience. As per the radiotelephony procedure, the control station on the radio net identifies itself by using the call sign of the called station. Something urgent must have developed as the call now coming in identified itself by taking my call sign:

'Delta 40 message for you. Over.'

'Delta 40 for Delta. OK. Over.'

I had correctly identified the voice of Lance Dafadar Daneshwar Nath, the gunner in Chiefy's tank crew. I waited anxiously to hear what Chiefy had to say. There appeared an unusually long pause before Daneshwar's voice, more solemn and sorrowful, came up on the blower again.

'Delta 40: Saab ab aur nahin hain. Over.'

('Delta 40: Sqn Cdr is no more. Over.')

I waited for the implication of this message to sink in. Daneshwar Nath was a talented Assamese who was extremely professional and had received outstanding grades on all his courses of instruction. He was meticulous and responsible. Notwithstanding his qualifications, the message still sounded absurd. The NCO was unable to provide the desired clarity and did not sound his confident self. His subdued tone and long pause were pointers of some serious development—a sinking feeling that a major calamity had occurred during the tank battle, which was still raging and had perhaps reached a critical stage. I refused to believe the obvious—no, this could not be possible. It was more likely that Chiefy was injured and needed help. There was no means of finding out except the radio, so I asked Daneshwar to repeat his message.

'Delta 40 for Delta: Repeat, I say repeat your message. Over.'

'Delta 40: I say again, Major *Saab ab aur nahin hain.* (Sir is no more.) Over.'

It was one of those messages, which you could not acknowledge without feeling the pangs of sorrow and personal loss.

For the next few moments, I forgot all about my gun, which was still out of action. I had pushed my headset further back as if to signify my disbelief at this message. Everybody in the squadron must have heard this message and regretted having heard it. Besides, this was the first death reported on the radio.

Each one of the crew must have reacted to the loss of his commander by a display of inaction, identical to my own, for it dawned on me that the squadron had suddenly stopped engagement with the enemy. This was the most critical moment for the enemy tanks were still in the vicinity. In a sense, I felt guilty at my inaction for not accepting immediate responsibility and reacting quickly under this grave situation, which might spell disaster for everybody. Somebody still had to lead and coordinate the actions of the squadron for the total annihilation of the enemy. Somebody still had to take decisions, to guide the troops, and tell them what to do and do it well. I could not let down my comrades in a crisis. I still had to acknowledge the last message received and steel myself to execute the higher levels of responsibility thrust on me by fate.

'Delta 40 for Delta: Roger. Proceed to regimental aid post forthwith and report. Over.'

'Delta for Delta 40: Wilco, repeat, Wilco, Out.'

'Delta 40 for all stations Delta: I am assuming control repeat assuming control, Roger so far. Over.'

'Delta 1: Roger. Over.' 'Delta 2: Roger. Over.' 'Delta 3: Roger. Over.' 'Delta 4: Roger. Over.'

'Delta 40: For all stations Delta, I have assumed control. Out.'

Precious moments had passed when I heard myself telling LD Daneshwar Nath, Chiefy's operator, that I had understood his message. The orders for him were to withdraw to the position occupied during the night and from there proceed to the Regimental Aid Post (RAP). I then informed all that in view of what had happened, I was assuming command. The message by itself would not have amounted to much but it had the necessary psychological impact to break off the phase of inactivity. I passed this message with little or no hesitation. I motivated myself into believing that destiny had entrusted me with a responsibility, which I must now execute with diligence and dedication.

Having passed the message, my first reaction was to pull out a packet of cigarettes and light up one of those lung busters. I offered Saighal, the artillery OP officer, one from the half packet I had borrowed from Chiefy the same morning, but he declined. Years ago, during commando training, our instructor had advised us that, faced with an adverse situation, one should sit back, relax, and think through the problem coolly. I was sitting on the turret of my tank watching the operator and gunner still engaged in removing the jammed round. Taking a long drag at my cigarette, I told them to dismount and use the long cleaning rod from the muzzle end and force the projectile out. The projectile was now lying halfway across the open breach block, half displaced but still unrelenting. With renewed vigour, all four flexed their muscles and hammered away until finally the projectile and the brass case ejected. With all the hammering and pounding delivered to this rebellious specimen, we expected acquiescence of the gunnery dictum 'ek gola ek dushman' (One round, one enemy), from the projectile in its burial state!

I got in touch with the troop leaders so that I had a complete picture of the battlefield. From their reports, it became clear that four to five enemy tanks stood destroyed. Approximately half the squadron was reported still active but withdrawn further towards the road axis opposite our squadron location. Having got into a battle position, my gunner fired off two rounds to reassure us that we were back in business. Though the visibility had improved, the likelihood of spotting tank targets was bleak, as enemy tanks had withdrawn into the khaji groves more than 1,000 yards from our location.

Digby called to ascertain the enemy situation, saying that his repeated attempts to contact Chiefy had gone unanswered, resulting in his now bad temper. I informed him that a squadron of enemy Chaffee tanks had assaulted our position. Out of the first wave of seven tanks, five or six had definitely been destroyed. Troops had reported heavy movement of infantry. Based on the reports of troop concentration, reported last night, it appeared we were under the well-planned, coordinated attack of the enemy. I then explained the circumstances under which I had assumed control. His radio reception was weak due to which he asked for frequent repetitions.

'Delta for Delta 40: Where is Chiefy? Over.'

'Delta 40 for Delta: He has kicked the bucket. Over.'

'Delta for Delta 40: What bloody nonsense are you speaking? Speak clearly. Over.'

'Delta 40 for Delta: I say again, he has kicked the bucket. Killed, repeat, killed in action. Over.'

I waited for some time thinking that Digby may come up on the air again. The silence continued. It was evident that the message had finally sunk in that Chiefy would never come up on the air again.

The martyrdom and sacrifice of Maj Daljit Singh Narag, killed in the tank versus tank battle at Garibpur on 21 November 1971, while in command of C Squadron, 45 Cavalry, would be written in golden letters in the regimental history. A grateful nation would soon recognize the exemplary courage and dedication of the officer and the Rashtrapati would decorate the outstanding officer with the nation's second highest gallantry award, the Mahavir Chakra, posthumously.

Movement of enemy tanks, earlier reported by Speedy was confirmed by reports of the other tank commanders also. A fresh look at the map and knowledge of the terrain and enemy deployments gave us a fair assessment that the eastern flank was the more threatened one. I informed Col R.K. Singh of my decision to outflank the enemy located in the grove further to the east such that I could get the enemy broadside in case they attacked. As part of coordination, it was essential that the troops be kept informed of their own tank movements so that the likelihood of fire from friendly forces could be eliminated. I decided on a quick manoeuvre:

'Delta 40 for Delta 1 and Delta 3: Orders. Over.'

'Delta 1: OK. Over.'

'Delta 3: OK. Over.'

'Delta 3: Outflank enemy position and deploy northeast, 1000 yards of his location. Delta 1: Advance figures 500 due east to provide covering fire. Delta 3 to lead. Over.'

The next message heard on the radio was from Speedy:

'Delta 40 for Delta 3: Wilco, out.' 'All stations Delta 3 follow me, out'. Speedy, forever alert and agile, was the first one off the block, his transmission reflecting the very spirit of the cavalry: 'Follow me'. The other troop leader took a little time to align himself to the new task. Speedy had commenced his outflanking movement but was followed by only one tank of his troop. His repeated attempts to get his third tank on the air had failed. It was important that these tanks get into position at the earliest as a cloud of smoke and dust was visible above the tree line, confirming enemy movement.

Ramparikshan, the troop leader, and Gogoi, his other tank commander, had reached the selected tank positions to my west. As we had been leapfrogging forward from one fire position to another, this was an automatic signal for Ramphal to engage the gear and put the tank into motion and quickly move into the pre-selected tank position about 70 yards ahead. My tank had covered more than half the distance to the next bound when four Chaffee tanks leapt out from amongst the bushes about 250 yards in front of our location.

Neither had realized how close they had come due to the limited visibility, undergrowth, and foliage. Both were denied the benefit of observation and detection, now resulting in complete surprise in close proximity of the enemy tanks. Tank to tank engagements since World War II had taken place over much greater distances. Our tactical doctrines had not visualized combat situations wherein armoured fighting vehicles would lock horns in close quarter battles. The situation was more like the Wild West movies where in a one street town, the mounted cowboys of the rival gang arrive outside the local watering hole to encounter each other. Not unlike the movies, the winner is the person who can shoot from the hip and leave the talking for much later. The Chaffee tanks, advancing like four Sumo wrestlers, broke into a sprint, discarding their battle formation. Watching them coming closer, I ordered my driver to turn left and stop. In the same breath, I yelled into the intercom, 'Enemy tank in front, fire, FIRE.' My eyes were transfixed on the enemy tank, which was speeding menacingly towards my position. The enemy tank which I had spotted earlier traversing the gun to target my tank, was now depressing the barrel to provide final correction before firing. It was evident that a moment later the enemy gunner would press the firing switch, scoring a bull's eye. Being at the receiving end, I could feel the air gushing out from my lungs. The thought that I had just looked through the muzzle end of an enemy gun levelled directly at me left my mouth agape. The enemy tanks were still on the move and now dangerously close. The downward movement of the gun had stopped. I could visualize the gunner having got us within his aiming arrow, awaiting the final order of 'fire' from his commander.

My own gunner, involved in a similar activity, had been given the order 'Fire', which I now repeated, 'Zero range fire; FIRE!' at decibel levels harmful to his tympanum. Whether this fire order would go down as 'the famous last words of a posthumous soldier' in regimental history now depended on providence, as also which gunner could press his trigger first. Suddenly, there was a deafening sound as two distinct near simultaneous blasts rent the air. My own tank carried out a convulsive movement and for one breathless moment, the thought that 'this was the end' flashed through my mind and with that I closed my eyes.

I do not recall how long I was possessed by this mental frenzy or how long it took for the mind to register the involuntary closure of the eyes to escape the danger perceived by the senses. The acrid smell of rubber burning soon reached my nostrils. Surely, my tank must be on fire! As if to confirm it, I peeped through my eyes. A cloud of heavy smoke and dust rose in front of me. I looked around but there was no fire. Slowly the realization came that I was still standing on my legs. I looked down and found both the gunner and loader in their places. A gentle breeze soon carried over the smoke and dust that still hung in the air. Not more than thirty yards away stood the Chaffee—burning. I heaved a deep sigh of relief and in the process, provided the life-saving oxygen to my lungs. I stretched my hand in relief and rubbed my eyes to ensure that what I was seeing was real and not a mirage. A feeling of joy, happiness and relief swept over me as I felt my taut nerves relaxing once again. A faint glimmer of a smile spread over my face as I congratulated my gunner for his excellent shooting. Just then, the driver of the enemy tank opened his cupola and straightened himself on the deck of his tank. For a fleeting moment, he stood there, providing an attractive target to my gunner who had him centred on the cross mark, thumbs carefully resting on the electrical trigger, urging me to let him fire a machine gun burst. I don't think it was a sense of pity or mercy that prevented me from uttering the word 'fire'. Perhaps it was gratitude, signifying celebration of life. I knew fully well that the figure looming large on the deck of the tank, now in the process of jumping to the far side, had no hope of survival for at that moment, his life was in my hands. I let the opportunity pass for I was still celebrating the experience of having survived.

The tactical advantage of 'one leg on the ground' was critical to the outcome of this encounter. Ramparikshan's and Gogoi's tanks were already stationary when the Chaffees broke through the hedge line to appear in front of them. The time taken for loading, aiming, and firing from a static tank and the accuracy achieved, gave no chance of survival to the enemy tanks, possibly still in motion. No sooner had they come into view that both R.P. Singh and Gogoi opened fire with a simultaneous announcement of 'one tank destroyed'. I looked in the direction from where the Chaffee had burst out of the bushes. Two more tanks were ablaze while the slow curling smoke was coming out from the third. Not far off lay one of their crew members, one arm blown off and body badly mangled. The body, covered with what must have been a black dungaree, badly soiled by mud and blood, was on fire. I turned my eyes back to the tank lying nearest to us. A neat round hole could be seen in the middle of the turret. As the petrol spread, the tank turned into a bonfire. Tongues of flame leapt skywards and enveloped the turret with bright red flames. The heat was becoming difficult to bear as the tank destroyed by my gunner had come to rest 30 yards from our location. The driver now put the tank in reverse gear and took the right stick to move to a different position.

While still on the move to the new location, I checked on the progress being made by Speedy. He had moved along the periphery of the grove by fire and got to the appointed place in the quickest possible time. As soon as he had moved off to the first bound and had taken up position, one of the enemy tanks fired at him. Having spotted the gun flash, he engaged the target, destroying it in the first round. His two tanks were moving forward to join him when the enemy knocked out one of them. After this, there was a slight hesitation on the part of the other commander to move forward. During this period, Speedy's tank lay exposed to the enemy's fire. While he was still entreating the commander to get a move on, an armour piercing shell penetrated the turret of his tank, killing the gunner instantaneously. Speedy himself, though injured, had a miraculous escape. The shell, after penetrating the gunner's chest, passed through between his legs, fortunately, leaving his testicles aside. Splinters and small pieces of shrapnel struck him on the inside of both his thighs and buttocks. After ordering the crew to bail out, he slid over the side of the tank and from there onwards, crawled to a position directly in front of our own defences where, from loss of blood and fatigue, he collapsed. One of the Sikh NCOs of the infantry, who till then was suspicious of this movement in front of his position as that of the enemy, recognized the faint outline of a turban on his head. Having identified him, he ordered a local ceasefire by his platoon and himself went forward to bring Speedy into the comparative security of his shelter, from where he was moved to the regimental aid post.

Chakraborty who had, before the outbreak of the battle, offered us a steaming cup of tea, now sprung a big surprise. He had been exercising good command and effective control as the firebase of the squadron. While watching the tank engagement in which I was involved, Chakraborty had spotted one of the enemy tank crew slide off the destroyed tank and crawl towards a nearby hedge. Taking the assistance of two infantrymen and his operator with an ANPRC-25 radio set, he dismounted from his tank and led a sortie to capture his prey who was apparently unarmed. Across in the adjoining bamboo clump, he chanced upon an assembly area of an infantry battalion preparing to launch an attack. Chakraborty directed his tanks to spray the area with MMG fire and informed the OP officer for intense shelling based on the grid reference provided. The dispirited enemy infantry, which had formed up in that grove to attack suddenly, took to their heels as they saw the tanks approaching. This was a harmless enough target so the tanks sprayed the compete area with machine gunfire.

Chakraborty arrived at the Squadron Headquarters (SHQ) accompanied by an infantry officer and a couple of soldiers. In their midst, stood a very crestfallen and dishevelled man, looking forlorn and lost. My interest in this man was enhanced when I spotted his black overalls, usually worn by the armoured corps. He belonged to 3 Independent Armoured Squadron of Pakistan. The squadron less two troops was to attack our position while the remaining two were to provide fire support. They were told that only a weak infantry battalion supported by a troop of tanks held the position. Out of curiosity, I asked him to point out his tank on the battlefield. He pointed at the tank destroyed by my crew at 30 metres. He confirmed that he was the driver of the ill-fated tank. Before they realised what was happening, the two leading tanks had become bonfires, still burning bright. While his tank commander had repeatedly asked him to stop, he felt that safety lay in flight. An attempt by his gunner to score a direct hit stood deranged as the driver panicked and refused to stop. The Chaffee tank does not have a stabilised gun, as such the gunner had little chance to score a hit. The cowardly act on the part of the driver had provided us the opportunity to fight and live another day. Further proof was evident in the manner in which the driver now denounced his officers. Cowardly or not, his decision had prolonged our lives. During this debrief, he received good treatment and was taken aback when tea and refreshments were offered to him. Somehow, the impression I developed from this experience was that the Pakistani officers do not understand that loyalty is a two-way commitment. This driver had entered the battlefield hungry for two days and still unsure if this was war or an exercise or part of internal security duties.

It was now becoming evident that the backbone of the armour assault had been broken. Radio transmission within the squadron had dropped to the barest minimum. Digby came up on the air again to inform that he had dispatched a troop to reinforce our location against enemy counter-attacks. Maintenance, rest, repair and recuperation would have to wait till the enemy was completely destroyed.

This done, I moved off to the Battalion Headquarters. Speedy was amongst the first I met at the RAP. He was lying on a stretcher, a white sheet covering his legs. On seeing me approach, he broke into a smile of welcome. Only a few hours ago, we had been standing together, chatting merrily and sipping tea. The picture of Speedy rushing to mount his tank, his sharp and clear radio messages, his cheerful voice, his rapid reaction when ordered to outflank surged in my mind. He explained that having destroyed one tank, they were targeting a second when their tank made a convulsive movement. The next instant, he felt as if somebody had fired a buckshot on the inside of his thighs, resulting in intense pain and his legs on fire. Panic overtook him as the precious symbols of his manhood hung in the same region. Though his legs were beginning to buckle, it did not deter him from conducting an immediate survey. As he loosened his grip on the tank turret to lower his hand towards his crotch, he realized that he had blood on his trousers. Suddenly, he felt weak and dizzy, darkness descending around him. He recovered from this blackout to find himself atop his lifeless gunner who had a large gaping hole in the middle of his chest. The tank driver had crawled into the fighting compartment and was now helping Speedy get back on his legs. Speedy finally pulled himself out of the tank, then slid over the sloping turret and hull to drop off on the far side, away from the enemy view. The JCO, after giving him a swig from the water bottle, got busy looking for the first-aid kit when Speedy found the strength to complete the aborted personal survey, feeling relieved, if not delighted, that 'his precious marbles' were intact. As he would describe weeks later, after he returned from hospital, the prospect of 'uncle being addressed as aunty' was indeed very real and horrifying. He would tell friends, over a drink, jokingly, that it was not Army training but his genes that had saved him. He would point towards one of the youngsters 2–3 inches shorter than his 6'1" frame and proudly ask a riddle, 'What would you call an uncle who had no balls?' Other than the immediate victim, tasked to solve the puzzle, all would have a hearty laugh and yell in unison, 'Aunty, of course!'

The doctor attached to 14 Punjab, Capt HC Vishwakarma, had a cheerful disposition. One could see him moving from stretcher to stretcher like a man possessed. As the RMO, he was responsible for proper first aid, documentation, and evacuation of the casualties. With so many injured lying around, I realized that identification was becoming a problem as most were covered in white sheets or bandages. An NCO of the squadron, whose wound needed only first aid and was categorized as 'walking wounded' by the medical fraternity, volunteered to accompany me. One tank gunner, S.K. Baro, an Assamese boy, had received severe body burns and had a point 30 Browning bullet embedded under his collarbone. Another young Bengali boy called Sinha had lost his sight due to the blinding flash. Pain and agony could be seen writ large on the faces of these young soldiers. Another casualty was R.K. Pegu, placed on the seriously injured list. Invariably there would be a message from the soldier, 'meri chinta na karen' (please do not worry about me) to be conveyed to his leader. Sowars Dharam Pal and Om Prakash had been killed. Their bodies had to be recovered for cremation.

The sound of gunfire and small arms fire continued unabated. I was planning to move away from the RAP when I noticed patients being transferred from their now messy stretchers into ambulances. I stood alongside, adding a word of reassurance or comfort, sometimes shaking a hand or giving a friendly pat on the back, wishing them speedy recovery. Just as one of the ambulances was about to drive off, Dafadar Rameshwar, one of the tank commanders, his face a picture of excruciating pain, suddenly caught hold of my hand, and with a tight, forced, smile asked me, 'Did I do all right, Sir?' It's funny how many of them would ask you this question. Especially the good ones who had done the task assigned to them to the best of their ability. It was as if an endorsement of it was in some ways, very important in their lives. 'Of course, you did well. Well done! Shabash!' A short while later, the ambulance drove off. Dafadar Rameshwar never returned to the squadron.

At the RAP, I had made enquiries regarding Chiefy from the doctor. I was quite distressed to learn that he had heard nothing about this casualty. Since the start of the tank battle, I had not seen Chiefy myself. It did not appear logical, for nearly six hours had passed since the message of his death was transmitted by his gunner, Dhaneshwar. I could find no justification for the delay. The possibility of the tank having been damaged or destroyed while on the way to the RAP could not be ruled out. I moved in the direction of my tank, to rejoin my crew.

My tank was still standing in a small *khaji* grove behind the RAP. To get rid of all the dark thoughts that were now entering my mind regarding the fate of Chiefy's tank, I directed Shibe Lal and Harish Chandra to contact Chiefy's tank crew or the squadron rover. However, no news came. The tank battle had already died down and except for sporadic fire, no major disturbance had taken place during this period of reorganization. Suddenly, a scary thought flashed in my mind, how did I know that he was dead? Like others on the radio net, I too had heard the message, responded, directed the crew to move to the RAP. I had not seen the body. Where was the tank crew? I had to get my hands on this crew. Muddled up, a little anxious, assured that no major blunder could have taken place, I yelled across to the operator, 'Trace that blessed tank crew and that bastard Upadhya, not a single message from him throughout the battle.' Immersed in these thoughts, I mounted the tank to convey my anger personally. Desperation and anxiety were not going to help me establish contact. I lit up another lung buster to release the mounting doubts within.

The operator had his ears glued to the radio so that he could keep me informed of any important transmission. Looking at his tired face, I asked him to increase the volume, then remove the headphones and hang these against the turret, midway between us, so that we could simultaneously hear the radio transmission.

The constant mush of the radio and steady flow of transmissions could be exhausting for the operator. He responded with a tired grin at the understanding gesture. A couple of minutes must have ticked away, when a booming explosion took place near the tank. It sounded too close for comfort. Dust, debris, smoke was all over us. 'Some asshole with a rocket launcher has attempted to knock out our tank.' The instinct for survival overtakes all thoughts of fear, danger, and death in such moments. The spontaneous reaction to this untimely threat to life and limb was to get out of the line of fire to save our pretty skins. The operator must have sensed the situation at nearly the same time. Instinctively, both of us jumped, not inside the tank, but off the tank, to seek shelter away from the direction from which the blast had delivered the shock waves. We hit the ground as the sound of another blast penetrated our eardrums. As we crawled into the relative security of the trench occupied by a Sikh soldier, he let off a long burst from his LMG announcing the arrival of dismounted cavalry. It took time to catch our breath. It had been a close shave with danger. One learns very fast when the bullets start flying. What good was a man, after all, who was very brave and very dead? One had to discriminate between an opportunity, which demanded bold offensive action, and discretion, against taking an uncalculated risk.

No sooner had we crawled into the trench, the Sikh soldier using the authority of his three stripes, cursed the enemy, using the choicest Punjabi expletives, 'Mother fucking son of a gun had fired his 106 RCL gun on the tank', 'lucky saabji, saabji very lucky', 'he must be changing position before firing next round as per drill'.

The intrepid enemy RCL gunner appeared to be merciless in his determination to destroy my tank—his chosen target. The next round from the RCL pierced a *khaji* tree standing alongside the tank, the upper half of the tree trunk now lying against the tank. The Sikh Havildar was on the radio, speaking to his platoon commander when, below the cloud of rising smoke and dust, we spotted two figures in black dungarees. Spontaneously, I looked into Shibe Lal's eyes who had read my thoughts: let us make a dash to the tank. Like desperados, caught in the crossfire, we swung into motion, each aware of the danger hanging in the air, rushing towards the tank which had now assumed our collective identity. Fear of the tank's destruction had united us in thought and action without a single word spoken. The crew was moving at lightning speed, determined to mount the tank and deliver itself from the humiliation of destruction, even at the risk of certain death. Each one had visualized that survival was dependent on speed to reach the tank, mount, fire, and move with clockwork precision before the RCL could align the cross-wire of his gun sight on the tank and press the trigger. No sooner had the gunner landed on his seat that he started depressing and aligning the gun in the rough direction of the RCL. The operator, who is also required to perform the duties of the loader in the tank, removed an HE round from the ammunition bin and after inserting it into the chamber, readied himself with a fresh one, just in case the requirement for the second one arose. While this was in progress, the driver started up the tank and engaged his gears, clutch pedal depressed for release as soon as he heard the sound of our gunfire. This complete action could not have taken us more than a few seconds but the looming fear of sure death made it seem unbelievably long. While waiting to hear the word 'loaded' from the operator, I had switched on the radio set and adjusted my headgear, at the same time, straining my eyes to search for the most likely trouble spot in front. I was so anxious to get over all this that I did not even feel it necessary to await the operator's announcement of 'round loaded', as I watched every minute movement of the crew inside. At the command of 'fire', the gunner pressed the electrical trigger and the same moment, the tank was in motion. We learnt subsequently that the arrival of ambulances and other vehicles of the F1 echelon had attracted the attention of the enemy. An unrelenting enemy, in spite of a bloody nose, had planned a small, audacious but unsuccessful raid over the RAP by a detachment of RCLs and MMG of the Reconnaissance and Support Company.

The search for the squadron commander's tank had ended. Standing before me was the gunner, LD Dhaneshwar, with streaks of dried blood clinging on to his black dungaree, along with the crew, looking crestfallen and dispirited. He reported that soon after Speedy and I returned, after meeting the squadron commander, the position of the tank was readjusted. Chiefy later mounted his tank to establish communication with Digby regarding the impending move of two tank troops. Some minutes must have passed before they heard the sound of gunfire. The initial reaction was that it could be a case of accidental fire when suddenly the sounds of artillery and tank guns firing were heard. Chiefy ordered his tank to move forward as heavy fog restricted visibility. While on the move, Chiefy spotted an enemy tank and gave fire orders. The first round fired was an HE round, preloaded in the gun chamber as per established drill. The next round, an armour-piercing projectile fired by Chiefy's tank, found its target but ricocheted off the enemy tank turret. He then fired a heat round. This found the target, as confirmed by the smoke billowing out from the enemy tank immediately after. With joy and excitement, Chiefy congratulated the gunner on the intercom by repeating, '*Shabash, Maro, Maro.* (Good job! Kill, kill!)' In that moment of exultation, he pressed the radio net switch, resulting in this transmission being heard by the complete radio network. Between the gunner and the loader, the next shell had been loaded while Chiefy was giving orders to traverse the gun, scanning the battlefield through his binoculars for a fresh target. 'Traverse left, reference last kills 11 O' clock, tank.' The gunner had got the target on his gun sight and was about to apply the fine correction by elevating the gun barrel while simultaneously tracking the moving target, to announce 'on target firing now', his thumb on the electrical trigger, itching to receive the final command 'fire' when he suddenly he felt a heavy weight on his shoulders and back. Involuntarily, he lifted his left hand and panicked at the touch of warm blood. The same instant, he yelled across to the operator but did not get an immediate response. Daneshwar reluctantly lifted his right hand from the trigger to reach out to the loader, who quickly replaced the shell held in his lap into the ammunition bin. The driver meanwhile crawled through the driver's compartment to reach the other crew members. Daneshwar directed him to return and position himself over the commander's cupola and help lift Chiefy. It must have been a herculean effort for the three to place Chiefy between the engine compartment and the ammunition bay. While a shooting war was raging outside this tank, the crew was involved in a heart-breaking battle inside the tank. They felt his pulse and heartbeat to see if there were any sign of life but alas! Chiefy had been killed in action by the MMG burst which hit his exposed upper torso. His last words were still ringing in the ears of his command 'Shabash, Maro, Maro!'

The regiment had paid a heavy price for a local modification carried out to facilitate induction of a fourth crew member into a tank designed for a crew of three only. Armoured regiments traditionally had a crew consisting of a driver, gunner, loader/operator, and a commander, all housed within the tank. Using the regimental carpenter, 45 Cavalry had voluntarily modified the gunner's seat, whereby, the tank commander, having lost his rightful seat inside the tank, could now stand on top of it with his torso exposed to small arms fire. The customized seat, due to the induction of additional crew, had the disadvantage that during shelling, air attacks, or flotation, the commander's cupola perforce had to be kept open, as the restricted space inside the tank would not accommodate all four crew members. All the tank commanders of this PT-76 Regiment fought the war standing upright, with torso and head exposed to small arms fire and shelling, whereas the rest of the crew enjoyed the protection against small arms fire provided by the armour plating of the tank.

LD Dhaneshwar having received radio orders to pull back and take the tank to the RAP for first aid, shared this order with the crew. Not being aware of the RAP's location and with the battle raging at high pitch, they decided not to pull back but continued to engage the enemy. In so doing, they paid the highest tribute to their late squadron commander. After all, these crew members were selected for their loyalty, steadfastness, and courage—qualities he himself displayed throughout his life. The other cause for inaction was the need for additional hands for removing the body from the turret compartment. The manifold difficulties due to the restricted space and the awkward position in which the body was lying made this a difficult task. I mounted Chiefy's tank to understand the explanation provided by the crew, as also assess for myself the effort required for extricating the body. Blood splashed across the gun controls and on the inside of the commander's cupola. Small, dried flakes were visible on the headgear and radio set. The body lay in a heap between the swivel seats of the gunner and loader, directly below the gun chamber. Rigor mortis had set in and the pool of blood spread across the tank floor. It was a ghastly site, borne in stoic silence by the crew. The crew had lived through a nightmare of watching their commander, dropping dead inside while a tank battle was raging outside, petrified, shocked, and scared. It would need extra crews as also some rope and pulleys to recover the body. The Rover crew, which had been hibernating in the location next to the night harbour of the tank, was commandeered to assist. While the crews got busy, I selected an open patch nearby and asked for a tarpaulin with blankets spread out for the body to be sent to the RHQ for cremation. Redeployment of the tanks and quick replenishment of ammunition was a priority before dusk. Inder, forever thoughtful and efficient, was on line to check the map reference for the dispatch of ammunition.

Lorries were already under move from the administrative area, and guides positioned to lead the ammunition vehicles directly onto the tank. Stacking of ammunition inside a tank can be a very tedious job for each round, is housed inside a bin, so that the assortment of ammunition can be easily identified under all battle conditions. This involved parking the ammunition lorry alongside the tank, transfer of crates onto the tank deck, carriage, and loading in specified bins earmarked for separate categories of ammunition and returning of spent shells. The PT-76 needed a variety of ammunition, besides ammunition for the co-axially mounted MG and turret mounted ack ack gun. Ammunition of personnel weapons comprised pistols and carbines, pyrotechnics, and grenades. Inder, realizing the effort involved, had packed spare tank crews in every ammunition lorry so that the tank crews could take some rest. RHQ staff, especially Chaks, the technical officer, was on the air, confirming our demand for spares while Inder and Digby wanted details of tank kills, and identity of enemy units and prisoners. These anxious enquiries had to be answered promptly as soon it would be time for submitting the daily situation report to their higher HQ.

In my first situation report to the RHQ, I reported complete annihilation of the enemy 3 Independent Armoured Squadron. Two infantry battalions, along with elements of the Reconnaissance and Support (R&S) battalion, consisting of RCL and heavy machine guns, were badly mauled. Six of the enemy tanks were by now bonfires, the flames and the thick black curling smoke visible for miles. Of the other tanks, four were lying disabled in the open. Three non-runners lay streaked in a single file, with their guns dipped, as if in everlasting salute to the gunnery skills of 45 Cavalry by the dismayed and disheartened Pakistani crews. The enemy troops had launched a well-planned attack with the support of tanks and artillery, and R&S battalion elements, under their Commander Brig Mohammed Hayat. This was the biggest attack planned by the Pakistan Army in East Pakistan during the 1971 War.

Digby informed me that the Kruppman bridge across the Kabodak river had been completed and sanction obtained to utilize a troop of T-55 tanks which was now being placed under my command. Lt Dubey, the troop leader from 63 Cavalry, reported the arrival with the news that another troop under the squadron 2IC, Maj Kewal Ramani, was under move and would soon come under command C Squadron for the battle ahead. A bold and enterprising higher command could have unleashed the reconstituted C Squadron to enter the deserted Jessore citadel the same night and brought the war to closure even before the declaration of war. This was an ideal setting for a truly lightning campaign never visualized in any war game at Command/AHQ; it did not figure in any corps/divisional plan either. We deployed the newly arrived T-55 tanks to zero their guns on the wrecked M-24 Chaffee tanks spread over the battlefield. Digby was obviously pleased with the performance of the squadron and wanted a few more rounds onto these tanked-up tanks.

By the time I finished answering the comprehensive enquiries of the RHQ, the body of Chiefy had been removed from the tank and placed on the tarpauline/blanket at the site selected. Chiefy now lay motionless in his blood-splattered black dungarees and radio headgear with his signature tank dust goggles. Both his hands were stretched out in front of him, his fist half clenched, as if he was holding on to the tank commander's cupola, while standing on the modified gunner's seat, overlooking the tank battle. One side of his face was smeared with blood, which had now dried forming a thin cake. On one side of his stomach, there was a large gaping hole by enemy point 50 MMG bullets. There was no sign of pain or agony on his face for it was still well composed and life-like. Death had obviously been instantaneous.

Seeing my old friend and comrade lying thus, tears started forming in my eyes. I controlled myself and ordered the tank crews in the vicinity to assemble so that we could give our

beloved squadron commander a military farewell. Raghubir
Chandra had come with the 'F' Echelon vehicle to accompany
the body and arrange for his last journey from the battlefield.
'Saab was a very courageous commander, the men loved him.'
Chakraborty who had found his way after replenishing his tank,
added: 'We will always remember him for his wit and humour.'
R.P. Singh chipped in, 'He was like a friend to us, *ab tutak
tutak tutiyan kaun gaye ga hamare saath'* (Who will sing folk
songs with us now?). One of the NCOs who had served with
him in the parent regiment, Deccan Horse, mentioned his feats
as a footballer. Gripped with these thoughts, I took refuge in
speech to escape the mounting tide of emotion: 'He lived like
a soldier and has died like one, spurring the men on to greater
deeds of valour and sacrifice. Chiefy has made the supreme
sacrifice. A brave and courageous comrade has done his duty to
his squadron, regiment, and Army, and through them, to the
nation. He died a soldier's death. Remember, he would often
use the phrase, "good man the lantern". The good man has left
us forever but will remain the guiding light (lantern) for us all
in the coming years.' Speaking had not helped in drying up the
tears that were beginning to form. After that, we loaded our
pistols and let go 21 rounds as our salute to the fallen hero.
Just then, the enemy fired a salvo, as if they had no desire to
be left out in paying a tribute to this brave heart. I helped lift
the body and placed it in the returning ammunition lorry. The
crew had thoughtfully placed his black silk scarf, wristwatch,
goggles, and a pair of leather gloves he was immensely fond of
near his shoulder. I picked up his gloves and handed them over
to his crestfallen tank crew as a memento. As the vehicle rolled
past, tank crews waiting on either side of the dirt track raised
their hands in a soldier's salute— their final farewell to Chiefy.

The crews dispersed while I stood watching as the vehicle picked up speed, kicking up a small cloud of dust rising skywards to mingle with the setting sun. As I turned around to return to my tank, I felt the tears welling up inside, seeking release. My self-restraint finally gave way, as the tears rolled down my cheeks, on to the earth below.

The battalion commander was extremely happy and proud of the tank kills spread across his battalion frontage. What had happened was that during the night, the battalion had sent out two patrols which drew a complete blank and returned without valuable information. Based on our report about the presence of tanks in the area, the Brigade HQ had directed 14 Punjab to despatch another patrol, led by an officer, to probe this report further. Capt G.S. Gill, commando platoon commander, and Capt R.P. Chaturvedi, FOO from 6 Field Regiment, were tasked to patrol the area around 0200 hrs. In the twilight, what the patrol saw at dawn must have brought their hearts into their mouths. They feasted their eyes on the assembled mass of enemy infantry and the tank concentration organized into sub-units lining up in assault formations. Soon after, the patrol leader passed on this vital information to the adjutant. Once detected, they were fired upon, some soldiers falling victim to a rain of bullets. A detachment of B Company had taken up a protective position northwest of Garibpur. Under cover of dense, heavy fog and a heavy artillery barrage, the enemy advanced unobserved. The visibility could not have been more than 50 yards. The enemy was soon upon the B Company detachment that had no time to prepare regular defences resulting in a mad scramble towards the main position as soon as the enemy was sighted. The sight of our B Company running encouraged the enemy to follow them in hot pursuit. Unwittingly, they were led into a trap for a hail of bullets greeted them by the Engineer platoon boys located close to the main position of B Company. The momentum of their attack could not be broken, resulting in a hand-to-hand fight. Both sides suffered heavy casualties. Our troops finally overcame all resistance. With this, the backbone of the enemy assault had been broken and their faith and confidence totally shattered.

The battalion commander was quite convinced that there was no chance of a major counter-attack. What was likely was that small tank hunting parties would launch a limited offensive during the early hours of the morning. The Battalion Commander Col R.K. Singh and I agreed that the maximum threat lay on the eastern flank. Accordingly, I agreed to deploy the T-55 tank troop on arrival to cover this approach while he would adjust his C and D Companies. Responsibility of further coordination and guidance would be with D Company in whose location the T-55 troop would deploy. The reason for deploying the T-55 troop was that it was equipped with an effective Infra-Red Device (IRD) for night firing, unlike the PT-76, which had IRD for driving only. Our main task during the night would be to provide protection to the defended sector. The infantry, besides providing early warning and local protection elements, would carry out aggressive patrolling of the perimeter. R.K. Singh received orders from the division, restricting further advance, otherwise Jessore would have been within striking distance the same day. After coordinating the deployment of tanks, I returned to my Squadron HQ. The troop leaders were kept informed about the positions they would be required to take up on receipt of the code word Pippa from me and need of coordination with the infantry companies in their locations. Half an hour after sunset, the code word Pippa for getting into harbour was issued.

Unlike older regiments where personnel were grouped into squadrons, based on a single pure class composition, the identity of C Squadron was different. 45 Cavalry had been raised with a class composition of two SIC Squadrons and one OIC Squadron. Many of the boys came from far flung areas of the seven north-eastern states, Jammu and Kashmir (J&K), Bengal, Orissa while others belonged to the Scheduled Castes and Tribes of India or unrepresented communal or linguistic groups from within India. This was in many ways a cross-section of the emerging face of India. Due to loopholes in the recruitment procedures, a small percentage of regular classes may have also secured recruitment under the OIC quota, using pseudonyms. This was the first OIC Squadron raised since Independence and a precursor to the 'All India All Class' composition for all newly raised units in the defence forces of India. This OIC Squadron had no colonial baggage of custom, tradition, history or battle honours earned during service under foreign flags. This sub-unit could take pride in its high standard of training, cohesiveness, and efficiency as an integrated fighting machine. It did not take cover behind battle-hardened customs or legendary bravery being the preserve of the martial classes. This OIC Squadron was a living example of how the service and patriotism of the non-represented classes, when harnessed as an integrating glue, could reinforce the concept of unity in diversity for India. The olive-green uniform of the Army served as a symbol of 'India First' to the citizens. This combined with military discipline and the unit motto 'Veer Bhogya Vasundra', grouped under the 'dull cherry and beige drab' colours of the regimental flag would serve as a new icon for the defence forces of emerging India. The sweat and toil of training during peacetime had amply prepared them to write about this day in the annals of India's history with blood and glory. Watching them dismounting from their tanks, dishevelled and untidy, tired and weary in body and limb, one could not help but notice the pride and supreme confidence written all over their faces. The calm, unhurried, professional manner in which they got around to perform the chores of maintenance, replenishment, and minor repairs of their Pippa tanks could be the envy of some of the elite and highly glorified units of the country. Today, they represented not just the changing face of India, but pioneers, and living examples of integration. At another level, they represented nature's law of 'unity in diversity'. These were my personal views and well known to them due to our long association. Providence had put us to test by providing us this opportunity to walk the talk.

The medium artillery Observation Post (OP) officer assigned to the squadron had not accompanied the tank column when we crossed the Kabodak river, though his detachment had arrived and mounted their radio equipment on one of the tanks. The officer, Capt Saighal, announced his arrival by reporting in on the radio set during the night. We recognized each other from our meeting in his Officers' Mess on the day I had arrived in Kanchrapara. Watching him now, crestfallen and silent, I sensed that something was disturbing him. On questioning, I found that he had received a 'rocket' from his commanding officer for his inability to direct medium gun fire on enemy tanks during those crucial moments of the tank versus tank battle. This had shaken him badly and his morale was now in his boots. I was aware of the desperate efforts made by him to get through to the gun end to direct the fire, but his radio had packed up. He switched frequencies and tried repeatedly using the tank ANPRC-25. By the time he got through to the gun position, the firefight had fizzled out. I tried to cheer him up by saying that I was a witness to his difficulties and he would get many opportunities in the days ahead to wipe off his CO's harsh assessment of his abilities. After all, it was not difficult for anybody sitting in the rear areas to pass judgement, as they were not exposed to the danger of the bullets flying around. While the infantry and armour had cover, an OP officer sits fully exposed to the dangers of small arms, artillery, and tank fire without even the advantage of firing back due to his preoccupation with the handheld radio sets and a personal weapon. Saighal, who sat exposed through all the shell bursts and gunfire during the intensive battle, had tried his utmost to establish radio contact with his gun position, but in vain. His sincerity and earnestness were, as far as I was concerned, beyond doubt. By the time the tank commanders started arriving for my briefing, he had shed his negative thoughts and pulled himself out of his current depression.

En route to the Squadron HQ, I felt a sudden urge to sit by myself for a few minutes, away from the clatter, commotion, and noise of the tanks' engines. I sat down, resting my back against a *khaji* tree, a cigarette in my hand, permitting random thoughts to float across my mind. At some distance, I could see the tank crews dismounting, to be soon engaged in essential maintenance, repair, and gun cleaning in preparation for the next encounter. The troop leaders would soon assemble now as part of my O group to take orders. The realization that I now had the responsibility of being the squadron commander was disconcerting. During the battle, taking charge had come naturally and unhesitatingly. While immersed in activity, there with no time for reflection. Now the truth of the additional responsibility began to materialize. I was still a substantive Lieutenant, holding the acting rank of Captain. The thought melted away as Digby would soon appoint a senior officer from amongst a dozen available in the regiment. Until that happened, how could I sit around and languish when my prime duty lay with the troops. Somebody still had to continue in command, provide the necessary leadership, and ensure that the squadron was ready before the next encounter. It was still early to throw away half a cigarette, but reluctantly, I got up and after a long drag crushed it under my boot.

The harbour drill SOPs specified the procedures that tank commanders had to complete and then assemble near the squadron commander's tank for the briefing. They were now trooping in. As they arrived to a warm welcome and a big shabash, each had a story to tell. R.P. Singh, easily the more expressive, was the first.

'I told you, those headlights were tanks.'

'Yes, that was our first information. Well done.'

'They came charging at us! Idiots, lucky for us.'

'My troop destroyed two tanks.'

'Well done. What range did you spot them?'

'First tank—400 metres. The second was much closer.'

Chakraborty spoke up to inform that some tanks were targeted by two or more tanks simultaneously.

'Yes, that is true; what is important is that we got the bastards.'

Chakraborty: 'We destroyed one tank at 80 metres after the outflank ordered by you.'

'Yes, that was very lucky indeed. Call it providential.'

'After that kill, we saw the infantry in their Forming up Place (FUP) ready for attack on D Coy location.'

'Must have run helter-skelter,' piped in Dubey who had just joined the group.

'Slammed them with HE, MG, and ack ack machine gun.'

'Fuckers will be counting their dead all night.'

'Is that when you caught the driver of the enemy tank?' questioned Pandey.

'Yes, we had seen him jump off the tank when it caught fire. Poor fellow, kept crawling towards our tank, surrendered meekly.' 'He broke down when you offered him tea and biscuits.' 'Yes. His poor training possibly saved the lives of my crew.'

'He was calling his officers womanizers and drunkards, one of them raped a woman inside the tank, then shot her.'

I complimented everyone present for the excellent performance of the squadron. To the best of my knowledge, never before had one squadron completely annihilated another squadron in a tank versus tank battle. More importantly, the OIC squadron had carved a place for itself in the history books of the country, and cracked the myth about martial classes, accepted for centuries.

The 'O' group came to order with the announcement of a one-minute silence for our valiant soldiers killed, and a short prayer for speedy recovery of the injured. Battle reports had to be collated, covering a wide range of operational and logistic data for onward submission to RHQ. This mundane activity was the foundation for maintaining the operational fitness at a peak level. Folk tales of how a kingdom was lost for want of a horseshoe nail are relevant and not treated as myths at the regimental level. Collection of even minute data is vital and becomes the bedrock for military planning. The number and type of ammunition fired from the main guns, co-axial guns, ack ack guns, or personal weapons of the tank crew, pistols/ sten machines, carbines or hand grenades or smoke bombs expended had to be reflected. This data would be fed into the supply chain to ensure that the correct amount, type, category of items are delivered through the A1, A2, and B Echelons within a specified timeframe. The same would apply for Petrol, Oil, Lubricants (POL) and replacement of hundreds of tote items on the inventory of tanks which may have been damaged or destroyed. Repair and recovery were the other critical matters that had to be undertaken on priority. Defects reported were those that were beyond the capability of the Light Repair Workshop detachment, consisting of technicians from the corps of Electrical and Mechanical Engineers attached to the sub-unit. The need for spare crews is desirable at this stage so that the tank crews can get some rest and relief to maintain peak battle efficiency. Food and individual needs of clothing, equipment, or emergency rations make up an exhaustive list to keep the military machine moving. The tank commanders dispersed on the arrival of the echelons carrying hot food and other soldierly comforts. Lt Dubey's T-55 tanks, fitted with the gunner infrared, were tasked to stand on an all-night vigil, guarding the eastern flank as the likelihood of the enemy despatching stray tank hunting parties or artillery shelling to recover dead bodies would continue during the night. The other big fear was of an early morning air attack for which plans and deployment had to be coordinated now. The moon was just beginning to rise over the horizon to spray a warm glow over the assembled troop leaders. In the limited light, I studied the faces of my troop leaders. They all seemed to be in good control of their nerves. Before closing the conference, I passed around a bottle of brandy from which Speedy had earlier taken a swig while lying on the stretcher in the RAP. The neat brandy created a burning sensation on the tongue, quickly rolled around the mouth and down the gullet, leaving in its wake a feeling of warmth and inner glow. We got up with a flush on our faces for the council of war had ended.

Night falls early in Bengal. It brought about a complete transformation of the battlefield. With nightfall, the noise and commotion of the battle died down. The muteness of a graveyard now enveloped the battlefield, broken now and then by a salvo fired by the guns to remind us that war was still on. The muffled sound of metal striking against metal indicated somebody was repairing his damaged tank track. I was sitting on my tank with my legs spread out in front of me and my back resting against the sloped turret. Ahead of me, in the area where the tank battle had taken place, could be seen a few bonfires. These tanks were still burning bright. The wild tongues of flame had now subsided giving way to an orange glow, which appeared brighter in the light breeze. There seemed to be a strange hypnotic charm attached to the bonfires from the tanks still burning for I felt my eyes getting transfixed on the orange and blue of the flames, forming a rich hue. I kept watching these for very long, oblivious of my surroundings. There was a feeling of happiness and satisfaction that the enemy tanks were burning. Perhaps many of those who were killed or wounded in today's action were still lying inside. My own fate could have been no different from what I was witnessing, had the Gods in heaven not been providing a protective umbrella for me. Amongst the many burning tanks, one at least was ours. The body of the gunner could not be recovered as the tank was in flames. This man was my responsibility and I felt disgust rising within me, trying to find some justification for the burning funeral pyre. Revulsion soon gave way to consideration, a sense of justice. Did not somebody say that all is fair in love and war? This was war!

I adjusted my overcoat around my shoulders, aware of the nip in the air. The thought of death crossed my mind. I had been face to face with death a number of times that day but even when I had come close to it, it eluded me. What amused me considerably was that the face of death held no special horror. The face of death in the early stages of the battle had invoked fear. This fear was no different from what one felt before entering the boxing ring. It was the fear of the unknown, which created a vacuum in the pit of your stomach, soon washed away after the first couple of blows are traded. The fear of death creates the same distressed feeling before the first few gunshots. This fear is apt to rise again whenever the mind and body are placed in a dangerous situation. However, the mind, having reacted to it earlier, learns to accept it with more grace under pressure. Death, once you have stared at it eyeball-to-eyeball, laughed in its very face or felt it brushing against you, creates no panic. It becomes a way of life. When I first looked down the barrel of the enemy tank, which was subsequently knocked down at a range of 30 metres, the same uneasy feeling in the pit of the stomach arose. This realisation was repeated a little later when accompanied by the tank crew we went charging down, to safeguard our tank. Why we rushed into the jaws of death was not because a tank was more precious than our lives but because along with it, our honour and prestige would have been blown to pieces. It is in these moments of existence that the true significance of life, discipline, loyalty, pride, honour, comradeship, sacrifice, and patriotism dawns on you. Based on one's individual experiences and consequent interpretations, evolves a new pattern of life. It carries with it liberal knowledge of the meaning of life and an appreciative understanding of one's fellow beings. Life in the possible contemplation of death becomes more enjoyable and more rewarding!

With a feeling of unease, I remembered that I had not met or spoken to the only other officer left in the squadron. This was a subaltern called Narain. This officer, a young sturdy Rajasthani, had been with the regiment for only three or four months, during which he had familiarized himself by reading about tank troop leading and the battle-drill pamphlets, besides receiving instructions and practical handling on available equipment, covering all three trades of driving, gunnery, and radio. The battle must have been quite an experience for him as he had never even fired the tank gun on the open ranges. He had learnt his drills from his crew members on sand models and hastily made diagrams on rough pieces of papers or chalk drawings on the ground sheet. I could not help but feel sympathy for him.

As war had been imminent, he could not attend the basic Young Officers' course. Until the successful completion of this course, such officers are not even addressed by their rank, but simply as a Mister. Even a junior soldier in the armoured corps takes delight in treating their rank with disdain for their limited knowledge of soldiering and regimental duties. Every officer goes through this phase, for though the one pip on his shoulder will ensure that his orders are obeyed, respect is something he cannot demand. For this, he will have to work hard and establish his own brand of leadership, based on professional competence and character. During this period, when he is striving to establish his identity, every action of his will come under scrutiny and observation before he is accepted as a leader. It is true that the President of India can give you a Parchment Commission but he cannot make you a leader. This remains your own personal battle, an endless process throughout your service career.

Exposure to death and danger in the battlefield need not be restricted to enemy action only. Carelessness of individuals and poor coordination amongst sub-units can sometimes bring untold misery and regret. Two episodes of the night held us spellbound. The first episode occurred in the early part of the evening and carried within it all the elements of an imperial flap. One of the tank gunners, while removing the 7.62 mm ammunition belt, fitted on the co-axial machine gun, lifted the metal plate, not realizing that a round was already inside the chamber of the gun. As he jerked the belt off the machine gun, the tracer round triggered and could be seen darting off in the direction of a group of riflemen of the Punjab Battalion. The sound of a shot within the harbour alarmed everyone. The situation could provoke retaliation if this bullet struck any soldier. Not waiting for details of how and why, I quickly contacted the anxious battalion commander on the radio. Even while I was explaining how the accidental round got triggered off due to 'hung fire', caused mostly due to an overheated machine gun, I knew that the worst was over for retribution is mostly immediate. The gunner carrying out maintenance had failed to observe the basic precaution of keeping the gun end elevated and pointing towards the enemy side as precaution in case of 'hung fire' accidents. The sound of a gunshot caused a general alarm amongst the troops and a very agitated company JCO let fly his full-throated Punjabi vocabulary. Incidents of this nature sometimes take an ugly turn resulting in friendly troops firing at each other. Later during the night, I had to cope with a far more sensitive situation.

Two troops of 63 Cavalry (D Squadron) had been placed under command C Squadron Capt P.F. Kewal Ramani, along with one troop of T-55 which was under move and would soon link the next morning. The T-55 tanks of 63 Cavalry under Lt Dubey were tasked to keep a strict vigil on the exposed eastern flank as remnants of the withdrawing troops/tank-hunting parties could infiltrate our defence area. They were assigned an arc within which they were permitted to open fire in case they saw any enemy movement. In the greenish yellow light of the gunner's IRD, it is possible to pick up a moving target but difficult to identify objects, especially at ranges of 500–600 metres as the intensity of light drops and only a blurred image appears on the screen. Around midnight, the gunner of a T-55 tank was watching this arc of responsibility allotted to him when suddenly the image of two suspicious figures sprang up on the screen of the IRD. The gunner promptly alerted the rest of the crew and had their gun sights tracking the two aliens. At any movement within this arc of responsibility, the tank commander could open fire without seeking the permission of his troop leader or the company commander. The alert commander, noticing that the infiltrators were proceeding in the south to north direction, held his fire, and chose to challenge these 'aliens': 'Stop. Raise your hands or I will fire!' The tranquillity and silence of the night suddenly broken by a threatening voice asking them to raise their hands must have come as a bolt from the blue to the 'aliens'. Without waiting a moment to assess the situation in which they found themselves, they made a dash, hoping to avert disaster under the cover of darkness. On the tank commander's order, the gunner who had been dutifully tracking the 'aliens', pressed his trigger and let go two short bursts. Even before the staccato of fire had died down, the infantry company closest to the two 'aliens' started cursing loudly in Punjabi, *'Banda mar dita, sadda banda mar ditta'* (they have killed our boys). The tank commander, having zeroed his target, could see the two 'aliens' now lying midway between his position and that of the rifle company. He realized in that instant that the aliens were friendly troops but demanded that they identify themselves, as trespass had been committed into a restricted zone without notice. Having directed his gunner to hold fire, he ordered the 'aliens' to raise their hands and advance towards his position. Meanwhile, a representative from the rifle company came up to identify them. The 'aliens' needed no identification for they were Sikhs soldiers, wearing patkas. They were part of an early warning detachment from the rifle company sent out to a listening post. Their immediate commander, a non-commissioned officer, had warned them not to cross the tanks' arc of fire for it would put their life in peril. The boys who had had nothing to eat since morning were finding it difficult to bear the cold winter night on empty stomachs. Having been relieved from sentry duty, they sought to venture across to fetch nourishment for themselves and the rest of the platoon. Instead of taking the safe longer route behind the tanks, they ventured across the arc of fire at a 'safe range' from the tanks, fully confident that the tank men would not be able to spot their movement on a pitch-dark night. What nobody told them was that the tanks were equipped with IRDs. Fortunately, for all of us, the bullets only grazed one of the chaps on his buttocks and burnt holes in the OG jersey of the other. The closeness of the bullets had made them yell out the choicest Punjabi curses in which the neighbouring company soon joined. They accepted the tragic event of the last few minutes with a broad grin on their faces realizing how close they had come to challenge their fate.

The rest of the night passed off peacefully without any untoward incident. A couple of hours of sound sleep in the driver's seat, wrapped in my overcoat and a blanket, using the 08 pack as my pillow, was relief. The early morning ritual of shit, shave, shampoo, a habit ingrained since the academy days and loosely referred to as 'morning prayers' had been completed. Tank crews are adept at brewing tea at short notice as also rolling out goodies like *shakarpara*, both salty and sugary. The simple Indian makes few demands on the logistics chain and is fit for another day of combat if these small needs are provided.

The operator Shibe Lal was already walking in my direction carrying his ANPRC-25 set. My guess was right, for Bains was on air:

Self: 'Pass your message. Over.'

Bains: 'Are you planning another hearty breakfast? Over.'

Self: 'I would love some real fried eggs for breakfast today. Over.'

Bains: 'Radio Pakistan has given extensive coverage to the Garibpur Battle in the news bulletin. Over.'

Self: 'Please provide details. Over.'

Bains: 'Paki Radio announced attack by Indian armoured brigade in Jessore sector. Over.'

Self: 'Go on, tell me more, don't have a transistor. Over.'

Bains: '28 tanks of 45 Cavalry regiment completely destroyed along with 10 other armoured personnel carriers. Over.'

Self: 'Pakis will be shell-shocked when they hear the truth spoken. Over.'

Bains: 'Yahya has announced a national emergency in Pakistan.'

Self: 'Oh, this is hilarious.'

Bains: 'Yahya is meeting a Chinese delegation today, big developments in the offing. Over.'

Self: 'The Chinese will never fight somebody else's battles.'

Garibpur, East Pakistan. Graveyard of
Chaffees, 21 November 1971

Lt Col DS Jamwal (wearing dust
goggles), briefing officer on his left
while Capt B.S. Mehta (seated)
looks on

Capt B.S. Mehta, discussing battle plan
with Lt Col D. S. Jamwal while Capt
Indrajit passes orders on radio

THE DEVIL FOR PAK CHAEFEES

Capt B.S. Mehta mounted on
PT-76 tank with his gunner LD
Harish. Photo with caption received
from 14 Punjab

Troops of 14 Punjab deployed at battlefield Garibpur

Married, 7 March 1977; Ahmednagar. Seated: Mother, Jayshree, Balram. Mother's right: Madhu with son Rohit; standing (left to right): Shamsher, Uncle Keshodass (KD) Surinder, Rajinder, Minoo, Narinder, Kusum, Kukkie (seated)

Newspaper Headlines;
Morning after Garibpur

Family in Shree Sahoo Palace, Pune 1949:
Father (wearing whites); Mother
(holding bouquet), with her sister,
brother and palace staff

2/Lt N S Mehta commissioned
into 5 Garhwal led a successful
company attack for capture
of Hilli and became a Battle
Causality within a fortnight
of joining his paltan

Victorious tank crews of C Squadron after the successful battle of Garibpur

Dhaka, 16 December 2015. Brig and Mrs Mehta with
the President and PM of Bangladesh on Victory Day

Nandini and Brijraj with Their Nani, Mrs Ghanshyam

Colonel Hardeep, 17H, with Sister Jayshree

Bains: 'There are reports that Bhutto is heading for New York to address the UN Assembly'.

Self: 'And what about the ugly American?'

Bains: 'They have stopped military aid to both India and Pakistan.'

Self: 'That's good for us. Over.'

Bains: 'I would say smart move, they will now encourage the mullahs of the Middle East to transfer weapons to the Pakis.'

Self: 'But what about Russians?'

Bains: 'They have a stiff upper lip, silence is golden. Be watchful today, air raids expected.'

Self: 'Thanks and out.'

A dense heavy fog enveloped the area, limiting the visibility to barely 50 yards. We positioned the tanks, making maximum use of cover from aerial view even at the cost of appearing non-tactical in the ground configuration. Camouflage and concealment against a possible air attack was the need of the hour. The infantry, meanwhile, were improving their defended locality by preparing overhead cover for their bunkers / dugouts, and laying anti-tank and anti-personnel mines to cover the exposed flanks. Responding to cheerful salutations of Sat Sri Akal, I asked the Sikh detachment commander why the mines were being laid when the cavalry was in the location. 'We love you, but we cannot trust you. One radio message and the cavalry will disappear, leaving us exposed.' His simple answer was logical and appropriate and brought much amusement to the mine-laying party.

Having checked the camouflage of the other tank troops, I finally arrived at Ramparikshan's location and found two tanks parked very close to each other. This was fundamentally wrong and unexpected of a tactically qualified troop leader. Enquiry revealed that Dafadar Dubey, one of his tank commanders, had refused to budge from this position. My first reaction was that it was out of character for a mild NCO like Dubey to countermand his superior's orders. As both were from Bihar, could this be a case of some private differences causing disharmony in their official dealings? As I was soon to learn, the reason for the discord was far more serious in this case. Ramparikshan confided that during the previous tank battle, when the outflanking move was ordered, Dubey had failed to accompany him. He had not made an official report, as it was a very serious development.

'What do you mean by serious development, it is a court-martial offence,' I thundered.

'I knew you would react strongly, also I had to verify the reasons before reporting.'

'Have you verified the reasons now?'

'He says that he could not comply with the order as his tank did not start.'

'You must have checked with the tank crew, what do they say?' 'Sorry to report, Sir, but they are all tight-lipped on this issue.' 'Get that rascal up here quickly.'

Dafadar Dubey arrived, on the double, to deliver a smart salute, and the traditional Jai Hind, his expression clearly indicating that he was prepared for the questioning.

Self: 'So how many tanks did you knock out yesterday, Dubey?'

Dubey: 'Two tanks, Sir. We got two.'

Self: 'From which location?'

Dubey: 'Sir, same location, as the present one'.

Self: 'But Dubey, Ramparikshan says you did not accompany him on to outflank move yesterday.'

Dubey: 'No, Sir, I informed the troop leader that my tank was not starting.'

Self: 'Dubey, when your tank did not start, what action did you take?'

Dubey: 'Nothing, Sir, we engaged the enemy from same current position.'

Self: 'This is poppycock. Your troop had a jump lead which could have been utilized to start the tank engine.'

Dubey: 'But there was no other tank in the vicinity.'

Self: 'All the more reason for you to inform your troop leader. Did you inform him?'

Dubey: 'I tried, but could not get through to him.'

Self: 'Is there any other problem you are not sharing?'

Dubey: 'No, Sir, all is well.'

Self: 'Dubey how many rounds did you fire yesterday?'

Dubey: '10, Sir.'

Self: 'And how many AP (T) rounds were fired?'

Dubey: 'Seven, Sir'.

Ramparikshan: 'Wrong, Sir, I checked only four fired.'

Self: 'Tell me, were all the rounds fired from the same position where your tank is now?'

Dubey: 'Yes, Sir, from the same position.'

Self: 'You never moved your tank to an alternative position while engaging enemy tanks.'

Dubey: 'No, Sir.'

Self: 'Because you knew that your tank had a starting problem!'

Dubey's vague answers and body language were beginning to reveal some strange nervousness that I could now fully comprehend. Was this incident evidence of the murkier side of his character? I was inclined to believe that a full investigation may be necessary to establish the truth. The number of rounds fired, the tank being a non-starter, the inability to use the jump lead to start the tank, non-compliance of orders, and failure to follow the troop leader's tank were confirming Ramparikshan's worst doubts about Dubey's strange behaviour. 'I never realized that you could lie to me, Dubey. I will see you later, meanwhile, move your tank away from that hut before you are spotted by the Sabres.' 'And you, Ramparikshan, make sure my orders are implemented.'

Having made a mental note of Dubey's conduct, I walked away to meet Col R.K. Singh at the Battalion HQ for a liaison visit. The chill of the morning, which had immobilized everyone, was beginning to loosen its grip. Daylight and visibility were beginning to improve. The sun had come through the winter clouds and was now shining brightly in the eastern sky. For the troops who had spent the night in the open and braved the cold, made worse by heavy dew, nothing could be more revitalising. Looking around, one could notice tank crews pulling off their jerseys and overcoats to soak up the warmth of the sun. That no air alert warning had been sounded was beginning to act as a further incentive to take things easy.

I spent some time at the Battalion HQ with R.K. Singh going over the events of the previous day. The mystery of half a squadron being withdrawn minutes before the start of the tank versus tank battle was still fresh in my mind. He attributed the snafu to poor staff work at Divisional HQ. While on this subject, his adjutant butted in: 'Sir, the Div HQ wants six-figure grid references of enemy tanks destroyed.' This really got him miffed and agitated as the battalion had already submitted a detailed report on this subject yesterday. The pressure of the last few days must have been telling on him as he got into a monologue. 'Staff exists for troops and not in spite of them.

Tell them to stop breathing down the neck of the CO, it is becoming bloody fashionable.' Standing there in his Battalion Headquarters, he spent many minutes imaging the sequence of action at the higher headquarters after the initial reports of the enemy attack had filtered through. 'Battling the enemy was easier than answering the rapid fire round questions raised by these staff types.' I sympathised, adding, 'Well, they have to prepare their briefs for the commanders'. R.K. Singh was not in a relenting mood: 'What the fuck will the commander do with the six-figure grid reference of enemy tanks destroyed—send it to his wife or shove it—'. The cheeky adjutant suggested a soft option: 'Sir, we will forward the coordinates of the square instead.' 'No, on second thoughts tell them that the armour squadron has been tasked to file the grid references.' My quick response was, 'Sir, their problem is trust. They think you are faking it. Better to invite them over for a *dekkho*.' It ended up in a laugh. RK Singh, equipoise restored, now spoke in glowing terms about the armour boys, while his staff dispersed to attend to other radio messages. He had received word that the corps commander and Army commander, were more than pleased and may even visit the battle location on clearance from Delhi.

Good staff work is an essential ingredient for success. 'Getting into the picture' and 'feeling the pulse' are important for commanders to make snap decisions. To the staff officer, a pause in the battle provides a brief though happy interlude to give full licence to a vivid imagination to identify tasks such as the present one which, even if provided, would reach the waste basket because more important events would occur. R.K. Singh agreed that the staff officers and commanders must have had their own compulsions. After all, we were not fighting in isolation and feedback of information was a responsibility of frontline soldiers.

We had barely moved out of the Battalion HQ when an urgent message came through on the radio. What we had been suspecting since the early morning now stood confirmed by the radio message, followed by the short shrill blasts from a whistle, which somebody was blowing impatiently. It was a signal, practised and rehearsed during exercises, to indicate an imminent air strike.

I elbowed my entry into one of the crowded trenches close to the Battalion HQ, as there was no way I could make it to my tank. The trench, designed for not more than three persons, was a small, ramshackle shelter with an apology for overhead cover consisting of small *khaji* saplings and dry twigs covered with earth to provide protection. On one side of the trench, a small aperture had been cut open through which its occupants could fire their weapons in case of a ground attack. Before I could adjust my weight on my feet, somebody inside yelled, 'Enemy planes are coming.' The four black dots had now grown much larger, their outline becoming more menacing. Soon, they were overhead, and started to circle over our position, to determine our defence perimeter within which they would select their targets to spell death and devastation. Their main effort was directed towards the tanks, being the more lucrative targets. Sitting inside the trench, packed like sardines, one could do nothing more than watch the aircraft, which we now recognised as the infamous Sabres. We had heard and read enough about these aircraft but all that knowledge was of no avail, since it had only acquainted us with the physical and technical features of the aircraft. What we were going to discover in the next 10 minutes or so would be its capacity for annihilation and its ability to create havoc amongst the ground troops. The cumulative effect of its monster-like presence moving around at supersonic speed, creating a blood curdling roar through its jet engines, the reverberation and echoes, plus the physical damage its cannon, bombs and strafing would create was something we would be compelled to undergo with our hearts in our mouths. While they were still high up in the sky, I ventured to count them, hoping to draw some consolation from their numbers: one, two, three, four—possibly some higher up in the sky. The Sabres were pulling up once again to gain height as by now they had completed a dry run. It would now be only a matter of moments before they swooped down, one after another, unloading their cargo consisting of bombs, cannons, machine guns, on pre-selected targets. I was still peeping through the small aperture when the leading aircraft started its dive. I felt a shiver go through my spine for I had feeling that the attack was directed against the position occupied by us. Watching the dive, one could observe two puffs of white smoke followed immediately by a deafening explosion as the ejected rockets found their target. The foundation of our shelter seemed to crumble like a mud pie all around us for we were all covered with flying dust and debris. The continuous pounding around us made the earth reverberate. The air was soon filled with dust, debris, smoke and the smell of burning cordite. When the magnitude of this sound and fury abated, even shortly, one could hear the 'rat-a-tat-tat' of the machine guns. Every now and then, amidst this pandemonium, the anguish of a human body which had fallen victim to this attack was translated through cries of pain, agony and wild shrieks, caused undoubtedly by some red hot metal or shrapnel ripping through the skin or a limb being torn away. The pitch of human misery and the mental anguish is difficult to describe in words. The experience has to be lived. The last aircraft had run over our position and could now be seen gaining height, to complete its second run. There would be a moment's pause before the first aircraft, having gained height, would circle to repeat its earlier performance. It appeared that by the time the aircraft finished their sorties, they would have razed everything to the ground. Close to our shelter lay a human corpse the only evidence of what was once a living being. The smoke and dust suddenly parted to reveal five soldiers carrying their comrade fully drenched in blood to a place of comparative security. By now, the second attack was already underway.

My thoughts so far had been confined to all the human despair and devastation I could see outside the shelter. Suddenly awareness of a sound, which I had not heard until then, distracted my attention. What I saw in front of me filled my heart with horror: a young soldier, not more than 19 years old, totally unnerved by the wreckage, death, and destruction all around him. His mental reserve and military training were insufficient to absorb the experience entirely. Something within him had snapped. He was 'shell shocked'. It lasts for a couple of minutes during which an individual loses complete control of his senses. Either he falls into total silence and is immobilized, or he starts crying and shouting, becoming hysterical. This young boy had obviously become hysterical, which was having an adverse effect on those who were trying to brave the ordeal by keeping their composure. A senior NCO, trying to calm him down, added further agony to an already unbearable atmosphere. The more devout were chanting some mantra invoking the assistance of a higher power to stave off the catastrophe. The devotion with which they were involved in prayer may have kept the bombs and shrapnel away, for we were very close to it all.

The air attack could not have lasted more than ten minutes though it seemed like a virtual lifetime. The Sabres had made repeated runs over our position reappearing to deliver the parting kick by discharging unexpended bombs, and announced their departure, the aircraft gradually disappearing into the direction from which they had arrived. One could, in effect, listen to the grant of a stay of execution when a few hoots on the whistle announced the all clear. Instantly, everybody rolled out from the trenches/shelters, as if the inactivity of the last few minutes had to be recompensed. The platoon commanders were soon barking orders for the air attack had taken a heavy toll of men and material. A facade of command and control had to take effect at the earliest so that orderliness would replace the pandemonium. Evacuation of casualties, first aid for the injured, readjustment of defences, patchwork on-field fortifications, which had crumbled under the shower of thousands of pounds of high explosives—all had to be completed in double quick time. One had to prepare for the next air attack, and no one knew when it would come. I stepped out of the shelter, cursing my luck for having been caught out in the open, far from my tank. I hastened towards it now, finding my way through all the dust and rubble. An NCO rushing past to fetch some water, noticing the black beret, informed me that a tank had been hit. Instinctively, I moved towards the source of black smoke in double quick time.

On spotting the tank, all doubts dissolved. This was Dubey's tank, the one I had ordered to move to a different position. I suddenly felt a twinge of sorrow and rising anger at myself. If only I had stayed on long enough to ensure that he had moved his tank. Dubey and the tank crew had paid heavily for their stupid fallacy. They had broken one of the first principles of concealment by taking up a position in the vicinity of huts that comprised the most prominent landmark in the area. I moved around the tank to assess the damage. The aircraft had scored a bull's eye with one of its rockets. The hull plate being just 13 mm thick had disintegrated around the point of impact. The intensity of the impact had thrown up Dubey from the commander's seat to a miraculous escape. He suffered some second-degree burns and a few broken bones but would live to regret the error committed. The driver had been oblivious to all that had taken place in the engine and fighting compartment. He remembered that during the air attack, the tank had trembled and for a moment he felt that it might turn turtle. He became unconscious and on surfacing, recalled trying repeatedly to get the crew members on the intercom but failed. Later, he opened his cupola to find the commander lying near the tank tracks. Only while jumping off the tank did he notice the smoke now rising from the rear of the tank? The other two crew members had been brewing tea when the air strike came. Finding it difficult to make it to the tank they had sought refuge in the huts where they received a fair share of the shrapnel flying around and now lay injured though not seriously.

With the diesel, having caught fire there was nothing we could have done to save the tank from further damage. The flames engulfed the area around, the soft breeze fanning them as if to hasten the process of destruction. At irregular intervals, a muffled explosion would take place, reminding us of the ammunition still stored in the tank. Ramparikshan from the adjoining tank came over to report that the other tanks of the squadron and the crew were safe. A few tanks had been under attack but the damage was limited to flying shrapnel. In the next few minutes, he recounted the sordid tragedy which had led to the tank casualty. While the aircraft was overhead, the pilot searching out for targets, through the dense foliage, fired a stray rocket, which fell between Dubey's and Ramparikshan's tank. The pilot using the hut as a reference point, registered Dubey's tank as a target when he fired his anti-aircraft gun. During the next run, the pilot had adjusted his gun sights on Dubey's tank. From the pilot's vantage position, this must have appeared as a sitting duck to score a bull's eye, hitting the tank broadside.

A tinge of regret and disappointment cast a shadow over me, giving rise to a feeling of guilt. Some unknown voice within held me responsible for the failure to move Dubey's tank away from the hut location in my presence. That I had made Ramparikshan, his troop leader, responsible to implement the change ordered by me, now did not sit easy on my conscience. I felt that I had blundered by not being firm and more assertive in accepting command responsibility. Like everyone, I too needed to learn from my own mistakes.

The second air attack came at 10.30 a.m. I had finished my round of inspection during which the tank crews were reminded to open anti-aircraft gunfire only when directly targeted, as premature firing would reveal their location to the pilots. Minutes after the air alert sounded, four black specks were seen, emerging out of the sun, coming towards our location. In a few moments, they would be on top of our position playing merry hell into us. While still on the move in my tank, I surveyed the area around, and realized, much to my distress, that the closest bamboo grove was more than 400 yards away. A shortcut through an area dotted with *khaji* trees was available which I directed the driver to take. Our dash to the grove selected was exhilarating, as I could perceive the fast-approaching Sabres getting closer while we sprinted for cover under the blue winter sky. We must have presented quite a spectacle to the pilots who would be hoping to lift their prey in one fell swoop! Ramphal, the driver, was a Haryanvi of slight build, not loquacious but a dependable and efficient driver. As a last-ditch effort to stave off danger, he pressed the accelerator pedal all the way down to find himself stuck between two stout *khaji* trees, barely 10 feet apart. His experienced eye must have told him that the tank could not go through but fear of the Sabres now overhead made him throw caution to the four winds. The *khaji* trees did not relent, resulting in the tank, its engine silent, now lying wedged precariously between two stout trees.

The efficient and well-trained driver wasted no time in fruitless explanations. Having recovered from the jolt delivered by the unrelenting trees, he immediately started the engine and applying the reverse gear tried to wriggle out. The track must have got embedded in the juicy trunk of the *khaji* trees for it refused to budge. Ramphal then jumped off the deck, axe in hand to hack one of the trees. Two infantry soldiers watching our predicament joined the tank crew in this valiant effort to set free the tethered tank. The enemy aircraft were now at the start of their attack run. One of them had targeted us. The white smoke indicated release of rockets followed by the reverberation of the strafing attack whizzing past. Deafening sound decibels and exploding rockets made the tank go through the motion of rolling and pitching, in spite of being shackled. While the Sabre gained height for a second run, operation hacking went into top gear. Vigorous and energetic effort had cut through more than half of the tree trunk when the driver returned to his seat. My eyes were still glued on the Sabre which had targeted us. Ramphal, meanwhile, revved up the engine and locking one stick swerved the tank in the direction of the tree that he had hacked. The battle for survival between the tank and the tree had commenced while the Sabre commenced swooping down menacingly towards us. The tank engine, on full throttle, was groaning as the revolution per minute of the engine intensified and the tank went through a convulsive movement every time the driver locked the right stick to apply maximum power on the gradually relenting tree trunk. The swan song of the tank was now blending with the decibels of the fast-approaching strafing attack and roar of the Sabre engines overhead. This would be recorded as one of those performances where the spectators would not be able to ask for an encore as the end would consume both the artists and the stage. The increased pitching and yawing movement every time the driver locked the sticks had increased, providing a slender hope that we may yet prevail. Suddenly, like a dam bursting, the tank swerved viciously into a spin, bringing down the tree trunk. The speed with which the driver released the locked stick made the tank leap forward in uncontrolled aggression for the long bitter struggle it had experienced. Like a bait released before being devoured, the tank, with the crew, sped into the nearest grove in celebration of the new lease of life while the rocket and strafing attack settled into a deafening explosion disturbing the flora, fauna, and ecology of the land. Our problems, however, were not over, for the other Sabres had reached the release point, but the apprehension that we were being targeted, compelled the driver to adopt a zigzag route, denying the pilot adequate opportunity to aim. It involved the tank driver alternatively locking left/right driving sticks and pressing or releasing the accelerator pedal. One pilot released his rockets but was wide off the mark, not finding a stationary target. This time, when the black underbelly of the Sabre went overhead, we knew that in this battle of wits, we had won the day for even while the aircraft was pulling up, we had entered the safety of a large bamboo grove.

The second air strike took its own toll of men and material. The tanks, because of wide dispersion and better concealment, had come out of it without further loss. The infantry casualties became evident from the number of persons being carried or guided towards the Regimental Aid Post. The question which everyone was now asking was: why had our aircraft failed to intercept the Sabres? Was it because our MiGs and Gnats (both a kind of fighter aircraft) had failed to give battle or was it due to the official policy to not permit aircraft to cross the Pakistani air space? The effect of two air strikes in quick succession had had a shattering effect on the morale of the men, besides causing heavy damage. It was difficult to explain to the men why the Air Force refused to join in what had so far been a ground battle for our troops. I felt convinced that the Army/Air Forces bosses must be seriously contemplating employing the Air Force not only to protect the ground troops but also to obtain complete air superiority in this sector. My explanation to the troop leaders that the Sabres would not bother us if we were well concealed and camouflaged, proof of which was the second air strike, must have fallen on deaf ears for they all left looking crestfallen and doubtful. Little did they realize that I was in total agreement with them, as the fact was that I was asking Digby the same question, but not getting a plausible reply. The most I could do under the circumstances was keep a bold front and hope that others would follow the example.

Higher commanders visiting the battlefield and exposing themselves to the dangers suffered by the common soldier acts as a morale booster for the troops. An experienced and astute military leader utilises such visits to get feedback as also feel the pulse of subordinate commanders responsible for execution of his orders.

A shrewd and perceptive leader can influence inter-arm/ Service cooperation by applying balm to trampled egos. After all, an individual with a toothache is more concerned about his pain than all the gems of tactical wisdom the commander may bequeath to him. Brigade Commander of HQ 42 Infantry Brigade, Brig Gharaya and Digby made an appearance at our location. Their hearty appreciation, cheerfulness, and composure soon endeared them to the troops. Gharaya, being a seasoned campaigner, had adjusted to the new environment with ease. They went around shaking hands with one and all, congratulating others they came across. They were both keen to see the Chaffee tanks which we had claimed as destroyed. It must have come as a big surprise that we had not exaggerated. The Chaffee tanks lay strewn all over the battlefield. Instead of following the cumbersome procedure of target indication, a quick burst from the LMG helped in pointing out the location of each tank. One could see their eyes dancing with excitement as they counted the rich bag of thirteen. The other fact which moved them considerably was the close range at which the tanks had been destroyed—the complete battle fought at ranges of 300–500 yards and the closest tank knocked out at a bare 30 yards! One question repeatedly raised by the troops was: why had our Air Force not been employed so far? Fear of fresh air attacks was still lurking in the minds of all. Considering that the time lag between the first and second air strikes was 2.5 hours, another strike was expected in the next 30–40 minutes. Either way, there certainly would be another strike before dusk. Both visitors tried to explain the official policy but it sounded hollow and unconvincing. The troops had suffered and were becoming vocal in their disappointment and wanted a firm commitment in this regard.

By the time Digby and the commander reached their HQ, the air alert was being sounded again. This time, I was in the squadron Rover, which had arrived with the A1 echelon vehicles after a long period of hibernation. Being in a wheeled vehicle, I followed the prominent track leading to my tank and did not risk the shortcut attempted earlier. On mounting my tank, I realised that the driver Upadhya and Signal NCO, R.N. Singh of the squadron Rover were following me. This surprised me considerably and I ordered them to camouflage their vehicle in the grove behind. Their reluctance to stay with the vehicle was in many ways indicative of the difficulty we had faced in establishing contact with both of them during and after the tank battle. I was determined to take the edge off their fears and ordered them to return to the jonga. The Sabre swooped down for his bombing run. I glanced back and saw the driver once again sprint from the jonga.

'Where are you going, you goddammed son of a bitch?!!' I screamed. The driver stopped dead in his tracks. He was equally paralysed by fear of me and of the marauding jets. I advanced on him and fear of me won out. He returned to the jonga.

Without saying another word, I pointed first to the jonga and then to a grove just 50 yards away where I wanted him to deploy. Having overcome their initial fear and hesitation, I must say to their credit, that their performance improved as the operation progressed. Later, I learnt that a bullet had grazed his temple after hitting the windscreen, which had unnerved Upadhya since the first day of battle. The four Sabres once again appeared on the horizon to play merry hell with our defences. The initial terror and menace which the presence of the Sabres evoked had to some extent been allayed. We had understood the pattern of their attack. The knowledge that the Sabres had a Time over Target (TOT) of 10 minutes did embolden us to suffer their presence with tranquillity and fortitude. Much before the TOT elapsed, their interest seemed to get diverted towards Chaugacha, about 2 km northwest of our location, as our FOO Capt Saighal had intelligently directed smoke shells fired on enemy gun positions. The pilots mistook this as a signal that a more worthwhile target existed, as indicated by their ground troops. Their attention diverted away from us came as a great relief. Not being in the line of fire, we could now throw open the commander's cupola to the fully open position to stand erect to witness the Sabres bombing their own gun position. I kept one eye on the TOT while watching the Sabres at play with a field battery of artillery guns and one of the air defence troops located in the area. The sound of explosions and strafing continued to pierce the air around us. Saighal was soon to announce that the countdown for the last 60 seconds had commenced. At best, they would make one more run before flying over our position on their way back to their air base at Jessore. The tenth minute ran into the eleventh and we were surprised when they pressed on with their attack into the twelfth minute. Sitting on our tanks, we could only attribute this extravagance (or was it arrogance?) to the realization that they were within their own air space and were confident that the Indian Air Force would not interfere with the proceedings. Our anger and disgust heightened when our watches told us that the Sabres had now spilled over to the thirteenth minute. They had undoubtedly overstayed their hospitality.

The thirteenth minute of time over target saw the Sabres making their runs at an excruciating slow speed and at low height, seemingly without a care in the world. While preparing to dive down on fresh targets from the start of the runs, two white specks appeared plunging down upon them from the heavens above. Before one could say 'Joi Bangla' the white specks had transformed themselves into two Gnats and were moving headlong onto the tails of the two Sabres in front. The next instant, the two Sabres were spinning down to mother earth, leaving behind a trail of thick black smoke. Somewhere in between the black smoke and the whirling aircraft, rapidly losing height, two parachutes ejected to reveal their pilots. Their descent would lead them to their destiny, witnessed by the troops of the Indian Army.

The Gnats of the Indian Air Force had struck like lightning from the blue. While the first two Gnats, having scored bull's eye, could be seen pulling up to greater heights, two more Gnats came diving down. The Sabres, no longer masters of all that they surveyed, took evasive steps to break contact. A dogfight ensued which was a treat for sore eyes. The aircraft were now directly overhead and to track them in the clear November sky was a gratifying experience in which the ground troops were engrossed. One of the Gnats manoeuvred itself onto the tail of the Sabre. Two puffs of white smoke discharged by the rocket fired were being viewed by a thousand pairs of eyes from below, ending in an explosion of joy as the collective chorus swept the sound waves, 'Look one more.' Before the echo could reach the eardrum, one could see thick black smoke rising from the fast-descending Sabre which soon burst open in the sky and came plummeting down, following the laws of gravity. It was difficult to imagine that the pilot would survive this ordeal. While we were focussed on the two descending pilots parachuting down to captivity, Saighal drew

my attention towards the eastern sky where a Sabre, with its
tail on fire, was being chased by our Gnats.

As soon as the aerial execution of the Sabres was completed,
a cry of joy and jubilation reverberated throughout the
battlefield. The battlefield appeared transformed. Many like
Chakraborty had left the comparative security of their tanks/
shelter to observe the dogfight in the open. The infantry had
virtually stepped out of the trenches to do the bhangra. Many
of them were now dancing around, asking their friends if they
had seen the spectacle of the dogfight with the Gnats shooting
down the Sabres. The pent-up anger and disgust at not using
our air power earlier, gave way to accolades for the aviators and
their lovely flying machines. So elated were their spirits that they
went about patting each other on the backs and, in so doing,
paying their own tribute to an exceptional performance put up
by the Air Force.

The meticulous planning and strategy developed and
carried out by the Air Force was remarkable in many ways.
What was puzzling was the timing and method employed. It
later transpired that the complete operation was masterminded
at Kalaikunda Air Force Base. The radar network established
around Calcutta had picked up the movement, flight path,
characteristics, and individual signatures of the Sabres after
they took off from Jessore air base on their first mission. The
suitability of the Gnats for counter-strike had to be evaluated
and comparative performance tables prepared. As the strikes
progressed, the Sabre pilots became lax in their vigilance for
they had by now convinced themselves that the Indian Air
Force would not interfere. This pattern was pinpointing
towards callousness for which they paid dearly. Soon after
the Sabres took off from Jessore, the Gnats took off from

Kalaikunda. The flight time and height at which they were to fly to avoid detection by enemy radars had been fine-tuned. The Gnats took the added precaution of flying at tree-top level to avoid detection by enemy radars and then 'reached for the sky' to hover, high up in the clouds while the Sabres continued to expend their TOT and staying power. Finding the Sabres lingering longer than their specified TOT must have gladdened the hearts of our pilots.

The implication of this was that they would have just enough fuel to return to base, thereby reducing their ability to take part in a dogfight.

Readers may sometimes get the impression that might makes right. However, the analysis above shows the intelligence that goes into victory. Experienced and knowledgeable men analyse every aspect of a fight. The facts are collated, analysed, and conclusions drawn. A commander needs to synthesise various inputs received to finalise a plan of action. He then implements a detailed plan of attack. The line officers then execute it with precision. The fight is won through intelligence, coupled with strength and daring, instead of mere attitude. This aspect of planning and execution makes this incident very meaningful for those who wear the uniform for national service and others who enjoy their freedom due to the sacrifices of the country's brave hearts.

More than three decades after the dogfight, I met Wing Cdr K.B. Bagchi who recounted in great detail what had transpired during this eventful period at the Dum Dum air base. As per his version, the embargo on use of air power had been lifted much earlier. Jessore airfield was within range of our radars and every take-off and landing was closely monitored. When the Sabres took-off, for the first mission, the order to 'scramble' had been given and four Gnat aircraft under a Group Captain were in the air when the mission was aborted due to hydraulic failure. When the Sabres came up the second time, the Gnats were 'scrambled' again. The mission leader, soon after take-off, reported trouble with the radio set, much to the disappointment of the other three pilots—Ganpathy, Massey, and Lazarus. With the mission aborted once again, the younger pilots found it difficult to hide their disappointment. The air traffic controller for this sector, Bagchi, as also the ground staff and technicians knew exactly where the problem lay. Like good gentlemen officers, they kept a stiff upper lip. The fateful last mission for which the Sabres took off a third time found Ganpathy as the mission leader. The rest is history. As per Bagchi, Lazarus was the first to spot the Sabres. While Massey was engaging a Sabre in front, another appeared on his tail. Ganapati asked him to take a break. Ganapati fired, and with the finger still on the firing button, flew through the wreckage of the Sabre. The debris of the Sabre caused damage to his aircraft and fuel tanks, which made returning to base and landing a problem. The Sabre, which was in Massey's gun sights, was damaged, but managed to return to Jessore. The three others were destroyed. As is customary, the pilots did a victory roll before landing. The entire Dum Dum base personnel came out of their houses and offices to greet the daredevil pilots. Bagchi too left his post to join the celebrations, having known the truth behind the earlier two aborted missions. While in the Officers' Mess, he received a call from the PMO (Prime Minister's Office). Sober and worried, he had the rare pleasure of receiving compliments from Prime Minister Indira Gandhi. She wanted the video recordings of the dogfight to be dispatched forthwith as she had an important announcement to make in the Parliament.

Three decades later, all the officers connected with this dogfight had retired. One reached the rank of Air Commodore before superannuation; one took premature retirement and went off to Australia; one committed suicide; Bagchi retired as Wing Commander and works for the Maharishi Shiksha Sansthan. One of the mission leaders who aborted the mission retired as an Air Marshal. *Life mein aisa bhi hota hai!* (Such things happen in life!)

The fog lifted early on 23 November, compelling us to disperse quickly. In a way, it turned out to be a blessing, for a large number of top brass was to descend upon us. This included amongst others the Corps Commander, Lt Gen T.N. Raina, PVSM, MV General Officer Commanding 2 Corps and Maj Gen Dalbir Singh, the Divisional Commander of HQ 9 Infantry Division. General Raina (Tappy to his friends) who wore a green patch over one eye, was a great one for details and any encounter with him meant answering a barrage of questions. He spoke in short, clipped sentences. He was from the Kumaon Regiment and later became Chief of the Army Staff. General Dalbir, on the other hand, was a down-to-earth soldier who enjoyed the good things of life. He belonged to the Jat Regiment, and had served with Chiefy's elder brother. With them arrived a cavalcade of jeeps and jongas bearing staff officers of all denominations. The entourage went around the battalion defended area where company commanders and troop leaders were introduced. R.K. Singh kept up a running commentary highlighting the salient points of how the battle unfolded. He finally came and stopped in front of the tank knocked off at 30 metres. Raina questioned me at length on how the amour action had been fought. He complimented us on the successful conduct of the tank versus tank battle. Brig Gharaya announced that permission to advance was withheld, otherwise the tanks would have reached Jessore on 21 November itself. This drew cheers from all present. The battle of Garibpur had become synonymous with victory to inspire an entire nation to rise as one man. Future historians would record it as the day when India transformed itself from a struggling, non-aligned third-world country, traversing world capitals with a begging bowl in hand, to a South Asian power, and an emerging world leader.

8

REST AND REPLENISH

The squadron had been in the thick of battle for over 120 hours and needed to be pulled back for rest and refit. Bains had deputed Naib Risaldar Mahato, the reconnaissance troop leader, to guide the tanks down the main Chowgacha–Jingergacha track to Bhadra, designated as the tank harbour. A troop of anti-aircraft guns was deployed to provide protection against sneak air attacks. The squadron A1 and A2 echelons were co-located. All field arrangements to welcome tank crews were in place in the harbour area.

While the boys from the administration troop were busy, helping out the tank crews with unloading and maintenance of tanks, the S/JCO Risaldar Raghubir Chandra accompanied me to meet the crew members. Everyone I met was cheerful, in high spirits and optimistic. Each had his own story to tell of how he sighted the enemy tanks and his own part in this decisive battle. They felt sorry for their comrades who had fallen but then a price had to be paid for victory. After all, this was a shooting war with no holds barred. Chiefy and all others killed in action had been cremated with full military honours. The regiment had dispatched the personal effects of the personnel killed to the next of kin, along with condolence messages from the commandant. Immediate monetary help to the bereaved families was arranged from within the limited pool of regimental funds available.

The details mentioned above may sound out of context here but those of us who lived and fought with those men understood that morale can be sustained only through such acts of goodwill, empathy, and understanding. Morale was, after all, a state of mind conditioned with the reassurance that the sacrifice of the dead would not be forgotten. To sacrifice his life for his country, his regiment, his officers, and comrades was a soldier's duty. The human relationship that exists between an officer and a soldier is completely different from, and cannot be compared to, that between an employee and his employer, union workers, or communal groups. It is a relationship of life and blood, and stays that way long after the bones have been interred.

The men having finished their errands, were moving off towards the langar to collect their mail and have their first regular meal. Raghubir Chandra guided me towards the squadron commander's caravan. This is a one-ton vehicle that serves multiple functions. During day-time it is used as a squadron-office-cum-operational room in which he can brief his 'O' group, hold briefings, etc. During the night hours, it converts into a retreat for the squadron commander. It is a functional vehicle, with a makeshift folding shelter consisting of strips of tarpaulins hung from the three sides of the vehicle, stitched together into separate compartments so that no artificial light can escape from the shelter. It provides a few hours of much needed solitude and rest for the squadron commander. I was about to step into the caravan when thoughts of Chiefy came flooding into my mind.

I pulled the tarpaulin aside to peep inside the caravan. Chiefy's personal effects had been removed and a fresh set of clean sheets and bedding placed. I must have stood gazing at it for a long time until my batman, Massey, brushing past me, went and placed my baggage inside. I suddenly felt the need to be alone.

Sitting under the huge mango tree, the events of the past few days went floating through my mind like a cloud being swept by the gentle breeze. The premonition I had had at Kulanandpur; the moment when I received the news of Chiefy's death; the ensuing tank battle; the sight of the Pakistani driver jumping off his burning tank; meeting Speedy and the other injured: the sound of the Sabres overhead—all these images zoomed through my mind. I drew solace from Rudyard Kipling's poem, 'If' in which, referring to victory and defeat, he mentions something about 'treat these two imposters just the same'. Somehow stepping into the caravan had been more difficult than taking command of the squadron during the tank versus tank battle.

It had been more than a week since I had bathed. Hot water and soap had a magical effect on bruised bones and torn muscles. Even while I was towelling myself, I wondered when was the last time I had felt so relaxed. I got into my sleeping suit, which had come in along with the rest of my luggage in the squadron's heavy baggage lorry. Massey, a resourceful batman, had procured a bottle of rum and was now pouring me a 'Patiala peg'. The combined effect of cigarettes and liquor had a wonderful stirring effect on both mind and body, when consumed in moderation. I lay back on the makeshift bed. Physical and mental exhaustion must have got the better of me as I dozed off into a deep slumber. I became aware of somebody standing close to me calling out in a monotonous tone 'Saab, Saab *utho*' (Sir, please get up). Massey had brought some hot, steaming food for which I had built up a large greedy appetite. The smell of meat curry was enough to make my taste buds start watering. The warm food in the pit of my stomach seemed to revitalize me with strength and vigour. I took a walk around the camp. Tank shelters had been pitched and the men, having finished their dinner, sat around in small groups, relating tales of all that they had experienced. These stories, with exaggerations, would be repeated, in the days to come and become part of the regimental folklore.

With thought of sleep far from my mind, I spoke to Inder and Bains. These two officers seemed to answer all calls instantly. Though it was a little late in the night, Inder agreed to send a dispatch rider with the squadron mail and a fresh stock of cigarettes for me. Bains likewise promised to hunt out The Poetical Works of Tennyson, something I had asked him to carry for me along with his maps and charts of the intelligence section before we mobilized.

I am very poor at keeping up with my correspondence. It had been months since I had written to friends or relatives. A letter for me, therefore, came as a surprise. Whoever could have thought of writing to me? Possibly one of my outstanding bills or a reminder to pay up my insurance premium from Mr Abbott from Ahmadnagar or was it perhaps Hira Bankers from Poona, very popular with hard up Army officers who had lost their meagre savings either on the Poona race track or due to extravagant tastes. I had always found it difficult to stretch a Captain's pay with my Colonel's tastes. It was from a sweet little thing I had met during my frequent visits to Ranchi. It was a letter that touched some soft spot in my heart. When would I return from the field area? She wanted to know how I passed my time and whether there was any truth in the news that war was imminent. She went on to mention that it was her firm resolve to enrol herself as a nurse in case war broke out so that she could be at hand in case I got injured. She had read with fascination a poem I had composed, passed on to her by one of her friends titled, 'For your eyes only'. She was keen to find out who 'your' was!

Tank crews maintain a stiff upper lip and rarely complain about the performance of their troop leaders but body language, poor response, and lack of excitement are indicators. Rum loosens the tongue and, gradually, word goes around, making change a compulsion. One of the troop leaders who had under-performed, was assigned administrative duties and a request was made to Digby to release Risaldar Limbu to take charge of the troop. Limbu was the only Gorkha JCO in the regiment. He was a cheerful figure, energetic and popular. I planned to assign a limited task at the next opportunity, so that they could develop self-confidence like the others. The transformation in this troop's outlook convinced me that the decision was fair and justified. A troop leader who is confident and possesses knowledge, makes all the difference between success and failure.

A troop of T-55 tanks was sent as replacements for the PT-76 tank casualties suffered during the last few days. This was unusual because as regimental officers, we were under the impression that sufficient numbers of replacement PT-76 tanks were available. In reality, it was a one-time buy, soon to be phased out; therefore, no reserves had been procured. The crew of the T-55 tanks was from 63 Cavalry. This regiment had a class composition of Sikh, Jat, and Rajput. The detachment, which came to us was from the Sikh squadron. In a clever move, they had asked the senior JCO to inform me that the main task of their sub-unit was delivery and not participation in battle, as they had not been placed under command. They were unaware that I had spent four days at their Regimental HQ in Delhi and was fully conversant with their charter of responsibility. The entire T-55 crew assembled and paraded along with their equipment for my inspection. It was then that I recognized my old gunnery instructor at ACC&S, Lance Dafadar Channan Singh, a sharp shooter and a very fine instructor. I briefly explained to them the tank battle that we had gone through and, notwithstanding their present charter of duties, asked for volunteers to operate the T-55 tanks and participate as crews. As expected, I got no positive response as their minds were already made up. I had no reason to blame them because if you are not with your own regiment in combat, there is no justification to volunteer for action beyond the call of duty. The attention was focussed on the problem of converting PT- 76 crews overnight into T-55 tank crews. I immediately sent word asking for volunteers from amongst spare crews of the squadron. A sufficient number came forward and explained that as both tanks were of Russian origin, they had undergone a number of combined classes/practical work and, with some training, would be able to handle the equipment with confidence. While the detailed crew list would be worked out later, I called for Dafadar Ramchander, who was from the Squadron Repair Organisation (SRO). He was a fine NCO and a good Driving and Maintenance (D&M) instructor, with good command and control qualities and capable of forming a team. I assigned him the responsibility to take over the T-55 tanks from the ADR Detachment and assist me in putting together the new troop.

I was extremely pleased with the early morning development and confident that we would be able to arrange a crash conversion course. For this, I needed the assistance and cooperation of

Risaldar Jagtar Singh, a white bearded, senior JCO, on the verge of retirement, and my old gunnery instructor LD Channan Singh and the SRO Dafadar Ramchander, to jointly prepare a training programme. While Jagtar would cover tactical drills and radio, Channan and Ramchander would cover gunnery and D&M, respectively. The volunteers were interviewed and selected, based on declared proficiency and grouped into tank crews. Day and night driving and recovery training, along with handling of radio equipment and practical gunnery could start forthwith. Zeroing of guns and firing of live ammunition was easy for us as we were in enemy territory with no restriction of 'Battle Zero' of guns. Worries about the number of rounds fired and accounting did not arise as long as the troop developed sufficient confidence to handle the equipment.

Logistics for the T-55 was being handled by the RHQ. I still had to provide leadership to this troop. Before raising the issue with Digby, I decided to call Narain as it was important that the person nominated be associated right from the beginning so that the entire training programme was conducted with him as the troop leader. I walked across to Narain's tank to find the crew busy with maintenance. Suddenly, Narain emerged from the driver's cupola: 'Hello Narain, good to see you.' 'Good afternoon, Sir,' he said, as he jumped off the tank to shake hands.

'You must be amongst the lucky few to have been bloodied in battle even before the YOs.'

His response was muted, whereas I was expecting excitement if not jubilation.

'Yes, Sir, it was a good experience.'

By now, the crew had also gathered around. 'So how many tank kills by your crew.' The crews had participated in the tank versus tank battle and each one gave his version.

What I found strange was that no one made a mention of Narain. This was unusual as tank crews take great pride in their officer. Addressing everyone present, I said: 'Narain Saab can now graduate as a troop leader before the next battle.' There was a sharp retort from the tank Dafadar; 'No let him learn to be a tank commander first.' Narain himself stood silent with a silly smile on his face. I knew the reason for my being soft towards Narain. I had a younger brother, younger than Narain, commissioned from the IMA Dehradun, a fortnight earlier. His request for being commissioned into the armoured corps was under consideration. Meanwhile, he had been ordered to report to 5 Garhwal Battalion, deployed under 20 Mountain Division in Hilli sector of the East Pakistan border on the same day.

A surprise, however, awaited me in the form of Risaldar Jagtar Singh.

'Sat Sri Akal Saab.'

'So what brings you back, some problem with training programme?'

'No problem, Sir, I have got them started. I have a personal request'.

'Sure Risaldar Saab, feel free to speak'.

'I want to first clear my conscience, I motivated the ADR detachment to say what they did, and they are now holding it against me.'

'I understand that a soldier wants to be with his regiment.'

'However, I was responsible for it.'

'Yes. OK. You have not committed an unlawful act. So cheer up. We got the crews, now train them.'

'If I train them, then I must lead them.'

I was very glad that a seasoned and experienced JCO belonging to another regiment had set an outstanding example of 'service before self'. By the time, Digby arrived, the crew list and training programme of the newly formed T-55 troop of C Squadron 45 Cavalry was well underway to the training area for a rapid conversion course.

It appeared that a major exercise was now underway to provide full publicity to the battles fought in this theatre. The photographer accompanying him had requested that a small part of the battle be re-enacted for the benefit of the larger Indian audience. The terrain conditions and the long haul of approximately 10 km presented numerous problems to the EME and Engineers. That much of this exercise had to be undertaken during night-time to avoid detection, demanded coordination for security as also secrecy at the regimental and divisional levels. After recovery, the Chaffees were rearranged to present a picture of tanks in an assault role towards our outpost at Boyra. The prisoners of war, weapons, and equipment and battle orders and documents supporting the attack plan of Pakistan were put up for display.

On the appointed day, Defence Minister Mr Jagivan Ram arrived to address a gathering of over 100 Indian and foreign journalists and explained to the world at large the suicidal attack plan of the Pakistani military junta. Tacit in this was the unsaid statement that India had resolved to invade and destroy the Pakistani forces and ensure the birth of a new nation— Bangladesh.

William Stewart, who visited Boyra soon after, quotes his briefer in his dispatch to the Times, 6 December 1971, thus: 'Proudfoot explains that Pakistani tanks have been probing the border near Boyra since Nov 17. On the night of Nov 20/21, a number of tanks were heard approaching Boyra. The tanks reached and began firing on the Indian positions. A squadron of

14 Indian tanks (Soviet-made PT-76) crossed into East Pakistan to outflank the Pakistani squadron. The battle raged four or five miles into East Pakistan. When the smoke cleared, three Pakistani tanks had been trapped in India, and another eight were reported destroyed. The Indians claimed a loss of only one tank.' The foreign journalists knew the truth but published this version as Pakistan had lost international goodwill due genocide and other atrocities inflicted on the refugees.

9

BELLICOSE BHARAT

Within the Indian defence establishment, the general feeling was that the 1962 War was a wake-up call for the nation. It shook up the defence establishment in many ways and prepared it for the 1965 War. After the war, reforms and restructuring of the defence establishment, military formations, and training establishments continued along with upgrading of the equipment profile and modernization which changed the outlook and thinking of the Indian Army between 1965 and 1970. The transition found India prepared for the 1971 War. Higher defence management, civil–military relations, inter-ministry coordination with the Services Headquarters was pursued with vigour and diligence. Political direction, intelligence gathering, and training of the para-military had received a major boost.

India had upheld its traditional values by keeping its borders open for refugees to enter and return at will. Imposition of refugee tax to share the burden of maintenance with Indian citizens reflected our deep concern for their well-being. The support provided to the Bangladesh government in exile and training to the Mukti Bahini strengthened their resolve to undertake this fight for liberation in conjunction with the Indian Army. The signing of the treaty of Peace, Friendship, and Cooperation with the Soviet Union was a masterstroke for which credit is due to Mrs Indira Gandhi's political acumen as also the wisdom of the civil servants, then at the helm.

As junior officers, we would often discuss role of outstanding personalities like P.N. Haksar, R.N. Kao, D.P. Dhar, T.N. Kaul, and Rustamji, loosely referred to as the 'Kashmiri Mafia'. Prominent Institute of Defence Studies and Analyses (IDSA) Director, K Subramaniam, a strategic thinker and visionary, had developed a sterling reputation for accurate analysis. Young officers of my generation who had grown up around the time of partition carried unhappy memories of the 1962 debacle, and the unfinished war of 1965. They were influenced by the leadership of military stalwarts like Gen Manekshaw, Gen Aurora, Gen Sagat, Gen Jacob, Gen Gill.

Operation Searchlight on 25 March 1971 was a military solution to a political problem which finally lead to genocide, rape, and plunder by the army. The Pakistani decision makers did not visualize probability of war when they unleashed Op Searchlight. They were satisfied that the 'traitors' and 'miscreants' along with other Hindu refugees had fled or were now dispersed. Thought of war in April/May was considered improbable. The picture changed during August/September/October due to activities of Mukti Bahini with tacit support and training from India, making war a probability but still avoidable. This was in sync with the commonly shared perception of the Pakistani governing elite that the international community would constrain any Indian propensity for aggression, and that if hostilities did commence it would be halted before Indian victory as had been the pattern of the three earlier wars fought during the first 25 years of independence.

Before Mrs Indira Gandhi commenced her visit to Europe and the USA in late October 1971, Pakistani attempts to dramatize their case before international communities and eagerness to reduce regional tensions increased manifold. On 12 October, Yahya announced plan for providing fresh constitution to Pakistan by 20 December 1971 followed by elections to appease the international community. In his address to the nation on 19 November 1971, Yahya Khan declared that Pakistan would defend its 'honour and territorial integrity at any cost'. The western press was beginning to see the incongruity of Pakistani declarations as also the plight of the 10 million refugees now residing in India. 21 November not only gave a bloody nose to the Pakistanis but also shook their misplaced belief in their cultural and historical superiority and proud heritage of having been the rulers of India.

What was the military leadership in Pakistan doing on the fateful day, 21 November 1971, when war broke out between the two countries? Excerpts from Niazi's book make an interesting reading (*The Betrayal of East Pakistan* by Lt Gen A.A.K. Niazi, 1998, p. 123).

On 21 November, my Chief of Staff rang up the vice Chief of General Staff at GHQ, Major-General Qureshi, and followed up with a written signal about the Indian invasion. I tried to speak to the Chief of General Staff, Lt. Gen Gul Hassan. However, he had gone to Lahore to celebrate Eid. Knowing that the Indians were going to attack East Pakistan on 21 November, I tried to contact Gen Hamid, COAS. He too was not available. I learnt later that both he and the President had left for Sialkot, ostensibly to visit troops but actually, for a partridge shoot – no C-in-C visits Muslim troops on an Eid day. The callous attitude of the three senior-most officers of the Army shows that they were not in the least interested in the affairs of East Pakistan or the integrity of Pakistan. Like Nero, they played, while Dhaka burned.

Mrs Gandhi made a statement on the incident in Parliament on 24 November:

On 21 November, Pakistan Infantry, supported by tanks and artillery, launched an offensive on the Mukti Bahini, which was holding the liberated area around Boyra, five miles from our eastern border. Pakistani armour, under heavy artillery cover, advanced to our border, threatening our defensive positions. Their shells fell in our territory, wounding a number of our men. The local military commander took appropriate action to repulse the Pakistani attacks. In this action, 13 Pakistani Chaffee tanks were destroyed.

On 22 November, the Pakistani forces called up an air strike of four Sabre jets on our positions. These were intercepted within Indian territory by our Gnats, which destroyed three Sabre jets. Two of the Pakistani pilots who bailed out were captured in our territory, indicating the Pakistani air intrusion into Indian air space. We regard this as a purely local action. (General Sukhwant Singh, *India's Wars Since Independence*, 2009, p. 124; *Asian Recorder*, Vol XVII, No 51, pp. 10511–10512).

Mrs Indira Gandhi announced in Parliament on 24 November that the Indian forces had been instructed 'to enter East Pakistan territory in self-defence. The military implication of this declaration was that after the night of 21 November the tactics had changed in one significant way—Indian forces and Mukti Bahini would not withdraw from areas occupied. A number of other formations, earmarked small tactical units to launch limited attacks to secure launch pads for subsequent operations. These were described as defensive responses to Pakistani shelling of Indian territory. These preparatory attacks used relatively small units causing uncertainty in Pakistan as to whether this was part of an all-out attack or a more limited campaign with the seizure of some territory as its goal.

Differences within the top military leadership became evident after the battle of Garibpur on 21 November 1971. Lieutenant General A.A.K. Niazi declared that for his Eastern Command the war had commenced. The C-in-C and his closest advisers estimated that India's move was a limited action and should be utilized to impress upon the super powers to contain India diplomatically. The strong sentiment of the Pakistani officer fraternity expressed itself openly when Gen Yahya Khan was greeted by chants of 'Allah-O-Akbar' while reviewing troops at Sialkot on 22 November. The assembled officers strongly pushed for declaration of war as a matter of pride, prudence, and necessity. Waiting for United States or United Nations to find a political solution was viewed as numbness and paralysis.

After the Battle of Garibpur, General Hamid called the Chiefs of the Air Force, Navy, and Chief of Army General staff and advised them that war with India had become inevitable. A national emergency was declared and the Air Force placed on 'phase two' alert. The commitment to prepare for battle is reflected in the message received from General Hamid commending Gen Niazi on 30 November: 'In meeting the latest challenge posed by the enemy in East Pakistan. The whole nation is proud of you and you have their full support. The gallant deeds of your soldiers in thwarting the enemy's evil designs have earned the gratitude of all countrymen. Keep up the noble work till the enemy's spirit is crushed and they are completely wiped out from our sacred soil. May ALLAH be with you.' General Niazi replied: 'reassuring you and pledging afresh at this critical juncture of our history we will INSHALLAH fully honour the great confidence that has been reposed in us and no sacrifice will be considered too great in defending our sacred fatherland.' General Niazi in his reply to letter from Gen Hamid wrote; 'Bharati onslaught has been blunted. God willing, we will take the war into Indian soil to finally crush the very spirit of non-believers through the supreme force of ISLAM. Pray and believe that the ultimate victory will be ours. INSHALLAH.'

Pakistani military leaders were under increasing pressure to declare war partly due to sensitivity to the adverse publicity in the western press—an image of 'nitwits and idiots' rendered powerless by India. Second, the aggression by India had not evoked any international response due to increased appreciation and sympathy for the refugee influx and human suffering. Third, Bhutto's caustic, graphic, and primitive details of what Mrs Gandhi was doing to the military leaders of Pakistan and threat delivered by him that 'lynching by the people' would be the only alternative unless war is declared by Gen Yahya Khan.

The Indian Army representative described Garibpur as a 'limited defensive action'. A correspondent of the New York Times described it as 'a policy of gradually increasing military pressure'. In Pakistan, Yayha Khan declared that a 'grave situation' had arisen following a 'threat of aggression' and soon after, proclaimed 'a state of emergency' in Pakistan.

On the morning of 22 November 1971, at the White House, Kissinger, relying on Pakistani radio broadcasts, informed Nixon about the attack 'heavily backed by the Indians'. 'It's a naked case of aggression, Mr President.' The next day, when told that a discussion at the United Nations was the only way forward, Kissinger snapped, 'Let's not kid ourselves—that means Pakistan will get raped.' The same day, Kissinger was directed by Nixon to 'lay it out thick' and suspend all aid to both countries, which would 'hurt the Indians more'. Nixon ordered Kissinger to 'tilt' their policy towards Pakistan wherever they could.

Kissinger, along with George Bush, Alexander Haig, and Winston Lord, were holding the first meeting at a Central Intelligence Agency (CIA) safe house in New York with the Chinese delegation led by Huang Hua, the new Ambassador at the United Nations, on the same day. Kissinger and Haig gave a military briefing, accusing Indian troops of attacking near Jessore and tantalizingly suggesting that India had left its northern border with China exposed.

The tank battle of 21 November 1971 had sent alarm bells ringing in the world capitals. The decibels multiplied soon after when Pakistan launched air attack on six Indian airfields on 3 December 1971. Kissinger told President Nixon that India had initiated fighting in the Western sector also. Nixon responded, 'It is a tragedy the Indians are so treacherous.' In the United Nations the exercise of veto by the Soviet Union was viewed as 'watershed' in the US–Soviet relations. The US encouragement to China to move troops and fear of Soviet reaction to China's gamble created a scenario where lobbying nuclear weapons or employment of conventional weapons began to be debated. Finally, the realization that China had no intention of moving troops and Soviet agreement of 'no more fist fights over Veto', and Pakistani surrender in East Pakistan ended the crisis.

Nixon and Kissinger felt that they had achieved the fundamental goal of preserving West Pakistan. The battle of Garibpur fought on 21 November 1971 represents a significant and radical change in the political and military mindset of the country. India had matured and was beginning to shed its 'historical baggage' to mould itself into an assertive and responsible regional power on the sub-continent. It was on this day, later adopted as the Bangladesh Armed Forces Deployment of troops in the 2 Corps Sector Day, that Mitro Bahini (Allied Forces) of India and Bangladesh was formalized to undertake joint operations in the war of Liberation against Pakistan under the overall command of GOC-IN-C, HQ Eastern Command, Lt Gen J.S. Aurora. This early victory served as a trumpet call across the globe, announcing the birth of a new nation— Bangladesh and India as an emerging Regional Power.

The US President Richard Nixon phoned Britain's Prime Minister Edward Heath and discussed the India–Pakistan situation. The US Ambassador to Moscow Jacob Beam visited the Soviet Foreign Ministry twice during the week to urge the Russians, who had become India's chief sponsors, to help stop the fighting. Zulfiqar Bhutto was despatched to UN Headquarters to salvage the country's reputation. A flurry of diplomatic and political activity was reported from world capitals, especially New Delhi and Moscow.

10

BURINDA BASH

A tank's attributes of firepower, mobility, and armoured protection are well recognized. Working with infantry battalions, we realized that the sound of the tank engines was an additional attribute which could be exploited as a tool for deception as also obscure the enemy's assessment of the tanks deployed opposite them. The mere sound of the tanks at night multiplied tension and the fear of localities being bypassed and routes of withdrawal being cut off. More than physical, it was a weapon directed at the perception of the enemy, causing alarm and trepidation in the enemy camp. It is very difficult to judge the size of a tank column, or the direction or distance of tank movement as the intensity of the tank noise varies with the changing wind direction and velocity-causing confusion. The regular movement of squadrons for limited operations between brigade locations during the night had deceived the enemy into believing that a tank brigade was opposing them when in reality it was but an armoured regiment.

The rest and relief for 72 hours had helped put body and soul together. With our human batteries recharged, we were ready for our next task. The newly composed T-55 troop had completed intensive training and appeared enthusiastic. Mujibur Rehman continued to be in jail, with constant danger of extermination. Bhutto, inducted as Foreign Minister, was heading to New York to present Pakistan's case in the UN General Assembly. The Bangladesh government-in-exile had become much more assertive and was making regular broadcasts, appealing to the world community, from a transmitting station off the coast in the Bay of Bengal. India, straddled with over 10 lakh refugees, had stopped issuing appeals for assistance. For once, India was fully prepared. The *jawan*, *kisan*, and *janta* (the soldier, the farmer, and the common man) were convinced that the cause was justified.

Our next assignment, announced by Digby, was to replace B Squadron under HQ 350 Infantry Brigade on the night of 2/3 December.

The Brigade Commander Brig H.S. Sandhu was a short, stocky Sikh who welcomed me in his tented office with a big hug. Brig Sandhu confided that the JAK LI battalion, which had gone in for an attack a day earlier, had suffered very heavy casualties. The enemy was well entrenched and occupying the high bund with good all-round observation and clear field of fire. To ensure success, he had proposed air sorties to soften the target, followed by carpet-bombing, if necessary.

His staff officer, Maj Reddy, fresh from Staff College, had taken over the appointment of Brigade Major. He provided insights into the failure of the earlier attack and made some valid suggestions about close cooperation with the battalion. The troop leaders and tank commanders who had accompanied me were despatched to meet their counterparts so that the process of 'marrying up' and taking over of 'operational responsibilities' could be completed and B Squadron relieved during the same night.

Relieving a squadron which is in contact with enemy defences is a deliberate operation, planned and coordinated with the battalion as it is subject to enemy interference and shelling. The two troops selected to relieve B Squadron were the newly converted T-55 troop and Risaldar Limbu's No. 4 troop. The battalion had planned a limited operation to occupy a portion of the pond near Matsarganya position to eliminate enemy observation of the minefield and fire from that area. The Limbu troop was tasked provide fire support and shoot in the infantry company.

The attack started at the given time. The enemy locality was plastered by artillery shelling to soften the target. The Matsarganya position was in reality a false front to deny observation of the main defences. The enemy, realizing that their objective of delay and denial had been achieved, quietly withdrew to their main defences. The engineers claimed that the tank lane clearance would take another half hour but the infantry lane was clear. I directed a stern message for Ris Limbu D for D4: 'Tanks will not cross minefield till my orders, Roger Over.'

'D4 for D: Wilco. Over', came the much-relieved response from Limbu. A visibly upset CO, supported by his battalion 2IC, an ex-cavalry officer, was up in arms: 'How dare you countermand orders of the CO,' barked the 2IC.

'This is an emergency; the enemy is about to launch an attack, move the tanks.'

'Why did you not move the reserve company after the infantry lane was cleared?'

'That was my decision, I am the commander.'

'Fine, but remember I am the tank commander here not your 2IC.'

A couple of minutes passed, all parties hot under the collar, when word came through the Engineer channel that the tank lane was clear for induction. The so-called enemy counter-attack turned out to be a red herring, a ploy to have the tanks inducted in an early timeframe to secure the much-coveted foothold.

I ordered Limbu to send a joint patrol and confirm that the tank lane was ready before induction. The adjutant was shocked that a junior officer could go against the orders of his CO. After about ten minutes, the tanks were inducted and the threat of an imaginary counter-attack set to rest. That the CO would consider my actions as an affront to his rank and authority is something I would learn next day from the Commandant 45 Cavalry.

Saighal and Narain were just preparing to have dinner when I joined them in the tank harbour. Before returning to my tank, Narain was briefed to keep in radio communication with Limbu and not disturb me unless, of course, there was a real emergency. Saying that, I entered my tank. There was a cosy little space on the left side of the driver's seat, where, if not full length, at least, you could crouch down into a comfortable position. The degree of physical exhaustion would determine the length and nature of sleep. My bed consisted of linear pipes housing cables running between the engine and the driver's compartment. The medicine and tank toolbox supported by the land and water gear lever made an excellent place to recline the head while lying on one side as if in a vice-like grip. The feet, in all positions, had to rest against the metal partition between the driver and fighting compartment. The stench of grease, engine oils, burnt diesel, and wet leather along with the disgusting odour of unwashed clothing, stinking socks, and bedding of the crews invaded the nostrils. The odd blanket or overcoat carried within it a bouquet of aromas of the countryside over which it had been spread, the smell of cordite and gunpowder emanating through the fabric. Individual body odours and hygiene, depending on dietary habits, were thoughts that never hit the conscious mind as physical exhaustion numbs and regulates the senses. Memories of having lived through difficult moments still resurface whenever a nostalgic mood sets in. It is perhaps true that when life itself is in danger, other hardships tend to disappear or else are tolerated with relative ease. Within minutes of entering the tank, I had created a hassle-free position and fell into a deep sleep. I came back to life only in the early morning, with somebody urgently nudging me. I rubbed my eyes to see someone holding the field telephone, plugged into the Battalion HQ exchange in front of me.

'Sir, the adjutant of 4 Sikh has an urgent message for you.' Capt Panag was a responsible officer, surely the message was important.

'Yes, Panag, what's up?'

'Sir, sorry to inform you, Risaldar Limbu is being evacuated to the Advanced Dressing Station (ADS).'

'Where is he now? Can I speak to him?'

'He wanted to speak with you. He is in the ambulance which will soon cross your location.'

I dropped the telephone and in a slow deliberate motion pulled myself out of the cupola and in the same movement, jumped off the tank. 'Narain, where the fucken hell is Narain.' My sense of disappointment and guilt got the better of me for I was now moving towards Narain's tank, angry, stressed, and yelling at the top of my voice at his not having informed me about the casualty. I must have sounded more like a battalion war cry while assaulting the enemy position. Two crew members leaped out of my path, leading me towards Narain's tank. Narain crawled out from under the tank to expose himself to a volcanic outburst 'you asshole, what were my orders?' He stumbled for words to explain briefly the circumstances and actions taken by him. I could see Saighal in the background, nervous that I may overstep my authority by getting physical. I turned around to face him when he tactfully reminded me that the ambulance was on its way to the ADS. I got into the waiting Rover to meet Limbu now en route to the ADS. Halfway through, I saw the ambulance and stopped to meet Limbu. It was a poignant experience meeting the ever smiling, cheerful Limbu, now in deep agony and pain. In spite of the excruciating pain which must be gripping his body, he tensed his muscles and let his smile spread to cover the fear in his eyes 'Saab, I did my best . . .' He stretched out to hold my hand and said, 'I will come back to serve with you again.'

What had happened was that after the infantry had firmed in, he had personally guided his tanks through the minefield lanes into new positions, keeping in view the deployment in the defended locality. As soon as the tanks started, the enemy began shelling the post. The shelling must have been heavy and well directed, possibly through a stay behind OP officer. Undaunted by this, Limbu carried on with his task until splinters from one of the shells struck him to tear up his chest and stomach. Fortunately, his injuries were not very serious though the bleeding and loss of blood had left him weak. I felt all the more sorry for him as I had specially asked for this full-blooded Gurkha to join me in battle. He was the only Gurkha JCO serving in the OIC Squadron, in fact, the entire regiment.

He had enrolled against some unspecified vacancy entitled to the northeastern states about 16 years earlier. The armoured regiments did not have Gurkhas in their class composition due to the recruitment policy as also the impression cultivated under the British that the Gurkhas could do wonders with 'a khukri in hand and *ayeho gorkhali* on their lips' after they were sufficiently packed with rum inside. I could not help but feel his departure as a personal loss. I wished him well and let the ambulance go.

The GOC arrived at the location of HQ 350 Infantry Brigade to finalize the attack plans. A long animated discussion on the attack plan followed the presentation made by Col Basant Singh. The Burinda defences were built around a series of ponds stretching approximately 400 yards and 400 yards deep, with high embankments. The enemy had prepared for all-round defence, covering the approaches with minefields and MMG fire. From whichever direction the enemy was approached, it would become a frontal attack. Absence of cover over the last 100 yards made the task more difficult. Artillery shelling had proved to be ineffective, as a majority of the shells would land in the pond itself, without causing any damage to the enemy defences. Air sorties and carpet-bombing were essential and inbuilt into the new fire plan. The armour would provide close support, with the troop of T-55 tanks shooting in the infantry. The PT-76 squadron less one troop would conduct an outflank of Burinda and establish a firm base on their withdrawal route. The capture of Burinda had become a prestige issue for the division as it was the shortest route to Jessore.

The CO, his 2IC, Maj Bal, and I sat together in the command post for Phase 1, listening intently to the progress made by the company commander. The infantry company commander, on reaching the launch pad, reported the enemy withdrawing. He did not realize that he had walked into a trap. The troops were caught in the open and came under intense fire of MMG and heavy artillery shelling. The leading platoon was pinned down and could make no progress. It appeared as if the entire company had been fossilized into inaction. From the messages now coming into the command post, it was evident that the company commander could no longer exercise command over the troops. The CO advanced Phase 2, ahead of the schedule, realizing the gravity of the situation. The likelihood of unbearably high casualties left me duty bound to rise to the occasion and comply with the diktat. I left the command post and made a dash to the tank squadron location for the commencement of Phase 2.

The area through which I was now sprinting to reach the tanks, approximately 600 yards away, was under artillery shelling. One would hear the shrill whine of the shells flying in the air to determine the direction in which the shells would burst and then quickly dive into the nearest ditch or tree, hoping like hell that it would not fall too close. I felt more like a rabbit hopping from one bush to another to avoid falling prey to providence. On two instances, the shell landed on the tree, with splinters falling around me. In another occurrence, the splinters came shooting into the little fold in the ground in which I was lying, my head rolled down, my hands on my ears, when pieces of shrapnel rolled on and struck my sides, their energy luckily spent out. It appeared as if I had crossed a time zone, though it was an experience stretching only a few minutes.

While panting for breath, I complimented myself on the distance and speed at which I had traversed the area between the command post and tank harbour without losing a limb or attracting too many flying objects. Waiting for the tank commanders to arrive for the briefing, I was thinking of how I should explain to the crews the critical situation in which the infantry company had placed itself, necessitating the change in orders. I felt it was crucial to brief them again about the extent of the minefield described by Lt Purshottam, an engineer officer, and carefully follow the outer periphery of the tree line, as mentioned in his briefing to us. The location of Limbu's troop, now being led by Narain, and of T-55 troop, west of our location, was indicated, and Narain informed about own move on the radio so that a misunderstanding and the likelihood of shooting at each other was eliminated. To ensure better coordination with the infantry, the company commander sent an officer so that we could coordinate our movement and cut off the enemy's withdrawal route at the same time. There were only about 10 minutes of daylight left when Phase 2 commenced.

As soon as the tanks spread out, one could glance back to see a column of tanks advancing, with infantry mounted, while the others moved in some tactical formation led by their platoon commanders. There was a gap of about 200–300 yards between the two tank troops that were following me. From a study of the map, we were aware that the axis of advance chosen would have to cross a large marshy area, stretching on either side of the axis. The infantry quickly dismounted and moved across to secure the only culvert over the bog and signal to us to advance. The culvert had seen better days when felled logs were used to construct this contraption for the loaded bullock carts to ply across for trade. My tank, being the first to cross, had the advantage of an experienced driver to negotiate the culvert whose width was a couple of inches shorter than the width of the tank. That it did not collapse under the dead weight of the tank was in itself a marvel. During less gruelling circumstances, we would never have dared to risk putting 14 tons of tank load on this ramshackle bridge.

Having crossed the culvert, we deployed briefly to guard against a surprise attack before resuming the advance. Having gone some distance, I looked back to find the last tank near the culvert. I felt happy that the creaking bridge was able to sustain the tank movement. I was partially wrong for shortly thereafter there was a radio message of Dafadar Ishwar to say that his tank had slid off, with the tank belly balancing precariously on the left half of the culvert. With dusk descending rapidly, it was important to get a move on. The crew of the last tank would do self-recovery or seek the assistance of the repair and recovery team following the tank column.

We were now going past the location occupied by Narain's troop in Phase 1 of the attack. It struck me that Narain had moved well forward of the infantry company commander who kept sending his guides rearwards to contact the tanks while sending incorrect messages to his CO that the cavalry had not caught up with him. I pointed out this fact to Purshottam and asked him to make a mental note of the tanks being well forward and not in the rear of this unfortunate company commander.

After sunset, a few minutes of light remains before darkness envelops the earth. This is referred to as telescopic light during which targets can be acquired and weapons can still use their direct sights to engage targets. In this fading light, with minimal visibility, a rocket launcher opened fire. The rocket launcher never got the opportunity to fire a second round as Harish Chander, my gunner, blew him up sky high, with his first round. The tanks behind me quickly took up position and drew enemy fire. It appeared that either we had hit right into the enemy prepared position or they had sidestepped some detachment to block our plan for outflank. My gunner had spotted movement 50 yards ahead in a well-dug-in bunker and fired another HE shell, followed by an MG in quick succession. As the tank charged towards the bunker, the occupants inside decided to withdraw. The gunner did not hesitate for he let go another HE, which must have blown the withdrawing enemy to pieces. Around the same time, I heard a big explosion from the tank on my left. There was no flash from the gun—that meant the gunner had not fired but I remembered seeing some black smoke coming from the side of the tank. I thought that another RCL / rocket launcher had fired and scored a hit. I ordered the gunner to let go a few rounds in the general area from where the fire may have come to settle scores. (Much later, I would learn the truth.) When I was moving off from this position I got a message from the CO that his company commander had reported that the tanks had still not arrived in his location. Instead of reacting to something so baseless, I simply asked him to speak to his battalion officer and Purshottam, travelling on my tank. This proved very effective, as I was never pestered with queries from the CO after that.

We now had to find a way through the village. Anybody who has seen the villages in West Bengal would understand the difficult task of navigating tanks at night when the enemy is creeping around every bush. Each family hutment has a shallow pond, while the village virtually lived off the main pond much larger than all the smaller ones put together. Added to this are the small, narrow winding lanes and mud-plastered houses. With an infantry platoon guiding the tanks, we managed, after much turning, twisting, reversing, and hitting into trees, to keep moving forward in total darkness. What was worse were the bamboos and overhead branches which kept crashing against the tank turret, sometimes like bent bows suddenly released to strike bodily parts like a whiplash, leaving tell-tale marks on the body and face. I felt acute pain in my nose, which had been bleeding after an unrelenting branch had struck the commander's cupola and broken the latch lock that brought the front edge of the cupola against my nose and displaced some of my front teeth. I could feel the swelling on my lips, making speech difficult. A stage arrived when due to loss of blood and intense pain I had to remove the headgear and ask the operator to man the radio. We finally traversed the route and reached the masjid area where we were to deploy. Somewhere between nursing my broken nose and stopping the profuse bleeding, I realized that no other tank had arrived at the location. The operator's repeated messages on the radio also drew a blank. However, considering the fact that as squadron commander I had reached the objective, justified my report to the CO that the squadron was on the objective. I then put Purshottam on the line to answer all the CO's queries and doubts so that he would end up fully satisfied.

The enemy had no way of knowing how many tanks had penetrated their defences to cut off their routes of withdrawal. The sounds of the tank engines and the roar of the guns were sufficient to demoralize his will to fight. The excellent company commander, Duggal, himself had to overcome great odds but was progressing well to finally link up. The infantry advance had slowed down as the enemy had started firing air bursts causing a large number of casualties. The enemy had cleverly withdrawn by pulling out under cover of darkness and artillery air burst, thereby, discouraging hot pursuit.

Totally overcome by fatigue and loss of blood, I found it difficult to even retain a thought in my mind. I tried cigarettes to keep me on my legs but found it becoming more and more difficult. Saighal who was watching this, agreed to take charge while I finally threw off my headset and slipped into the driver's seat, watching an airburst directly overhead and with that, I passed out.

The catnap, in spite of the pandemonium all around, had done some good and revived me physically as also stopped the dripping blood, though the pain persisted. I met Duggal, the company commander and tried to extract information regarding the tanks but drew a blank. Having again failed in my attempts to communicate, I told him that I had to get back and trace my tanks as all communication had been lost. I left Saighal in charge of the tank, asking him to continue in the same locations. The Phase 2 success signal had been given and soon the 'F' echelon would fetch up. Duggal had been good enough to lend me his civilian guide, a local of the village, who knew the tracks and routes well. This young Mukti Bahini guide led me on the track out of the village, where earlier we had blown off the rocket launcher and MG post. The moon had come out from behind the clouds, spraying gentle light over the battlefield, helping me follow my tank tracks backwards to unveil the mystery of the now silent tanks.

We did not have to go very far as within a few hundred yards we identified the silhouette of the tank, which I had crossed earlier after destruction of the rocket launcher. Absence of smoke or fire renewed hopes that all was well. We quickened our pace to the extent possible under the circumstances. A little further, a second silhouette appeared not very far from the first one. I had the uncomfortable feeling that the tank was far too close to the first one, which was tactically faulty. Two tanks, two sets of tank crews and no sign of movement or recognition by them sent my spine tingling. Something was seriously wrong. By now, we had reached within shouting distance of the tanks and expected to spot some movement or sound or at least acknowledgement of our presence. It struck me that the angle at which the gun was pointing could not be real, as direct firing weapons never elevate guns higher than say 30 degrees whereas the tank gun in front of me was well beyond 45 degrees. I was getting annoyed at this scene and also desperate and worried to unravel the mystery of the static immobilized tanks and no crew response. I had taken may be just two or three steps forward, hoping to mount the tank and shake the crew when the civilian guide caught me from behind and pulled at my jacket, bringing me to a sudden halt. He was mumbling something in Bengali, which I could not understand. But, I could sense the urgency in his tone and voice. As I turned to look at him, he pointed to a small harmless fold in the ground, just where my next step would have landed. He then pointed to similar mounds in the vicinity of the first one. In the moonlight, the little mounds did not appear unusual or even alarming. I asked him what he meant and with his hand extended fully forward, he pointed in the surrounding pattern of small uneven mounds set apart every 3–4 feet. Never having seen a minefield or a live mine, having skipped the field engineering classes earlier in the academy days I had closed my mind completely to such a possibility.

Like so many others from my batch, we would talk and discuss mines without having handled them. The civilian guide by pulling me back at that critical time, had saved my life or possibly saved me from getting maimed or losing a limb or two, coming under the blast of an anti-tank mine which invariably had an anti-personnel mine attached to discourage deactivation. In the same instant, it became clear why the tank next to me was lying immobilized like a badly beaten Sumo wrestler with the gun dangling at an unnatural angle. I felt sheepish at my ignorance and stupidity but then I had never seen a sight like the one I was witnessing under the moonlight. The moment the tank stepped over the anti-tank mine, a big bang would have thrown it up in the air, damaging the tank tracks and bogey wheels, possibly penetrating the hull plate. The impact would lead to damaging the gun control and engine compartment sufficiently to put the tank out of commission. The crew inside would be lucky to survive but would definitely receive injuries, depending upon the point of impact and the position of the crew inside the tank at the time of the blast. I thanked the civilian guide and asked him to retrace his steps, back to the path where we had left our own tank tracks. The thought that our tank tracks had passed through the same minefield, and that too intact, was a very humbling experience, making us realize the old soldier's belief that the bullet that gets you will have your name written on it. Call it destiny, fate, luck, kismet, whatever, for the difference between the martyr and the fighting soldier is sometimes as fine as the one we had treaded. Fate had conspired to move us through 800 yards of an anti-tank minefield of density two, having a high kill probability of 66 per cent, to reach the objective only to return to test the limits of luck once again. Was I being guided by the hand of the Mukti Bahini guide or was it the hand of God providing the protective umbrella?

We kept following the tank tracks, making very sure not to miss out even an inch after the recent brush with destiny. With every step, my weariness seemed to be multiplying. The loss of blood, the physical fatigue, combined with the tension of tracing elements of my command, not knowing their safety and well-being, was beginning to wear me down. In spite of the early morning chill, I felt the need to remove the overcoat, as it was beginning to weigh a ton. We had slowed down considerably but not quite given up when another silhouette appeared in front of us. The first thought that ran through the mind, conditioned by our more recent experience, was fear of yet another casualty. A little closer and the cloud of doubt gave way to jubilation as a feeling of relief came over me when I saw somebody getting out of the tank. The crews soon gathered around, including the crews of the two disabled tanks. The worst affected was the troop leader Chakraborty who had suffered concussion and needed to be evacuated to the ADS but refused, confident that a few aspirins and a bandage would see him through. Chakraborty was tall, of slight built, mentally and physically fit, and as tough as a nail. He was a fine regimental football player and basketball player of merit. Qualities of courage and personal example are more easily imbibed by sportspersons. By not taking the easy path to the ADS, he would set an example for others to follow, including certain officers of the regiment.

The loss of blood had made me so weak that even the short walk had drained all the energy from my body. I remember that even making enquiries needed a special effort. I felt cold sweat forming on my brow and my legs gradually giving way. I placed my hands on the tank to prevent myself from falling. Suddenly, everything around me was beginning to spin, and the thought that this was a blackout crossed my mind. The next thing I remember was somebody holding a mug of water to my mouth. Those around me got worried thinking that I had been hit and were about to evacuate me as I straightened out and told them that in another few minutes, I would be okay. I did not have the will or the desire to get up, so I reclined against the bogey wheel where I had fallen to let the cold sweat evaporate and the blood circulation revive while my heart regained its normal rhythm. Soon enough, I was up on my feet, mingling with the crews. The anxiety over whether we had suffered tank casualties was everybody's concern. The paramount thought that it remained a creditable performance could not be overlooked as Burinda was finally ours. The operation had been successful in the sense that the enemy had been evicted from the stronghold but this had been at a tremendous cost in both men and material. I was later to learn that the infantry battalion had about 40 soldiers killed and about 80 seriously injured. My own losses had been two tanks blown up by mines and one knocked out by a rocket launcher. The Pakistani commander had put up a glorious fight, shown courage, and put up some very stiff resistance from their well-dug-in defences. The resistance had been tough and the fighting extremely bitter, but we had finally managed to overwhelm them. The battalion had paid an unreasonably high cost for a pyrrhic victory. That we had at least managed to win the psychological initiative once again was true. The sacrifice made by the battalion would be judged by future regimental historians to confirm if it was in keeping with the sterling reputation for glory of this battalion.

The thought uppermost in my mind was that the immobilized tanks, capable of repair after recovery, must be protected. I then approached the Brigade Major who read the situation right and agreed to divert all available resources. In addition, I instructed the T-55 tanks to position themselves at the mouth of the minefield so that they could dominate the areas. The next task was to put the functional tanks and crews together and induct them through the minefield to deploy beyond the objective. I made a quick count of the tanks available. My good

friend and knight in shining armour, the civilian guide, was still
with me, to guide me back to the waiting crews. We had not
advanced more than 200 yards when, in the stillness of the night,
we froze in our tracks on hearing the blood curdling metallic
sound of somebody cocking LMG. A booming voice challenged
us, '*Thumb, kaun jata hai, pechan ke liye aage badh*' (Stop, who
goes there, step forward for identification). Another audible
voice saying, '*Jaldi load kareen*' (Punjabi for load quickly),
followed and I stopped dead in my tracks. I looked back to
see the shadow of two Sikh soldiers in their shallow trench. I
yelled back saying we were friends. I do not think this sounded
convincing enough but at least it had the desired effect and the
NCO commander decided to hold his fire. He ordered us to
raise our hands. We stood there frozen stiff with apprehension
until he asked us to move forward for identification. While still
walking, I decided to fire a volley of the choicest Punjabi abuses
throwing in the names of his CO and 2IC for effect. '*Bara tej
banda lagda hai*' (this guy appears to be extra smart) is all I heard
in reply. When we got closer, he ordered his sentry to stand
down: 'Sat sri akal saab ji', he greeted us with aplomb. He said
he became suspicious because of the civilian and would have
opened fire without batting an eyelid. It was evident that the
company occupying the defences had no idea that this civilian
was a Mukti Bahini guide provided by Duggal's company. As
I had to traverse through the defended sector occupied by the
Sikh battalion, it would have been pragmatic to have a Sikh
guide. My ability to curse in Punjabi had released the pressure
from the nervous trigger finger of the sentry, otherwise who
knows what would have been the outcome. Knowledge of
Punjabi expletives has its advantages! We started off once again,
taking the added precaution of keeping the Sikh guide in the

rear just in case some overhyped sentry got the idea that the Sikh was being taken away as a captive.

On reaching the tank location, the crews gathered around to discuss the move of the remaining tanks across the minefield. It was evident that the only safe lane across the minefield were my tank tracks. A guide was to be positioned on each track and ordered to use a torch to illuminate the track and help the driver in keeping the correct alignment. The tank commander would sit near the driver's hatch to keep a watch on the track and guide the driver from drifting away by exercising control, till the tank had crossed the minefield. The most experienced driver was to take charge.

The tanks started rolling forward in a slow deliberate manner. Dafadar Ramnath's tank was in the lead, followed by Narain's. Some initial nervousness led to lack of synchronization between the driver's ability to follow the torch signals from the two guides and blend with the verbal instructions of the commander. This was overcome. Steady progress was now evident and they were now moving through the 800 yards minefield, in a slow controlled manner. By that time, Dafadar Ramnath had cleared the minefield, Narain's tank was only 200 yards behind. I had briefed Narain personally to ensure that no latitude was given to anybody regarding the mine drill in view of the inherent dangers. I left him in charge to meet Saighal who had sent word through Dafadar Sharma that while relocating my tank, it had bellied and needed recovery urgently. 'What happened?' I asked Saighal, who appeared crestfallen. The driver, while attempting to manoeuvre over the narrow embankment of the pond, lost control, resulting in the tank virtually sliding into the pond before it bellied. One of the T-55 tanks along with a section of engineers would be required to recover it, with the help of some of the infantry and engineer boys. Our bag of woes was not packed to capacity yet and greater challenges lay ahead demanding the immediate attention of the squadron commander.

'It does not rain, it pours', when things begin to slide out of control! Our run of luck now confirmed this belief.

After my departure, overcome by fatigue, cold and all the other hazards of soldiering, Narain, contrary to orders, found it prudent to hand over charge of guiding his tank to his NCO and stepped into the warmth of the fighting compartment with a blanket wrapped around his shoulders. In his own words, he was taking a short nap when there was a loud explosion that flung him upwards against the turret. He felt excruciating pain in his legs and body as if shock waves of high intensity had passed through his body, leaving him paralysed. The impact of the blast was strong enough to carve out a huge hole, about two feet in diameter, in the bottom armour plate. In an effort to make himself comfortable, he had providentially moved some distance away from what was later to become the point of impact. The timely movement had certainly saved his life, however, things were bad enough as he was in agony and had to be lifted out of the tank and rushed to the ADS. The tank had lost two bogey wheels and the right track was lying all twisted and splintered with some of the track pins spread around the tank. Ramnath's tank had successfully negotiated the minefield and joined up with Dafadar Ishwar's tank which had stopped near the wooden bridge at the commencement of Phase 2, raising the total number of PT-76 tanks operational to three, besides the T-55. With two troops deployed before first light, the threat of a counter-attack had been eliminated.

I accompanied the commander to see the defended locality of 12 Punjab Company (Pak) which had put up such formidable resistance against repeated Indian attacks. Going around the defended locality, one saw the well dug and correctly sited trenches for all round defence. The enemy, in total departure from conventional military wisdom, had not provided any depth to the defences, as in their scheme of things, Burinda was, at best, a delaying position. It was a hard nut to crack. Burinda became a symbol of the Pakistanis' ability to stand up and fight against heavy odds, not witnessed elsewhere in East Pakistan during the 1971 War.

The Pakistanis fought very courageously; here Shakespeare's lines reflect the experience one lived through: 'Like flies to wanton boys . . .They kill us for their sport.' This thought was floating in my mind while I was getting off my tank, to stretch out on the sun-drenched battlefield, for a quick catnap. In the background, I could hear the sound of artillery guns blazing away, in support of trustworthy, devout infantrymen charging into the jaws of death, with regimental war cries on their lips, not knowing 'for whom the bells toll'.

With the capture of Burinda on 5 December 1971, the focus shifted towards the 9 Division attack on Durkabarkati, using the 32 and 42 Infantry Brigades. As complete air supremacy had been achieved, it was decided to launch the attack at 0800 hrs on 6 December, with air support. Due to heavy fog, the aircraft could not take off and the attack was postponed twice. The attack was finally launched at 0930 hrs, without air support. While 9 Division was preoccupied with the breakthrough, the squadron had the opportunity for rest and refit. The Engineers' mine clearing parties breached the minefield to facilitate the recovery of the tanks. The EME boys then got working and established new standards of field repair by carrying out gun tube replacement and changing complete engine assemblies. Welding of armour plates, cracked sprockets, and idler wheels, once considered base workshop tasks, were undertaken to the complete satisfaction of the users. Working under pressure made us aware of each other's points of view. Close camaraderie developed, leading to mutual appreciation and better understanding. Preventive maintenance tasks were completed speedily and minefield damage repaired within a short span of time to make the tanks battleworthy once again. It is unfortunate that the services rendered by the Army technicians and logisticians do not receive due recognition for their contribution to war effort.

The 350 Infantry Brigade did not have to wait long for even while the last phase of the divisional attack was in progress, the green signal for the advance to Jessore was given. The advance from Burinda to Jessore was virtually a non-tactical one. The troops, mounted on local civil lorries and other forms of public conveyance, were followed by Mukti Bahini personnel on cycles and rickshaws. As we passed through the village, the elders, women, and children would step out of their houses to welcome us. In a few cases, they would stop us to offer cigarettes or *daab* (coconut water) and provide information about the common enemy. In a few cases, they would reveal the hiding place of some Razakar who had killed or raped somebody in their village. The locals would refer to the Pakistan Army/Razakars as Punjabi, and then provide gruesome details of the atrocities committed on their families. Many of our soldiers who were from Punjab were amused at the Bangladeshi needing the help of another Punjabi to seek revenge on his behalf.

Except for problems relating to passage across culverts or bridges blown up, or damaged by, the retreating Pakistan Army, no other difficulty or opposition came our way. The Mukti Bahini had become our eyes and ears and were cheering and waving us through the narrow roads. Moving through this sea of smiles and miles of human habitation, we had entered Jessore, the fortress city, evacuated by the retreating Pakistan Army, by nightfall.

Time's William Stewart, who rode into the key railroad junction with the Indian Army's 9 Infantry Division, wrote: 'Jessore, India's first strategic prize fell as easily as a mango ripened by a long Bengal summer. It shows no damage from fighting.' The Bengalis, shouting 'Joi Bangla' and 'Indira Gandhi Zindabad' cheered the Indian Army everywhere.

Since the death of Maj Narag on 21 November, I had been performing the duties of the squadron commander. Decision-making was not dependent on officers volunteering for this post, it was incumbent on the commanding officer to appoint an officer. In retrospect, it appears strange that from the same regiment, an officer, Maj Amrik Singh Virk, while on staff of HQ 1 Corps, used his personal influence to find his way back to serve with Col Hanut, his professional guru, commanding Poona Horse. Indrajit confided that Digby turned down his request as he was filling the important appointment of adjutant. No replacements for the two officer casualties, Speedy and Narain, were provided, even though we had two young officers attached as liaison officers with the Division Headquarters. Major Gulati, posted from the Infantry School Mhow on 1 December, was appointed to take over from Maj S.R. Chakraborty, OC B Squadron. Another officer, Maj Surinder Singh inducted from 14 Horse (Digby's parent regiment) was empanelled into 45 Cavalry, but granted leave of absence, and finally reported on 7 December to take over as OC C Squadron.

11

OUTFLANK RAMNAGAR

The armoured columns had deployed south-west of Jessore and in so doing, provided some protection against any enemy action from the south and southwest. No fresh task was set for the squadron, so we got back to maintaining our tanks and catching up with sleep when news of Maj Surinder's induction was made known.

Wartime handing/taking over of command was free of all ceremony. Inder had briefed Surinder thoroughly at the RHQ in Jessore. The introduction started with his tank crew, followed by squadron appointments and, finally, the troop leaders who covered the state of equipment held and the morale of the troops. His brief opening remarks shocked all present as he explained the reasons for proceeding on compassionate leave even though war had been declared. This disclosure had a negative impact amongst the troops who had foregone the luxury of leave over four weeks ago. Death/sickness within the family touch all individuals and are borne stoically, without public display. The first impression he created was one of insecurity and caution where decision-making would not be spontaneous but calculated to create despondency, 'And if the trumpet gives an uncertain sound who shall prepare himself for the battle?' Simply put, the executive commander has to be positive, self-reliant, and decisive to lead.

The overall division redeployments and revised responsibilities after the capture of Jessore were as given below:

(a) HQ 9 Infantry Division: Jessore Cantonment. All administrative echelons were ordered to concentrate in Jessore.

(b) 32 Infantry Brigade: Jessore Cantonment, including the airfield, and to guard against any threat along the Jessore–Khulna road

(c) 42 Infantry Brigade: from Churamankati to Jessore city (inclusive), and to guard Jessore against any threat from the north and northeast.

(d) 350 Infantry Brigade to concentrate along the main Bangaon–Jessore road, southwest of the water channel at Mandalganti, and to guard Jessore from any threat from the southwest.

In the next phase of the divisional plan, the C Squadron was placed under command HQ 32 Infantry Brigade commanded by a cavalry officer, Brig K.K. Tewari. For the initial briefing, he had called for both Surinder and me together. Unlike other commanders, before giving out his formal orders, he sat down to informally discuss the task assigned to him and how it could be best executed. He questioned me at length on the experience gained over the last few days, and on the capabilities of the PT-76 to negotiate the terrain.

At the end of the discussion, he formalized his plan to our complete satisfaction, leaving us with the feeling that the operational plan had been prepared by us. Working with him was a learning experience.

Squadron Commander Surinder, speaking to the troop leaders before kick-off, asked them, 'So, are you all ready for the next battle?'

'Yes, Sir,' was the muted response. 'So, Mehta, who is leading?'

'Chakraborty, initially,' I replied, a little perplexed as this had been ordered by him as squadron commander.

'What compass bearing are you marching on till the first bound?'

Chakraborty rattled off some figure. Not satisfied, he asked for the troop leaders' route chart. An argument soon developed as a miffed Chakraborty replied, 'No route chart has been prepared but compass bearings and distance between bounds has been recorded in my diary.'

'So, you do not have a chart, OK, so, show me your diary.'

Chakraborty, now a little hot under the collar, as his verbal assurance had been doubted, responded, 'Here, Sir, please see for yourself.'

The atmosphere suddenly became electrified and tense. Not satisfied, he cross-checked with the others present, to learn to his horror that other than his driver, nobody had prepared the night chart/route chart. Surinder lost his cool on something as insignificant as the preparation of a chart. While the others listened in silence Chakraborty spoke up to say that they had 'never felt the need to prepare charts as the local Mukti Bahini guide was our compass.' This further infuriated the squadron commander who felt that his authority was being challenged.

He now ordered all the troop leaders to prepare route charts and advanced the start time. A sulking bunch trooped out feeling more like boy scouts than professional soldiers who had been fighting a war for over 15 days!

The route turned out to be a tank obstacle course, consisting of waterlogged paddy fields with high embankments, village tracks sinking into village ponds, and deeply rutted bullock cart tracks where the tank would belly before the driver realized why his engine was stalling. Moving tanks across water channels with a sheer fall on the reverse bank or moving over culverts, designed for light vehicles, not knowing when it would collapse due to the weight of the tank, was a nightmarish experience. The driver was the worst off. While driving at night, headlights off, gazing through a night vision device throwing up a greenish yellow light across 30 degrees of a blinkered field of view, revealing only a hazy unnatural shadow visible at limited range is every tank driver's nightmare. The mounted infantry had to suffer the effects of the rolling, pitching and yawing of the tanks, besides inhaling the diesel fumes and swallowing dust. Many fell victim to low hanging branches or thorny bushes tearing away pieces of flesh and fabric. The radio operators were constantly at risk of tank antennas striking power lines to see sparks overhead or may be smoke rising from their radio sets. The tank commander and troop leader had the added responsibility to dismount and guide the tanks across vulnerable areas with his feet, boots and socks wet, shivering in the cold winter night, or searching the route for a bypass, reversing the tanks, and sometimes towing them out of the marshes and bogs. All thoughts of consulting the route chart, prepared under duress, remained pocketed for posterity.

The doggedness and determination of Chakraborty and Mahato brought us within 15 km of the objective when we finally hit the road-track junction at twilight. The radio crackled to Chakraborty's voice, excitedly announcing, 'Now on Ramnagar road.' 'D 40 for all station's Delta: Well done, Chakraborty, well done Mahato, well done boys, we have made it. Full speed ahead now, out.'

A decision to shed the original cross-country route and take the road route turned to be the correct one as time was more central to success than the direction from which we were to approach the enemy. With no traffic on the road, the tanks flew out of the dirt track to swing onto the tarmac. Before the drivers could switch gears, a smiling S/JCO Raghubir Chandra stood before them with his one-ton vehicle suitably parked to deliver packed breakfast and lunch packets. Capt Saighal summed up the gratitude and appreciation of all when he said, 'Sardaron ka Sardar hai tumhara Risaldar', as we moved forward after a warm handshake with Raghubir.

'Well done, Raghubir Saab, you have set a fine example.'

'Good Luck, Saab, *hum sub saath hain*.'

He had ventured on his own, cutting across village tracks, keeping a check on the progress of the squadron outflank and had homed onto the road track junction, to ensure that the tank crews receive their packed meals before going into battle.

The tank drivers switched gears rapidly to put their Pippas to a speed test. I cannot recall any moment more exhilarating, before or since, when the C Squadron tanks were virtually galloping at speeds between 30–40 km per hour, having shed all fear of encountering the enemy. Looking back from the lead tank, one could see the tanks column against the backdrop of a cloud of dust and smoke rising with the first rays of the sun. The early morning breeze was stimulating, the speed exhilarating, as if we were engaged in some speed test. The roar of the powerful engines discharging energy to the tank sprocket to propel the tank track, metal against metal, to provide revolution to the bogey wheels, burning the tarmac below was all that was important. The mounted infantry was wide awake and desperately hanging on to the railings, helmets, and jungle caps. The metallic sound of the tank tracks biting into the tarmac, every time the driver took the sticks to steer the tank to the middle of the road, gave a strange overwhelming sense of raw power.

The enemy detachment operating along the main Jessore–Ramnagar axis had stalled the advance of 63 Cavalry and 7 Punjab ahead of the Ramnagar crossroads. As no immediate threat was visualized to their position, the sound of an engine noise coming from an unexpected direction must have created panic in the enemy ranks. The rapidly advancing squadron of tanks, main guns blazing, stormed into the enemy defences at the crossroads with the confidence that a target spotted was a target destroyed. I do not recall how much time the leading tanks took to overwhelm the enemy at the crossroads, because well before the last tank reached the objective, the engagement was over. The enemy troops were in turmoil, running helter-skelter. The early morning calm had given way to mayhem, havoc and chaos. Enemy RCL guns and jeeps attempting to escape were quickly destroyed. After the first few rounds, terror must have seized the enemy as we could see them stepping out of trenches scurrying around like chicken avoiding a speeding truck and making a dash for safety. The light machine gun and ack ack gun were very handy weapons to spray the target area. The fire-fight lasted only a few minutes, as groups of soldiers abandoned their weapons and sprinted across the railway line to the safety of the rail embankment. Our arrival at the roadblock site had resulted in the capture or destruction of approximately 60 Pakistan vehicles, four heavy mortars, some RCL guns, and a large quantity of ammunition, besides the enemy dead or wounded.

The T-55 tanks were held up en route as the ground conditions were impeding their movement. Tank crews were busy brewing up tea to enjoy the *aloo–puri* packed breakfast after a thrilling chase and a successful outflank.

Saighal was sitting alongside on the turret, complementing the tank crew for the piping hot tea and *shakarparas* when some shells landed in the adjoining area some distance away. The tanks which were bunched up, quickly pulled back along the road on which we had advanced due to the marsh on either side of the road. Shelling of our position only suggested that the enemy was keeping us under watch. Saighal advised that the enemy guns were beginning to register our area. He suspected that the enemy FOO was hiding in the vicinity and directing the gunfire. While the proximity of the shell was worrisome, more alarming was my coincidental observation of the shells that burst at the tree level directly in front of my tank.

'Hey Saighal, did you notice the last shell burst?' 'No, I could not, but it was very close.'

'It fell on that bloody tree in front.'

'Yes, enemy guns are registering our location.'

'No dammit, I saw that big branch flying off toward of enemy direction after the burst.'

'Nothing unusual, can happen.'

'How can both the shell and branch fly off in the enemy direction, after impact?'

'You have a good point but . . .' I cut him short, a little rudely. 'Dammit the sound of the shell was heard overhead before the bang. How do you answer that?'

As the process of registration was still in progress by the enemy, another shell landed behind us.

'The bastard has bracketed us, watch out.'

Saighal suddenly jerked my hand: 'The last shell was definitely fired from a medium gun.'

'So what does that prove'?

'The enemy does not have any medium guns in this area.'

Alarm bells began to ring, setting in the fear that the area occupied by us would be plastered by a heavy artillery barrage. From our own guns!

The process of registration of the target by artillery, usually carried out by a single gun, had been completed. It was not difficult to visualize that the gun position officer would now be applying whatever final corrections were necessary before ordering the guns to commence engagement. Our only hope was Saighal and his ability to get through on the artillery radio net and stop the Gun Position Officer (GPO) before the guns were ordered to fire. He was intense and desperate as was evident from the tenor of his voice and the repeated attempts to get some response from the GPO or control on his radio net. I was simultaneously transferring my panic to the adjutant on the radio:

'Delta 40 for Delta 25: Urgent. Fetch lion. Own medium artillery fired on our location. Stop, repeat stop. Over.'

'Delta 25 for Delta 40: Fetching Lion. Over.'

I quickly reached out to the other ANPRC-25 radio link tuned on to the 63 Cavalry frequency to contact Kewalramani, my counterpart advancing with 63 Cavalry Squadron.

'Mehta for Kewal, Urgent: own medium guns, suspected firing on our location. Stop, repeat, stop the blighters.'

'Kewal for Mehta: understood, checking, wilco, out.'

Inder had, meanwhile, come up on the other set in response to my call. Our appeals for quick intervention were still being processed when pandemonium broke loose. The clear whistle of shells flying through the air, followed by a heavy crunch and ear-splitting blasts covered the area with flying dust, debris, and smoke. The collective efforts of Inder, Kewal, and Saighal were not all in vain, as their efforts silenced the guns soon after. War reports and regimental histories of the units involved will mark the failure of coordination between advancing troops, staff, and gun positions, leading to avoidable deaths and casualties.

To fall victim to own guns is a tragedy of great magnitude and deep sorrow. Unlike us, not everybody was lucky to escape the disaster. The accompanying Madras Battalion was the worst hit as the first volley had caught them in the open. Soon after the fire stopped, I saw a lone figure running down the road coming towards my tank. He was dressed in *khaki,* side cap in his hand, oblivious of the unnecessary dangers he was exposing himself to, as *khaki* was the dress code of the Pakistani troops. He was a very spirited Forward Air Control (FAC) of the Indian Air Force attached to the Madras Battalion for the period of outflank operations. He told us of the heavy casualties suffered by the Madras Battalion and wanted an ambulance to help the wounded. S/JCO Raghubir had followed the tanks and represented the only vehicle available for evacuation, as all B vehicles had been shed before commencement of the outflank. The S/JCO, with his 1-ton under command, took on the new role of evacuating casualties to the battalion RAP. I ventured forward on foot along with some tank commanders to look at the now silent battlefield, splattered with dead bodies, burning vehicles and a wide array of weapons and personal effects. Unlike Burinda, the defences here had been hurriedly prepared as part of a contingency plan and with little or no coordination. The accompanying crew counted at least 60 vehicles of varying tonnage and capacity, many of them riddled with bullets or blown to bits. Amongst the most gruesome sights I came across was a cluster of jeeps with the crews burning alongside. The driver of one vehicle had got roasted and was stuck in his seat, the engine still purring away. In the adjoining jeep lay a figure fully stretched out, in his full battle dress, clutching on to his throat through which bullets had created a large gaping hole. Bullets had entered his neck and the riddled body was washed in blood. I felt no hatred or anger towards these soldiers. They were no longer masters of their own souls or of their destiny having enrolled in the armed forces. Due to partition of India in 1947, my parents were compelled to migrate. I had been now fighting for the rights of other refugees to return to their homeland. I could not help notice that many of those dead and dying belonged to the undivided Punjab where I was born. I was a soldier performing my duty to the country and the larger humanitarian cause.

12

ADVANCE TO KHULNA

When we enter Khulna, the country suddenly becomes very marshy. On one side (east) of the road to Khulna is the river Bhairab, one of the biggest tidal rivers, with a width of 200 yards and a tidal rise and fall of over 10 feet. As one keeps approaching Khulna to the south, the Bhairab is fed by more and more rivers and streams, till midway between Jessore and Khulna, it is about 350 yards wide and its tail bore is even higher. The road itself is at places only 300 yards from the river. To the west are the swamps of Sunderbans. These swamps are characterized by quagmires, densely foliated mangrove swamps and deceptive *bhils* (lakes) covered in cactus lily. The next position of the enemy was at Naopara area, about 15 miles further south of Ramnagar. In order to deal with this position, C Squadron was grouped with 13 Dogra and tasked to proceed via Manirampur, then cut due east towards Pachabaria–Chombardhaga, and hit the main road south of Naopara.

The tank columns arrived at a midway mark called Mani Rampur by about 0230 hrs when the leading columns came to a halt as the terrain limited further movement. What lay between us and the roadblock site selected was a formidable water obstacle that we had to go across to reach the main road to Naopara. The difficulty was finding a crossing point for the tanks for entry and exit across the obstacle. Three search parties scanned the water line to agree upon a crossing site, technically unsuitable and risky, but accepted, in view of the operational exigency. It must have taken at least 90 minutes for all the tanks to cross over. The infantry in the meantime had begun crossing over from the bamboo bridge in the area, and established a firm base. I put Risaldar R.P. Singh in the lead tank to perform all the navigation tasks while I had a good snooze to regain my energy levels inside the tank, while on the move. The tacit understanding with the operator was that a call for me was to be given the stock reply, *'Mehta Saab ground recce par gaya hai'* (Mehta is conducting a ground recce). Surprisingly, it worked very well!

Not many had seen Surinder dismount willingly from the tank to guide or encourage the crews. How I wished Surinder would take on the role of a squadron leader instead of a squadron commander and set an example of leadership. The tank columns had come to a halt again. This was probably the last obstacle between the Naopara objective and us now. Dawn would break within an hour. Now was the time to have some fun by adopting a simple ruse. I passed a message to Surinder that a site had been found but we were not sure if the risk would be justified. As time was critical, he fell for the bait and quickly came in to view a site which, if approved, would have been a grave risk for the men and the equipment. His rejection was a foregone conclusion which had triggered me to suggest that he may consider selecting a site on the left flank of the obstacle to save on time as R.P. Singh was covering the right half. There must have been something in the manner in which I said this, in the presence of the tank crews, that compelled him to accept the challenge. I still sometimes wonder why I made him do this because it is not part of my intrinsic nature. The thought uppermost in my mind then was that the soldiers should never be provided an opportunity to raise an accusing finger against an officer for something he had avoided or shied away from. He returned after half an hour, head hanging low, saying, yes, I had been right and the terrain around was murderous. The accompanying crew was to share their experience of the half hour spent in his company. Much of it remains unworthy of print as these were reactions of soldiers 'fucked and far from home', battling the effects of weather, enemy, terrain, fatigue. The positive impact of this ruse was that the members of the recce party witnessed their new squadron commander sharing the problems and difficulties with them while on his maiden reconnaissance mission under battle conditions. The mission was aborted when word from the commander confirmed that the enemy along the main axis had started withdrawing from Naopara towards Khulna.

Just before we resumed the advance, a middle-aged, short-statured, dark, stocky cyclist, frantically waving a paper in the air caught my attention. On getting off his bicycle, he saluted to announce that he was an ex-sergeant of the Pakistan Air Force.

'Anything I can do for you?' I asked.

'No, Sir. you are already doing everything for us. Give me a chance to serve you.' With that he handed over the paper he had been waving earlier. It was a chargesheet in which his name, rank, and the offence of inciting mutiny was mentioned.

'So were you cashiered or dismissed from service?'

'Neither, I have been declared an absconder, to face court martial, if caught.'

'Do you belong to this village?'

'Sir, I belong to Naopara, I was born here.'

I told him, more in jest, 'But we will not carry your bicycle.' He burst out laughing, 'No problem.' He yelled across in Bengali for two boys to appear and carry his cycle away, adding: 'Tell them, I will stay with the tank regiment till war finishes.' Although initially sceptical of his claims and talents, with the passage of time, I realized that my doubts about trusting an absconder were baseless. He turned out to be a devoted patriot and a big help. Being an ex-Service man, he understood and willingly accepted the discipline imposed on him. He soon merged with the tank crew and even learnt to load the gun and help the crew with odd tasks. His knowledge of the local terrain and cross-questioning of locals to verify and sometimes extract information proved invaluable. This devoted airman, true to his word, stayed with us until the end of the war to share with us the dangers and experiences, without making any claims or demands. On one occasion, he even suffered minor burn injuries from the tank exhaust. On yet another occasion, finding the .30 MMG unmanned, he fired on the retreating enemy infantry. He was with the tank column on the day the surrender ceremony took place at Khulna. We congratulated him on the victory of the allied Army and tears rolled down his cheeks. He did not want any certificate or citation for his contribution towards the war effort.

The novelty of armoured vehicles arriving in remote areas always drew swarms of humanity towards us. The entire village, including elderly men and women, would gather around to offer their reserves of the available food and supplies. There were many times when we would refuse these offers, being aware of their meagre rations, undernourished appearance, and the hardships they had suffered. Sometimes people would gather around and take out a procession carrying flags and shouting anti-Pakistan and anti-Yahya slogans. Much as we appreciated their gesture of welcoming us, from the operational and security point of view, it became difficult to control them. No matter how we tried, they would at the most move away but never leave for long. It seemed cruel to ask them to leave knowing what their freedom meant to them.

No let-up was allowed to the enemy and his next well-fortified and prepared position for the defence of Khulna was at Siramani. Syamganj position at Daulatpur was contacted the same afternoon. This position extended from village Syamganj. These positions had extremely well dug in trenches and bunkers, particularly on the sides of the high embankments of the road and railway line. The position was held with LMG, MMG, and dug in RCL guns, with fields of fire extending up to 900 yards. The main road in addition was held by a troop of Chaffee tanks and any move frontally would have brought down accurate and heavy fire. Probing attacks by 26 Madras and 8 Madras supported by C Squadron on 11 December 1971, on the main road, failed to make any headway. It was then planned to carry out a double outflank of this position, as it was obvious that the enemy would fight a last-ditch battle, since no further withdrawal was possible.

It appeared that as we were nearing Khulna, the units of the HQ 9 Infantry Division were gradually reverting to the main Jessore–Khulna highway. The reason was evident as cross-country movement was difficult, especially for A and B vehicles and guns. One of the major tactical implications was that the mobility of the tanks was restricted due to the terrain. The battle would now be dominated by the infantry, with the advantage quite naturally lying with the defender. The battle in the air had already been won. Sufficient resources were available to humble the enemy in conjunction with well thought out ground attack plans combined with the support of the artillery.

Having analysed that the halt would be for an extended period, I detached myself from the crowd around my tank and walked off about 100 yards away to where a small building was facing the road. This had seen better days as a police outpost. Peace, solitude, silence were luxuries for which the time was premature as I had spotted a delegation being led by someone wearing a suit and tie, and 5 or 6 other elderly people in tow. Their speech and appearance indicated that they had all seen better days. They came up to me with folded hands as I got up to welcome them and offered them seats. They wanted to distribute the little that they had and express their gratitude to the soldiers. I permitted them to distribute to the tank troops which was done efficiently and quickly by one of their senior members. Meanwhile, hot sizzling mugs of tea prepared by the tank crews were served to this delegation.

As the conversation picked up, I asked 'x' about his earlier employment.

'I was Principal of a Girls College in Jessore district.'

'Tell me all these stories about Razakars, are they true or propaganda?'

The person 'x' authoritatively silenced the others to narrate his version: 'Sir, I can narrate only the experience I have lived through . . . rascals, animals, not human at all, devils.' Obviously worked up, he paused for breath and looked around for reassurance.

'Something happened in your presence?'

'x': 'I was about to enter my college when an ex-student warned me that the police and an Army vehicle had entered the college campus along with local bazaar leader, a known *goonda* and troublemaker. I hid behind the wall to witness all the male teachers being ordered outside my office. They waited, perhaps for me to arrive. Soon, all had been pushed into the adjoining room and locked up. I thought maybe they would leave after some violence.'

'Then what happened, did they . . .?'

He interrupted me to say, 'No, those animals had vicious plans. They sent the Razakars around the classes and forced the female teachers and girl students out of the classes into two civil trucks.'

'But surely they would have resisted?'

'x': 'Yes, they did, many tried to escape, but were chased and caught by their long hair, beaten up and pushed, some dragged. Sir, some had their clothes torn off, while one was completely naked.' He was on the verge of a breakdown now.

'My God, swines of the worst kind.'

'x': 'Sir, amongst the teachers was my own wife, I saw it with my own eyes, her blouse in complete disarray, that bastard bazaar leader was taking revenge on me. I was watching but unable to do anything.' I could see tears rolling down his cheeks, his eyes bloodshot, his voice quivering at the memory of recalling this painful experience. He removed his glasses, wiped his eyes dry, before starting again.

'x': 'The Army men left early, but the police escorted the trucks out of the campus. There was nobody to help the crying women and girls whose lives and honour were in peril.' 'Was the Army helping the police?'

'x': 'No. The police only used them.' 'How was that done?'

'x': 'They waited for the Army personnel to leave and then showed their true colours.'

'What happened afterwards?'

'x': 'As the trucks rolled out, the police set fire to the room where the male teachers were locked, and they were roasted alive.'

'And what happened to the women and girls?'

x: 'Sir, you will not believe this, but I know it to be true. They were taken to some unknown destination. Raped and pushed into brothels. The young ones were despatched to Chittagong and, finally, to Pakistan to be sold as prostitutes.'

'And what about your wife?'

x: 'Like many others, raped by the bazaar goonda, the Razakar leader, till she finally committed suicide rather than live in disgrace.' His eyes rolled back as if he was relieving the horror of this experience. The tears continued to roll down. Then he composed himself, and in a voice still choking, he told us that he had taken a vow never to mention this experience to anybody, not even his closest friends, but somehow the smell of freedom and the presence of the Indian Army had given him the courage to seek revenge from these bastards. Saying this, he broke down and started weeping again.

The terrain astride the road on this axis was marshy. The enemy had occupied delaying positions and demolished a large number of bridges and culverts during the withdrawal. However, the delaying positions were pushed back one by one. The Pakistanis had apparently intended to fight to the last in this fortress. The capture of Daulatpur and Khulna, consequently, turned into a hard slogging match. Up to the morning of 16 December, the division had managed to capture only three of the forward enemy localities at Siramani East, Siramani West, and Syamganj. The first crossing was made with the help of the Mukti Bahini on the night of 13–14 December. The brigade moved south up to the river junction without much opposition. During the second crossing, however, they met with stiff opposition.

Over the next two days, due to the nature of the terrain, little or no headway was made by the troops in contact. The overall impression the junior commanders got was that detailed planning for the capture of Khulna had not been undertaken. No plan of action or strategy was available to guide the commanding officers who, true to form, ordered a company level attack while remaining sheltered in the comfort of a dugout themselves. Another serious malady that had crept into the operational planning and execution at the battalion level was viewing 'inching forward' as success, after every attack. The reality was of commanders sitting in barren operational rooms, bereft of original thought or innovative ideas, staring at maps and situation reports, to which they had no answers. Different battalions at different places and times, experienced sudden change in plans for the assaults to 'inch forward' and show progress, at great cost, and loss of valuable lives. On paper, therefore, 9 Infantry Division was making great progress, as evidenced by all the successful after-action reports and situation reports emanating from the Battalion and Brigade Headquarters. Few, if any, were counting the number of dead and wounded or the actual progress made by the formation to bring the war closer to culmination, or even the actual enemy territory captured, and damage inflicted to the enemy war machine, or the punishment meted out to break the enemy's will to continue with war. Ordering repeated attacks, not leading to substantial results, was being criticized.

The presence of Gen Dalbir at the Battalion Headquarters reminded me of what I had read in one of the books at Ahmednagar as a young officer in which a seasoned soldier, going in for assault says, 'Why, the Colonel was up in the fighting line just like one of us! We didn't want him there, we wanted him back behind to send us reinforcements!'

A commander has no business to be in the actual fighting line until he goes in with his last reserve. It is not possible to say exactly as to what size force a commander can, to a certain extent, exercise personal influence over—only circumstances and conditions can decide this. However, I am of the opinion that when it is possible, without the risk of losing touch with the rest of the force, he should, like a huntsman does with his hounds, draw near to where the greatest volume of the 'cry' comes from, i.e., to where the pressure seems to be the most severe. In doing this, the commander must not to get 'hung up' anywhere, because if he does so, one, or all, of the following things may happen:

(a) He may be killed, and, though the next senior officer may be a better man, a commander's death during the fight, will probably cause dislocation, may cause failure in the attack, or if the crisis is acute, even a disaster.

(b) If he is actually in the fighting line, he gets his impression from part of the field only, and, thus, if things are going well there, he may be too optimistic. If, on the other hand, things are going badly, many men being hit, ammunition running short, no water, etc., then, generally, any man, no matter how good his nerves are, will doubt if it is possible to 'hold on', or in other words, will be pessimistic.

(c) A force commander, who is 'hung up' in the firing line of any one part of the force, is not in a position to 'send us reinforcements'.

In the present case, it was proved right. While the battalion attack turned into a failure, with high casualties, Dalbir had a bullet grazing his large bottom.

The RHQ with which we had been in radio communication so far, moved up just 2 km behind the squadron location. Before nightfall, I had the task of selecting and marking the tank harbour. Having started early, I found time to visit the RHQ located atop a school building for a good view and possibly better communication with the squadrons. The general atmosphere appeared tense even though the humdrum work of messages, reports, and log messages continued. Inder, instead of his usual cheery smile and welcome, placed the draft report on which he was working into my hand. The subject heading was sufficient to send a shudder of shock and disbelief for written in bold block letters, underlined and marked secret was: THE KUSHTIA MASSACRE.

13

KUSHTIA MASSACARE

I quote Gen Niazi on what, in his opinion, led our troops to Kushtia: 'After Magura, 62 Indian Brigade advanced to Madhomati. The purpose of the move was to capture Faridpur after clearing Madhomati. Our intention was to divert the enemy forces in another direction. Our troops at Kushtia succeeded in luring the Indian division to the north. Jhenida–Kushtia offered a lucrative target. Our troops in Kushtia could now cut the Indians lines of communication in area Jhenida. Brigadier Manzoor at Kushtia was told to cut the road but before he moved, the enemy started moving towards him. General Barar, fearful of the flank threat from the north to his overstretched line of advance to Jhenida and Madhomati, ordered 7 Mountain Brigade to attack Kushtia. By getting drawn towards Kushtia, the Indian troops went off on a tangent, thus, giving us sufficient time to organize and readjust our defences at Faridpur and Golando. The diversion of the Indian forces to Kushtia proved fatal for the Indians—they got bogged down there, and the threat to Faridpur and Dhaka was reduced' (*The Betrayal of East Pakistan* by Lt Gen A.A.K. Niazi, 1998, pp. 147–148).

The A squadron had been detached from the regiment at the beginning of the war and placed under Command HQ 4 Infantry Division for Operations. Major P.K. Batra, along with three other officers, had been detached. Batra was a very considerate and thoughtful officer who ran a happy team. Initial reports of progress made by HQ 4 Infantry Division indicated that they were making steady progress. The Squadron 2IC, Capt H.S. Puri and a subaltern, Harsh Vardhan were not available when the demand for detaching two troops of tanks for Kushtia was received by the Squadron Commander. The corps commander 2 Corps and the divisional and brigade commanders were conducting an aerial reconnaissance of Kushtia and the adjoining areas to speed up the flagging advance of 4 Infantry Division. The divisional commander, having seen off the corps commander after the aerial reconnaissance, returned to his headquarters to give the final orders for advance to the Brigade O group which now included 2/Lt Sam Chandavarkar. The rosy picture painted was that Kushtia was not occupied and that the brigade must undertake rapid advance, taking full advantage of the tanks.

Sam had done only a few months service in the regiment. He had not done the basic Young Officers' Course, which qualifies an officer for tank troop leading. It would be fair to assume that he was the junior-most officer in that gathering of unit/sub-unit commanders, possibly for the first time in his life. Being an intelligent officer, he had digested the briefing provided by Batra. In addition to study of the map and route, he had discussed the movement plan with the more seasoned and experienced Naib Risaldar George. The consensus that had developed was that in view of the terrain configuration and built-up area, the advance should be led by the infantry. The tanks could under no circumstances advance tactically and would be restricted to the line ahead formation, like a convoy, as the ground on both sides of the road was marshy. Confident that he had done his homework, Sam, as he was popularly called, proceeded to the Brigade Headquarters to receive his formal briefing.

In Army parlance, the commander (at all levels) is referred to by the moniker 'Tiger', especially while using the radio telephone. The Army has evolved its own hierarchy of Higher Tiger and Higher Higher Tiger. In the instant case, the Higher Tiger (divisional commander), having seen off the Higher Higher Tiger (corps commander) at the helipad, accompanied the Tiger to his den for a cup of tea and *gup-shup*, chit-chat. Into to this none too friendly circle, Sam the dashing young cavalier was summoned for the privilege of briefing by the Higher Tiger. This was to be followed by a formal briefing by the Tiger. In the present case, Sam, after being told that the advance to Kushtia was a cakewalk and that the family of three Tigers had this confirmed through an aerial reconnaissance, bluntly told them that his information from the Mukti Bahini indicated a strong presence of enemy in Kushtia. Also, his analysis of the terrain/route ruled out an advance by the tanks. The roar of the tigers must have left him dumbfounded and confused. Those present were to later tell us that this Brigadier went to the extent of using unparliamentary language and made a personal attack on the ability of Sam to lead a tank troop, alleging that he was scared stiff. In a final display of his rank, authority and age, he mocked this intelligent young cavalry officer, saying, 'You can't be soldiering with the Beatle type haircut, looking like a Bollywood extra.' The personal hurt, abuse and challenge to his courage and integrity, done so ungraciously in public, would have set any young officer's blood boiling. Sam kept his cavalry cool and instead of retaliating, repeated his logically analysed reasons for not leading with the tanks, long hair notwithstanding. He had committed professional deceit when he made up the statement that the corps commander had told him that Kushtia was unoccupied and that there was no enemy for miles around. As events were to unfold, a very heavy price had to be paid in life, limb, and tarnished reputations, besides affecting the operational plans at the corps and command levels.

The dice had been loaded against this tank detachment by the very man responsible for leading them to success. As is the military custom, once the order has been delivered, there is no more discussion—thereafter, it is 'but to do or die!' Sam returned to brief the crews and caution them about the inherent dangers and additional security drills that his young mind could comprehend. The GOC placed George, his most experienced troop leader, to lead the column and took his rightful place behind the leading troop in the order of march. A little before they were to enter Kushtia, there was a prominent bend in the road with heavy foliage restricting visibility, which they had correctly identified as a bound. As the infantry grouped with the tank column was marching behind the tanks, Sam decided to adopt the blind corner drill in which the movement of one tank is supported by the firepower of the other two stationary tanks as they move across the bound to security. George as a Dafadar had often practised this drill along with me when I first joined the regiment in 1966. I knew him to be an alert and cautious tank commander. The three tanks traversed through the road bend and deployed to signal the remainder to follow. Sam ordered his troop to follow while keeping an eye on the location of the last tank of the leading troop. Sam tank crossed over and deployed ahead of George, followed soon after by the tank following when, at point blank range enemy tanks and RCLs opened up just across the road bend. The fire was opened just when the last tank was approaching the road bend. As per a first-hand account of the crews who survived, the very first shots would have scored direct hits, as the distance was not more than 200 metres. The effort made by individual tanks to break through brought about another salvo, until suddenly everything was mayhem and murder. Even as the last tank was turning to make a getaway, some tanks were on fire and the injured were making a desperate bid to jump off the burning tanks to what they felt may bring them safety. The Pakistani commander of this detachment had shown exemplary control of nerves as also fire control of the highest order in ensuring that this ambush become a complete success. Worse was to follow as the moment the firing finished, an infantry company launched an attack to kill or capture the crews. The tank attempting a getaway did not have far to go as an RCL round fired from close quarters punched a large hole into its right hull side. The crew that included Dafadar Cherian dismounted and hid in the bushes, close by to watch the events unfolding in front of them. As per his debriefing report after this ambush, all the tank crews, less killed, were made prisoners of war after they were physically captured. He distinctly remembered Sam being pulled out of the tank. He appeared badly bruised, and had lost one arm. Sowar Lazarus was chased for some distance, and badly roughed up by the Pakistanis. Cherian from his hiding place was able to see and clearly identify them. After nightfall, he overheard the soldiers talk about five Indian prisoners but he never saw them with his own eyes. Sam was easy to identify as an officer and got the most inhuman treatment from the Pakistani troops. He was tied to a tree and for each question that was not answered, he lost a limb or organ. As per Cherian, he could hear and feel his terror and pain but was in no position to help. The cruel inhuman conduct of the Pakistani troops in the presence of their officers, appears in sharp contrast to the manner in which we treated our prisoners. The Pakistani JCO in charge started by chopping off the ear lobes, fingernails, toes, and fingers and finally gouged out his eyes before shooting him in the chest. LD Puthran refused to give out information other than his name, number, rank, unit, and blood group as laid down in the Geneva Convention. The treatment meted out was similar to what they had done to Sam. LD Puthran bore the pain and agony in a stoic, composed manner until the very end. A young soldier—he could not have been more than 24 years old—he refused to provide any information other than laid down in the Geneva Convention for prisoners of war.

The enemy assault was not limited to the tank troops only. Having demolished the armour, they pounced upon the unsuspecting infantry columns lulled into believing what the senior commander had said, that there was no enemy around Kushtia. The sudden appearance of the enemy found them breaking ranks and running helter-skelter. Frenetic messages for help filled the air but these cries in the wilderness remained unanswered. The local enemy commander must have given specific instructions of 'no prisoners', with the result that even those who surrendered were shot dead. As news of this catastrophic event travelled rearwards, panic gave way to flight and, finally, a complete rout, with the other battalions, not in contact with the enemy, reacting in a knee-jerk fashion. The pliant brigade commander who had wilfully misled the troops into committing this abominable blunder, was himself now leading the shameful, hasty withdrawal of his brigade, to wear this cross of shame and betrayal to his command for a lifetime. The after-action reports of the formation as also the official history glossed over this major reversal, by holding back the actual figures of the dead and wounded in this catastrophic retreat. The responsible media too, did not play up the truth due to censorship as also to protect the guilty. The officers holding important posts at battalion level and upwards, permitted it to be recorded as a footnote to the glorious victory of the Indian Army without ever bringing the guilty to book. As revealed by subsequent books and articles published, this incident was big enough to send a shiver through the corps commander who found it necessary to call for a hurried meeting of his staff in the operational room. The corps level operational plans that were modified, reflect the magnitude of the massacre at Kushtia and other ill-fated consequences.

The only battle fought by 57 Brigade took place south of Kushtia on 9 December, when a company of 18 Punjab and two troops of tanks took on and held 22 Rajput. Artillery, automatic and recoilless guns opened up simultaneously creating a devastating effect. Only one Indian tank managed to get away. The rest were either knocked out or captured. The leading battalion suffered heavy casualties. The unexpectedly strong reaction by our troops, their violent and fierce action, created panic among the Indian troops. The first wave of the enemy bore the brunt, and those who could were forced to withdraw. The Indians literally ran from the battlefield. The troops in the depth and the reserve likewise ran for safety. The Indian Corps Commander pulled back another brigade from Jhenida to Kushtia, followed up by 41 Brigade also, leaving only one battalion on Madhumati. Thus, the entire division had been drawn in front of Kushtia by 10 December (*The Betrayal of East Pakistan* by Lt Gen A.A.K. Niazi, 1998, pp 109–111).

The author of *Surrender at Dhaka*, Gen Jacob has this to say for the negative impact of Kushtia on the overall operational plans:

> The 4 Mountain Division thereupon overreacted, and instead of pressing on with the advance on the thrust line across Madhumati on 9 December diverted to Kushtia. When the Hardinge Bridge was contacted on 12 December, it was found that the Pakistanis had withdrawn and partially demolished the bridge. The Hardinge Bridge could have been taken intact and the withdrawal of Pakistani troops across the river would not have taken place. More serious was the delay caused in getting the Division back onto its original thrust line. When I asked Raina to concentrate on his main thrust, he replied that he was not aware of the quantum of troops diverted by 4 Mountain Division from their primary task. Consequently, the advance to Faridpur was delayed by at least three days and the contingency plan of crossing the Padma at Goalundo Ghat to Dhaka could not be put into effect. The delay caused on this axis by the failure of 2 Corps to control 4 Mountain Division and to acquiesce to 9 Infantry Division's diverting troops from the thrust line Jessore–Magura to Khulna, together with the non-utilization of their Inland Waterways Flotilla cost us the chance to take Dhaka from this thrust line.

Every word that I read, made my heart bleed—so horrendous and reprehensible an act, even in war-time, could not have been done by an enemy but by sub-humans. The cold-blooded gruesome killing was not part of the training and discipline of honourable men in uniform. Our own soldiers, under the careful charge of their officers, had treated prisoners of war in a very civil, humane manner, at worst like criminals in a police lock-up in extreme cases where emotions ran high due to loss of comrades. To me, it appeared that the Pakistani military officers had lost their moral authority over the men they commanded. Acts of uninhibited killing could not be possible without the acquiescence of the educated officer class. It was difficult to believe that a tragedy of this nature and proportion had happened to one of our own. A polished charming young subaltern was received by me, as was the regimental custom, on his first reporting to the unit, and introduced to the regimental officers and ladies assembled at Gulati's house for a dinner party on the evening of his arrival. He had charmed everyone with his polished manners and personality. George Thomas was the first NCO I met when I joined the regiment in 1966. Later, as part of the same troop, he taught me how to drive the tank. Both of us played football for the regimental team and worked together on various regimental tasks. He had only recently been promoted to the rank of a JCO and had taken two months leave with furlough to get married. Both these fine human beings and dedicated regimental officers would no longer be with us. In addition, what about Lazarus, who even in his dying moments, stuck to what we as officers had taught him: to reveal only his name, number, rank, unit, and blood group if ever captured by the enemy. The raw courage, fortitude and stoic manner in which he held his own speaks volumes of his soldierly qualities and character. He stands out as a fine example of a soldier who lived and died upholding the soldier's oath. There have been many others like him whose acts of valour and bravery have been overlooked and not recorded, but that does not make their sacrifice any less, for they died for their comrades, squadrons, regiments, Army and nation, unhonoured and unsung, to abide by the soldierly oath and their allegiance for, and sense of duty to, the country and the regiment. I returned with a heavy heart at this dreadful loss of friends and comrades in arms. During the journey back to the squadron, the words of Omar Khayyam came to my mind as if to calm the soul in turmoil: 'The moving finger writes and having writ, moves on, nor all thy piety nor wit, can lure it back to cancel half a line, nor all thy tears wipe out a word from it.'

14

ACROSS BHAIRAB RIVER

The stalemate at Khulna had become evident as little or no progress appeared possible. The disruption in the progress of 2 Corps due to the Khustia fallout and the blowing up of the Harding Bridge had ruled out the likelihood of the corps making a thrust toward Dhaka. News broadcasts, specially from BBC, gave us some insights into the international and UN efforts towards a ceasefire. A gradual sense of urgency had gripped the military leadership to finish the war at the earliest as the Russians had virtually announced their ultimatum to comply with the Security Council verdict. A flurry of activity was evident at the formation headquarters level, but that was unknown to us. What was part of common knowledge was what was announced on All India Radio (AIR)/BBC.

The Army and the country knew that it was a race against the global verdict on the war, reflected in the voting, where 104 countries cast their votes against India, supporting the 7 December 1971 resolution in the UN General Assembly. India had been abandoned by Yugoslavia, Egypt, Ghana, and

Indonesia of the non-aligned group. While the vote was not binding authority, it was a tremendously humiliating experience.

Earlier, on 10 December, in yet another secret meeting, Huang Hua, heading the Chinese delegation in the UN, met Kissinger who had told him, 'Though illegal, they had asked Jordan, Iran, and Saudi Arabia, and would tell Turkey to ship the US arms to Pakistan. The President wants you to know that if the People's Republic were to consider the situation on the Indian subcontinent a threat to their security, the US would oppose the efforts of others to interfere in the People's Republic.' After the meeting, George Bush wrote that he was uncomfortable to be 'in close cahoots with China' (China responded by calling up reserve troops for its mountain divisions). The Soviet Union had already utilized two vetoes in the Security Council against an 11–2 verdict. The Russians had given a clear signal, 'No more veto.' Panic and crisis began to surface in Delhi.

The USS Enterprise group was sailing fast across the choke point of the Strait of Malacca, heading for the Bay of Bengal. The Enterprise is a nuclear carrier and was accompanied by the rest of its formidable task force: the helicopter carrier USS Tripoli, seven destroyers, and an oiler. An Indian sailor called it a nuclear-studded armada, including the most powerful ships in the world—five times larger than India's INS Vikrant. R.N. Kao of the Research and Analysis Wing (R&AW) was submitting regular reports on the movement of the Enterprise group that had entered the Bay of Bengal. While it was still 1000 miles away from Chittagong, rumours of bombing were beginning to spread. 'Don't let them touch our hilsa' was the war cry heard across Kolkata. On a more serious note, India had been tipped off by an American source that the task force had three marine battalions and planes ready to bomb India's communications and establish beachheads. As per Samuel Hoskinson, a close assistant of Kissinger, 'To my way of thinking, it was a brilliant strategic move. It stopped Gandhi in her tracks.'

General Manekshaw sent a note asking Gen Niazi to surrender, 'For the sake of your own men, I hope you will not compel me to reduce your garrison with the use of force.' On 13 December, the Indian Army was closing in on Dhaka from the north, south, and east. Niazi had approached the American Consulate in Dhaka for a ceasefire. A point had been reached where a ceasefire had become inevitable and the survival of West Pakistan a foregone conclusion, with Kissinger praising Nixon for having 'put it right on the line'.

Night in the tank harbour was spent without a wink of sleep as we kept turning and tossing to the music of the guns and the background score of rat-a-tat-tat of the MMGs and LMGs. On 13 December, with the first few rays of the sun, the radio began to crackle and soon Digby was on the line with an important message. The essential outline of the new plan envisaged half the squadron consisting of one troop each of B and C Squadron being placed under my command to report to the 42 Infantry Brigade. The rest of the C Squadron consisting of one troop, would remain under Surinder, the T-55 troop having transferred to Capt Gupta of B Squadron. This bit of news was music to my ears as the assignment once again put me in a position of greater responsibility and independence, where I could be free to exploit tactical opportunities to help win the war. The news that Capt Bhandari and Lt Mishra would link up soon was a relief. The weight of the divisional main thrust had swung in the direction of 42 Infantry Brigade, now tasked to secure Khulna from across the Bhairab river.

Our immediate task was to link up with HQ 42 Infantry Brigade as they had concentrated across the Bhairab river. We were guided to the waterline by our very reliable reconnaissance troop, led by Mahato. Our training and experience had been limited to small rivers with placid water, canals, streams, and ponds only, where the speed factor was not so relevant. River crossing operations of such magnitude as that of the Bhairab river, though visualized, had not been practised in the regiment.

Standing in front of the mighty Bhairab river, with the current speed above 5 knots, presented difficulties of drift and negotiating the far bank. Failure to cross the far bank would open the extreme possibility of the tank sailing downstream to finally arrive at the Bay of Bengal to battle the sea waves. The likelihood of a tank floating down the river in full view of the enemy entrenched on the far bank of the Bhairab river was a dangerous and distinct possibility.

Keeping in view the multiple difficulties in crossing the Bhairab, I decided that it would be best for me to lead the way. May be somewhere in the subconscious, the virus of command responsibility had germinated. In spite of the crews being trained, the level of nervousness and anxiety increased the moment one left terra firma to float on water. The change could be seen on the stressed faces of the crew while afloat. The creased line of worry on the forehead would disappear every time the tanks rolled back onto firm soil. The half squadron deployed along the water line was busy carrying out an inspection of armour plugs and rubber seals located on the deck and tank floor to remove all possibilities of leakage of water into the tank compartment.

The PT-76 has three gear positions: land; land and water; water.

In the first position, land, the power of the engines is transferred through the sprocket on to the tank tracks and drive achieved. In the second, land and water, the tracks and pumps operate simultaneously. This gear provides smooth movement to the tank after its entry into water, until it begins to float. In the third position, water, the power is transferred to the water pumps, which suck in water and then discharge intake rearwards, through water propellers, at a rapid speed to provide forward propulsion. A speed of 3 knots can be achieved by a tank while afloat in the water.

Inspection by the crew completed, Ramphal came up loud and clear to announce on the intercom;

'Tank ready to enter water, Sir.' 'Confirm all armour plugs checked.' 'Confirmed, Sir.'

'Harish, elevate gun, crew, prepare to advance, advance now, out.'

Ramphal slid the tank into gear and the tank rolled forward. Within a couple of minutes, we were at the water line moving forward smoothly. Like me, the crew was anticipating that very soon Ramphal would shift the gear to the 'land and water' position. The water level had reached the bogey wheels and we were waiting to hear the typical metallic sound of gears meshing together. Unknown to us, the path along which the tank was progressing had a vertical drop a few metres beyond the water line resulting in the tank taking a nosedive into the water. A blood-curdling scream of a man possessed pierced through the intercom sounding like a Mach 3 jet breaking the sound barrier. A watery grave was the first thought that flashed through the mind. The sharp plunge by the tank had unbalanced me, resulting in being flung forward onto the commander's cupola, hanging on for dear life. Ramphal, dripping wet, recovered from the shock and fright of water gushing over his head, for a moment submerging him. The suspense that we would sink with the tank took the wind out of our lungs. Before we could get hold of our senses or even react to this situation, both the gunner and operator were screaming of ankle-deep water inside the tank. The sudden start of emergency water pumps inside the compartment to discharge the water, added to the confusion and chaos. The tank had resurfaced to float. Our blood circulation and breath gradually revived to take stock of the desperation and shock we had experienced. Ramphal, in a squeeky voice, was on the intercom, explaining a little ruefully, 'Sorry, Sir, I forgot to close the driver cupola.' I was on the verge of blasting him with a few choice expletives when I remembered that it is the joint responsibility of the driver and the commander to check that all the hatches are closed before entry into the water. 'Had a good bath, I hope, you rascal,' I said, and let it pass. The other crew recovered quickly though it did dampen the spirits somewhat.

Recovered and now afloat, the driver tried to shift the gear lever from land directly to the final position, 'water', to move the tank forward under its own propulsion. We could hear his repeated attempts, as the gears did not mesh, causing perceptible tension as the tank was now drifting with the current. Thinking that the driver may still be in a state of shock I tried to boost him with words of encouragement. 'Hello, Ramphal, all well, what is the problem?'

'Sir, I think the gear has got jammed but I will manage.'

Another few futile attempts before I tactfully asked the operator to provide a helping hand but to no avail. My tank driving skills were no match of that of the experienced crew, especially on water. Ramphal, now in desperation, decided to use the age-old universal principle of delivering a few well-

placed blows with the heavy hammer but it only ended up in a
slight variation in the clattering sound of the uncompromising
gear. With each passing moment, we were sailing closer to the
Engineers bridge, under construction. This was creating a lot
of anxiety and apprehension, as evidenced by wild gesticulation
and hollering of the Sappers and tank crews, fearing a likely
collision and collateral damage. Bhandari, watching this drama
from the banks of the river, displayed imagination and initiative
when he had one of the Armoured Fighting Vehicle (AFV)
technicians advise Ramphal, on the radio, how to repair and get
the gear lever working. Nothing appeared to be working right
and we were now 'totally at sea'. The gravity of our predicament
became apparent when Harish Chandra, looking concerned,
handed over the life jacket for me to put on. Was this a signal of
despair or a reminder that wearing a life jacket was compulsory
for tank crews during flotation?

The tank and tide were carrying us closer towards the
belligerent looking Sappers, determined to protect their
bridge. The Engineer detachment commander, hovering close
by, immediately ordered his men to lift the cable and let the
tank through. I do not know whether it was ignorance or sheer
desperation, for like the proverbial drowning man, we clung on
to the cables and gripped them so hard that the knuckles turned
white. The simple law of physics that mass x velocity= force was
re-learnt on the high sea when foolishly and quite thoughtlessly,
like jokers in a tv commercial, we attempted to anchor the tank
with muscle power by not letting go of the life-line we were
holding. The effortless ease with which the tank moved with
the current made our Lilliputian effort dangerous for had we
not released our grip we would have been left behind like some
homemaker's washing hanging to dry in the winter sun.

Hope vanished like straw in the wind. Desperation must have activated unused brain cells to find a way out of this catch-22 situation. Could the velocity of the gushing water pouring into the tank disturb the gear lever alignment, resulting in the present crisis? Looking back towards the bridge, which was looking like a small toy bobbing in the water, the rapidly diminishing mass of humanity waving frantically in alarm at our unceremonious farewell, possibly wishing us bon voyage and the widening expanse of the water all around made me realize for the first time in my life, the true meaning of fear.

The sound of metal against metal seemed to distract me. The driver had begun to sledgehammer at the gear lever and after every blow, he would check if his efforts or our collective prayers had worked when possibly both blended to produce the heavenly music of propellers suddenly coming to life working full steam, as the 'water' gear slipped into position. No one bothered to see how close we had arrived to the enemy position or if we were under his observation for we were overwhelmed with joy by this miraculous change of direction. The scowl on the face of the Sappers was replaced by beaming smiles when they welcomed us back warmly as they lifted the cables one last time for us to start the river-crossing operation once again.

The return to the proposed site was not free of problems, as repeated attempts were made to align the tank and get across to the far bank. The credit for this goes to the grit and determination and driving ability of Ramphal. The next tank was already in the water when one of the crew suggested that we use our tank as an anchor and extend the long self-recovery rope to the incoming tanks. This would have the advantage of arresting drift as also facilitate alignment to the crossing site.

This local innovation was helpful in ensuring problem free movement of the remaining tanks across the Bhairab river.

Once across the river, the crews recouped to overcome the tension of crossing the tidal river and reorganize for the link up with infantry. The terrain in the area ahead was murderous. As we progressed through these villages, the path became restricted and the vegetation more dense. We were advancing through low-lying areas, which gave the appearance of having a firm crust, and dried surface but were virtual tank traps. The complete journey was in bounds, from one bogged down tank to another. There were places where the track had disappeared completely and the tanks had to go bulldozing their way through bamboo groves. While no serious casualty took place, each disembarking passenger, covered with dust, soot, and bruises, would recount this backbreaking experience to his comrades, invariably ending with the advice that it was better to walk than mount a bucking horse.

A large section of the rural gentry had moved back into the liberated villages that we passed through. Most of the rural folk had their families and meagre personal belongings loaded on animals or carried these on their person. The largely poor villagers had been forced to abandon their limited earthly possessions. It was a continuous flow of men and women, old and infirm, sick and weak, suffering from malnutrition. Just as we were nearing a village, my eyes fell on an exceedingly charming and beautiful young face, heavenly and angel-like. This girl, aged around 20, was with her husband, dressed in spotless white. She herself was wearing a simple coloured cotton sari and had her hair done up in a single plait. For a moment, our eyes met and then she turned to look at her husband who smiled back. Once again, she looked back, raised her hand, and waved briefly. The smile that accompanied the wave was like the sun coming out from behind the clouds. The gesture of raising the hand and slow motion of the nod reflected poise and charm. The gentle frame, gait, and carriage confirmed good breeding. The twinkling eyes and hidden mischief in her youthful looks could have made a sinner out of a saint. That a soldier stood exposed to such grave dangers in enemy territory while leading a column of tanks made mockery of Cupid's sense of justice. I was placed in that awkward position where I could not yell, tell, or even stare any longer at her. Looking on with an amused expression was not only the face of Saighal but other crew members also. She had said all that a woman need say and much more in that graceful unforgettable moment. With nothing more than a glance exchanged and a wave of the hand, thoughts of love, gratitude, and admiration filled the heart and mind. Neither rational nor logical, I have no explanation of how or why the persona of that passer-by should remain embedded in the software of the human mind. With the advantage of the internet, may be, someday, perhaps, . . . alas!

The link up with the infantry took place as scheduled. Next morning, Bhandari and Mishra moved off early to establish liaison with the 14 Punjab and 2 Sikh LI battalions of 42 Infantry Brigade inducted earlier. The new brigade commander of 42 Infantry Brigade had called for his O group. The brief meeting was, however, conducted by the Brigade Major as the commander was attending an operational conference at the Divisional Headquarters. The tentative task was spelt out to the O Group so that ground reconnaissance and marrying up by the units could be completed. The bridge across the Bhairab was expected to be completed during the day after which the F, A, and B echelons of the combat units would be inducted into the area.

Bhandari was waiting for me at the given RV. After a quick rundown of his interaction with the battalion, Bhandari took me to a vantage point overlooking the river to indicate the enemy positions that had come alive. None of the enemy bunkers was visible but from time to time, the movement of soldiers had been noticed and a few had opened fire. The Bhairab was much wider here as it seemed to stretch for over a kilometre. Khulna town was an important full-fledged port town and commercial centre with high-rise buildings and factory chimneys reaching out to the sky. It was like some of our own coastal towns and would not be an easy nut to crack, in spite of complete air superiority. A string of boats and launches could be seen at the far end of the river line, close to which were the interior water transport jetties. Mishra, the other officer, joined us to tell us of the reconnaissance conducted by him. He had met some of the brigade staff who told him that while a few infantry companies had concentrated, the rest of the troops, including the new brigade commander, would arrive during the night. This suited me, having gone through a gruelling day, and we retired for the night.

I was ready early morning when word was received that I was to report to Brigade HQ by 0900 hrs on 14 December. I learnt that only the Rover group of the commander had come across the river on rafts as the bridge was still under construction. The staff and vehicles of the brigade would come only subsequently as the concentration of troops had not been completed so far. The new Brigade Commander, Brig Kochhar, belonged to the Rajputana Rifles. He had moved from the Staff College, Wellington, where he was the chief instructor. He was a distinguished soldier who was professionally very sound and had achieved distinction on all the courses of instruction he had attended. When I first cast an eye on him, I was definitely impressed by his cool, reserved manner, and ability for clear thinking and sound decision-making. He gave us a rough outline of the way he had planned the river-crossing operation and attack. He wanted us to think it over, as he would be doing just the same, for it needed approval by the divisional commander. He planned to hold a meeting again at 0700 hrs the following morning at which he would give out his preliminary orders. The commander then met me separately and explained that I was required to select the crossing places for my tanks, while carrying out a joint reconnaissance with CO 14 Punjab battalion, earmarked by him for leading the river-crossing operations in the Brigade Phase I.

I had taken Bhandari along with me for the reconnaissance. On reaching the battalion, I met my old friend A.B.C. D' Mello, sitting like a mother hen along with a caboodle of staff and attached officers. His knowledge of the deployment and likely enemy strength was summed up in one sentence, 'My company commander Maj Sidhu will brief you!' Locating Sidhu was not easy and we had to seek the assistance of the local Mukti Bahini as he had deployed way beyond the grid reference given to us. When questioned, Sidhu started rattling off the enemy locations he had sighted and reported to his CO. A little perplexed, we asked him to check his location. It soon became obvious that the company had been reporting activity across the Atai river and not the Bhairab. This was sure to raise a stink with D' Mello. We left on the gentlemen's agreement that we would remain silent on this issue and let Sidhu handle the redeployment and the amendment to his earlier reports. Mistakes in navigation and deployment are commonplace but this was worthy of being recorded in the Limca Book of Records!

Bhandari accompanied me to the 14 Punjab location. We followed the tree line along the banks of the Bhairab until we reached Chandi Mahal, the crossing site recommended by CO 14 Punjab. The local company commander pointed out the enemy bunkers, kept under watch, but enemy activity was not seen in the area. The presence of two khaki-clad civilians detected near the entrance gate of the big factory made us curious. We pulled out our binoculars to observe the two men disappear into a building shortly thereafter. The binoculars soon revealed a different picture. Above the same building, we spotted a camouflaged canopy but no unusual activity. My interest in this area was flagging when suddenly a flash of khaki appeared on the eyepiece. One of the two men in khaki spotted earlier, entered the canopy by opening a door, behind which one could see a mounted MMG before the door was shut once again. The company commander was witness to this chance observation. A more detailed scrutiny revealed a sinister pattern of gun placements in the brick and concrete towers and canopies across the river. The realization that we were witnessing an elevated defended locality of the enemy came as a rude shock. The crossing of the Chandi Mahal had ominous implications if accepted as only a river-crossing site.

I sent a note, through a runner, asking him to request Col R.K. Singh to see the enemy dispositions before issuing his orders. Bhandari raised the issue while the CO was giving out the preliminary orders for an assault across the river explaining that a weak enemy was incapable of guarding the complete river line as our major force was simultaneously attacking along the main axis. He silenced Bhandari by an angry wave of the hand, demanding silence. Soon after the briefing, the CO made a hasty retreat to the Brigade HQ. The company commanders, however, accompanied Bhandari to the vantage position to see for themselves the enemy bunkers and form their own opinions. The manner in which Col R.K. Singh had silenced Bhandari made them realize that something was amiss. What they witnessed now convinced them that if the plan announced were to be executed, the casualties would be very high, as they would be attacking coordinated, well-prepared deliberate defences.

Vishwanath, who was senior and more defiant, spoke with bitter criticism of the highhanded, indifferent manner in which the CO had given out his orders, without carrying out a proper reconnaissance. His sudden departure after the orders had made them suspicious. The other company commanders spoke their minds and soon tempers flared up at the method adopted by an ambitious CO. Any hasty or extreme step would invite provisions of the Army Act and court martial for disobedience of orders. I requested the officers to be patient and continue with the reconnaissance as the attack plans had yet to be formalized by the Brigade HQ. As far as I was concerned, I would raise this issue at the brigade O group. I was confident that the brigade commander would take a balanced decision.

The two infantry battalion commanders, D'Mello and R.K. Singh, and the OC of other supporting arms had already reached the makeshift Brigade Operations Room, located in a small school building on 15 December. The commander, after a few pleasantries, was briefed about the reconnaissance conducted. D'Mello was the first. He apologized, admitting that the company commander tasked had committed a faux pas, for which he accepted responsibility, and requested additional time for submitting his plan. Kochhar's language and demeanour gave no indication of the disappointment at such a setback and was truly commendable and deserves mention. R.K. Singh was carrying a marked map of the area reconnoitred and highlighted the enemy positions identified. He then went on at length to explain his plans for the crossing, saying that instead of at night, it could be a day operation in view of the enemy strength the commanders' questions were meaningful and thought-provoking for which the replies were not convincing, and the doubts remained. It was getting into an interesting stage when he got up and said that he would accompany us on the reconnaissance next morning to see the enemy positions indicated.

I was returning to the tank location when a staff officer informed me that the commander wanted to meet me. Other officers who had come for the meeting had left. The commander pointed to a vacant chair, signalling to me to sit down while he continued studying the operational map. After a long pause, he asked if I was in agreement with the assessment of CO 14 Punjab. The discussion continued for about 20 minutes during which I gave him my frank, candid view. At the end, he wanted confirmation that the report I had shared with him was based on personal observations. In my presence, he lifted the receiver and asked to be connected to the GOC. While the line was being put through, he told me that he would soon be requesting for postponement of the river-crossing operation by one day in view of the information provided. A decision of this nature called for moral courage and character, a genuine love and regard for the soldiers, who unaware of the mix-up, would have still obeyed orders. This was a difficult decision, as a change in plans demanded integrity of character and professionalism of the highest order.

I could not help but reflect on the contrast in character of the senior officers and the orders being issued by them. The actions of the commander are always under the scrutiny of the subordinates for whom aberrations spell life-and-death situations.

Mishra, who, after finishing the reconnaissance, was to have moved his tanks and married up with the Sikh LI Battalion, had not responded throughout the day. Knowing that the terrain was tricky could be the probable reason for the delay, but his failure to respond on the radio was now causing concern. Around 2000 hrs, a very dishevelled, tired, and morose sounding Mishra established radio contact to explain the harrowing experience he and his tank crews had undergone, as two of his tanks had had a track shed. I had heard of, but never seen, a track shed before and was amazed to hear of the damage. After the track shed, the tank continued to stand majestically with its skirts up. It would need at least four hours to get it rolling again. The badly mangled and twisted mass of tank track, idler wheel, and sprocket, badly intermingled, presented an ungainly sight. I empathized with him but wondered why he had failed to communicate. I was standing around discussing this with Bhandari when the brigade staff officer tapped me on the shoulder saying that the brigade commander wanted me at his HQ. It must have been extremely urgent for he had sent his own jeep to fetch me.

On reaching the HQ, I was taken into the Operations Room where the commander was already briefing Col D'Mello. He briefly explained to me that there had been a change in orders and that the GOC insisted that a battalion must get across the Bhairab along with a troop of tanks that very night. The alternative crossing site in the Sikh LI location proposed by Mishra to D'Mello had been approved. The site, incidentally, was in the B Company new location of Sikh LI, commanded by Sidhu. The commander asked me a few technical details regarding the tank's capability and the gradients that the

PT-76 could surmount at night, which I explained to the best of my ability. I, however, stressed that I had not carried out any reconnaissance of this ferry site and would have to cross check with Mishra who had conducted the reconnaissance. The commander agreed with the suggestion that Mishra be called so that doubts, if any, of the crossing site could be resolved before the commencement of the operation. Like all great commanders, he refused to come under pressure and though not too happy with the decision enforced by the divisional commander, he was ensuring that the troops were not launched at any tactical disadvantage.

'Mishra, my compliments for the selection of the crossing site.' Mishra missed the sarcasm, but replied, '2–3 sites were discussed but not finalized.' The sarcasm was intended to make him aware that I had not been kept in the loop. 'Well, good luck, the brigade commander wants to meet you.' During the journey to Brigade Headquarters, I explained to him about the crossing site being used for the launch of Brigade Phase 1. Noticing his hesitation, I advised him to be 100 per cent certain of his facts as the plan hinged on his ability to take the tanks across from the site selected. He should, therefore, have no hesitation in expressing his doubts or his confidence on the suitability of the site to the commander. When confronted by the commander, he appeared undecided as to whether he should commit himself or not and was attempting to dodge a definite answer. I felt that the situation was getting to be an embarrassing one and asked him in unambiguous terms whether the tanks would be able to cross the ferry or not. He gave it a reasonable thought and in his slow drawl, barely audible, confirmed that the tanks could cross. It was past 2200 hrs and crossing had to commence at 0200 hrs, barely enough time to reach the ferry site. Unknown to us,

D'Mello had expressed confidence on his battalion undertaking Brigade Phase 1 operations if the tanks were provided. The die was cast!

Mishra had stepped into a situation where he had equal opportunity to speak the bare truth and take the rap on the knuckles by denying that he had recommended the crossing site when, in reality, he had only discussed the probability. His acceptance established a flaw in his statement overlooked by me earlier. Mishra's reply now made me responsible to help him for the success the mission. My ego state had reacted to a subordinate going over my head to undertake such a significant decision. Notwithstanding the uneasy feeling in my mind, I was now devising practical ways of what could be done under the circumstances. One immediate step was to ask Mishra to do a quick reconnaissance if he still had mental reservations about the crossing site. He requested for transport to carry two crew members with radio sets to conduct a route check and survey of the crossing site. Bhandari would guide his tank troop and meet him at an RV before the scheduled hour. Mishra was grateful for such an opportunity and got cracking while I started scouting for a jeep/jonga to transport him on this clandestine mission. Meanwhile, Bhandari reported that the tank, which had shed track, would be ready before 0100 hrs. We could now sit back and await Mishra's confirmation of his final reconnaissance of crossing at the ferry site. Things were falling into place.

Around 0130 hrs on 16 December, firing from the direction of the ferry site alarmed us. As the intensity of firing increased, my first thought was for the security of Mishra's reconnaissance party. Was it possible that their movement in that area had been observed? The time was already 0145 hrs, so when the operator announced an incoming call, I took it for granted that it would be Mishra. No, the operator clarified, this was straight from the brigade commander who announced that the Brigade Phase 1 had been aborted on the orders of the Division HQ. Mishra returned around 0300 hrs, looking tired and dejected. He had had an unusual day, followed by a night of high drama. Next morning, over an *aloo–puri* breakfast, he narrated to us in his own unique Oriya Hinglish the secret behind the aborted attack. It transpired that once D'Mello returned to his battalion, he briefed Sidhu about the orders he had received regarding Brigade Phase 1. The ferry site to be utilized for crossing by the tanks was in his area of responsibility, as such he was expected to perform a number of actions to assist the assaulting echelons. As had been observed, by the others also, there was no love lost between the two. When the task was spelt out, Sidhu reacted violently. He was not only critical of the tasks allotted but had turned abusive, causing acute embarrassment to all and sundry. D'Mello, diminutive in size, was a pleasant easy-going man, popular with the troops, with whom he enjoyed an easy understanding and affectionate relationship. His anglicized Punjabi and unlimited capacity for Punjabi abuses was what they looked forward to, especially under the tension that prevailed. D'Mello was not going to let this tantrum get past without sending a clear message to everyone present. Unperturbed, he repeated his orders, adding that any act of non-compliance would result in his putting the officer under close arrest. This had the desired effect on Sidhu, and realizing the consequences of his outburst, he apologized.

Sidhu was firm in his conviction that these attacks were no longer necessary, as it was now just a question of time before the enemy would buckle. This was a view which was shared by a large number of officers and possibly some subordinates also.

In some, it appeared as if battle fatigue was manifesting itself. A less generous view was that some commanders were pushing for self-glorification. Sidhu, a very intense man, must have started devising means of scuttling the plans even before he left the CO's shelter. It was well past 0030 hrs when Mishra met him to seek assistance for his reconnaissance. As per Mishra, Sidhu was already in a 'happy' state, having emptied half a bottle of rum. In a spirit of bravado, he told him, '*koi attack shatack nahin ho ga!*' (There will be no attack!) He thrust a glass of rum into his hands and bragged about the devious master plan he had evolved. He drew inspiration from the regular 'soldier to soldier' radio calls broadcast by Chief of the Army Staff Gen Sam Manekshaw, 'Should you not heed my advice to surrender to my Army and endeavour to escape, I assure you certain death awaits you.'

A little before 0100 hrs, he appeared to have sobered up, and looked as if he had to perform some important mission. He asked Mishra to accompany him, as also his company Subedar. They did not have long to wait for the plan to unfold. He stepped into the nearest LMG pit and fired a long burst at some imaginary target across the water line while issuing fire orders to his company to open fire. The rest is now history. The heavy volume of fire triggered the enemy to respond, soon escalating into the entire river line coming alive, followed by the expected artillery duel. A radio message to the Battalion HQ transmitted over the 'red hot' humming wires was transmitted verbatim on to the intervening Brigade, Division, and Corps HQ. Unaware of the ruse that had been played out, the unsuspecting staff briefed their commanders to abort the mission, and soon after, communicated this to us. Sidhu no longer needed the support of the rum bottle that he was carrying for what he had done was more intoxicating than power—a display of power!

On the following morning, I had to leave early to accompany the commander for a joint reconnaissance. On reaching the Chandi Mahal crossing site, Col R.K. Singh briefed the commander about enemy dispositions on the far bank and the feasibility of a daylight crossing. Based on his individual assessment on the suitability of the crossing site, the commander agreed, and approved the plan. The company commanders were in an aggressive mood but stayed silent, not expressing their reservations in the presence of the commander. Aware of the simmering anger amongst some of the officers, I thought it best to leave so that they could resolve their differences in-house.

It was not long before an urgent message summoned us to assemble at the Star Jute Mill, a three-storeyed building overlooking the Bhairab river. We were all huddled on the terrace, some crouching, and some sitting while others took up various positions so as to avoid being spotted by the enemy from across the river. The second-in-command of 14 Punjab had in a moment of sudden inspiration, uncovered an ideal crossing site visible from the vantage point, where we had now assembled. He took time to explain the many advantages this crossing site had over the Chandi Mahal crossing. R.K. Singh was present but had suddenly lost the sheen and bubbling enthusiasm for combat. He would have been aware of the task entrusted to his 2IC before the morning briefing. I listened carefully to this alternative plan and appreciated that the site selected had the advantage of good approach and negotiable river banks. The proposed crossing point was located on the river bend, making the wet gap twice as large. The commander must have read my thoughts, as I heard him telling the assembled gathering that 'ideal situations rarely exist and calculated risks have to be taken in life and war to progress and move on.' He then announced that as commander he had taken a final decision to cross the Bhairab. The time set was for 1400 hrs, 16 December 1971.

During the night of 15–16 December, the F and AI echelon vehicles of the squadron, along with the squadron Rover had been inducted through the recently constructed bridge. Ravi Bhandari had taken charge of these vehicles to ensure that the tanks were topped up with POL and ammunition, and maintenance tasks were completed. The last 72 hours had been tough on the troops as they had to survive on crew cooking and emergency rations. Soon after receiving the commander's orders of the Brigade Phase 1 being launched, I was able to inform Bhandari and Mishra. They were to move to an RV from where guides of 14 Punjab would lead them to the assaulting company locations. Before leaving for the RV to switch over to my tank, I stopped over at the Brigade HQ to confirm the move of the tanks to the ferry site. I found the commander sitting outside in the sun with his staff and Col Dutt standing around trying to listen in on the telephone. I joined them but could hear nothing at all. None of the other officers around was moving and there was pin-drop silence. I must have stood around for at least a minute in silence. I visualized that some important announcement was expected. The BM was standing next to me so I nudged him, saying that the tanks had reached the water line along with elements of two Sikh LI and 14 Punjab, to cross the river Bhairab. Before he could reply, the commander gestured by a motion of his free hand that the earlier orders had been cancelled. My expression of surprise at the cancellation made him repeat the gesture and, at the same time, put down the telephone. He got out of his chair, pulled himself up to his full height, a picture of grace under pressure and exemplary character. With a smile beginning on his lips, in a flat tone, he announced that ceasefire had been ordered and the surrender would take place shortly. There was no emotion in his words, just a hint of happiness as he made this announcement in a matter-o- fact way. He then asked me to revert the tanks to the Brigade HQ location and shook hands with everyone present before walking off towards his caravan.

An air of jubilation spread among the tank crews. Everyone wanted to know the latest of how and where the surrender would take place. Tank radio sets, instead of being switched off, were now being tuned into All India Radio, BBC, and even Radio Pakistan. It was reporting stiff battles and determined resistance being put up by their soldiers, with claims that Pakistan would never cower down to the kafirs, even as a surrender of arms was in progress by the Prisoners of War. After a couple of minutes, the soldiers switched over to AIR and BBC. What we were able to gather and share with others were the developments between 7–16 December that made us realize the gravity and tension our political masters and military leaders had undergone while we contemplated the capture of Khulna.

A sea of humanity had suddenly appeared. Men, women, and even children had come out of their houses to shake hands with, and express their gratitude to, the soldiers. The old, infirm, and weak, doddering, with sticks in one hand, and the flag of Bangladesh in the other, flocked together, shouting, till their throats became hoarse and dry. The tanks or 'chain gadi' as they came to be called, drew large crowds for they had never seen such equipment before. Many jumped onto the tanks and danced around, cheering and kissing the Indian jawans. They stuck marigolds in their gun barrels and showered them with garlands of jasmine. *Daab* (tender coconuts) were hurriedly plucked from trees and offered to soldiers. Cigarettes packets, biscuits, and whatever little eatables they could organize, were being distributed to the soldiers. This exuberance and happiness exploded in an ecstasy of hard-won elation. From the banks of the Bhairab river, from the emerald rice fields and mustard-coloured hills of the countryside, from the countless villages came the cry 'Joi Bangla!' 'Joi Bangla!' (victory to Bengal, victory to Bengal!) There was wild gunfire in the air, impromptu parades, hilarity and horn honking, and processions of jammed trucks. They danced on the roofs of buses and marched down city streets, singing their national anthem 'Sonar Bangla'. They brought the green, red, and gold banner of Bengal out of secret hiding places, to flutter freely from buildings, while huge pictures of their imprisoned leader, Sheikh Mujibur Rehman, sprang up overnight on trucks, houses, and street corners. Three cheers for the Indian Army, three cheers for Indira Gandhi, three cheers for Mujibur Rehman, it went on, and on, and on.

On 17 December, at 1400 hrs, Brig Hayat Khan, commander, 107 Infantry Brigade, along with seven Pakistani Lieutenant Colonels surrendered to Maj Gen Dalbir Singh, GOC, 9 Infantry Division, at the Khulna Circuit House. In a brief ceremony, the instrument of surrender was signed. The following Pakistani troops surrendered at Khulna:

Officers	81
JCOs	130
ORs	3476
Others	207

Our major partner in this success was the Indian Air Force which managed to wipe out the Pakistan Air Force in the east within two days, giving India control of the skies. In the Bay of Bengal and the Ganges delta region as well, the Indian Navy was in unchallenged command. Its blockade of the Chittagong and Chalna harbours cut off all reinforcements, supplies, and chances of evacuation for the Pakistani forces who found themselves 'fucked and far from home', trapped in an enclave more than 1000 miles from home bases in West Pakistan. The support, help, and assistance provided by the Mukti Bahini and the people of erstwhile East Pakistan hastened the freedom of Bangladesh.

APPENDIX

RECOMMENDATION FOR GALLANTRY AWARD
IC-16957H
CAPT. B.S. MEHTA, 45 CAVALRY FOR
MAHAVIR CHAKRA (MVC)

AWARDED: MENTION-IN-DESPATCHES

CITATION

1. Capt BS Mehta was the 2IC of 'C' Squadron 45 Cavalry. At about 0600 hrs on 21 Nov 1971 when the Squadron move to suitable loc to counter the threat posed by the enemy tanks, Capt. B.S. Mehta was in Command of the right hand group of the Squadron.

2. He effectively controlled his group of two troops on the right flank and opened fire, knocking down one tank with his own tank. In this tank to tank battle when one enemy tank tried to encroach further into the FDL's Capt. B.S. Mehta again engaged the tank and knocked it out. The enemy

also brought down heavy concentration of arty and SA fire, Capt. B.S. Mehta held his ground and kept on directing his group to effectively continue engaged by two enemy tanks.

3. It was at this critical stage of the battle that the sudden news of the demise of the Squadron Commander Maj. D.S. Narag reached Capt. B.S. Mehta. The officer was undaunted and unnerved by this loss and promptly assumed Command and control of his Squadron. He encouraged his troops with fine example of personal courage and leadership and led them on to the final destruction of the enemy squadron. The task was completed with in a short period and the Squadron accounted for 10 enemy tanks. The Officer displayed fighting spirit, courage and leadership qualities in keeping with the highest tradition of the Armoured Corps and the Army.

GLOSSARY

ACC&S: Armoured Corps Centre and School.

Ack Ack: Anti-Aircraft.

ADS: Advanced Dressing Station. This is the first link in the chain of evacuation of battle causality.

All India All Class: Units in which troops of all classes/ communities can be recruited. After the 1971 War, most units raised were on All India All Class basis.

Annexe: Officers' Institute at ACC&S. In earlier days, it was an annexe to the Officers' Mess. The name continues.

ANPRC–25: Versatile radio set of American origin which provided dependable communication.

Armd Regt: Tank regiment.

Armoured Delivery Regiment (80 ADR): See reinforcements.

Battle Drills: Battle contingency that had been rehearsed to maintain cohesion in combat.

Brigade Major: General Staff officer at Brigade Headquarters.

Bhangra: Dance form of Punjab.

Cavalier: Journal of ACC&S.

Cheshire Trust: An international trust for assistance to war wounded.

Class 9 Road: Military classification of road/bridges.

Combat Team: A combined team of all arms placed under one commander.

Driving/Gunnery/Radio: Three separate trades in which Sowars (soldiers) of the armoured corps are trained. Preference of trade determines the period of training in each trade.

Dungaree: Overall combination.

EME: Electrical and Mechanical engineers, responsible for repair and maintenance of military equipment and vehicles.

ETA: Expected time of arrival.

FDL: Forward Defended Locality.

Forward Concentration Area: A pre-selected area outside enemy observation and medium artillery range from where troops are launched into battle.

GOC: General Officer Commanding.

Harbour Area: A selected area where tanks can carry out repair and replenishment without interference from the enemy.

HEAT, HE, AP: High Explosive Anti-tank; High Explosive; Armour Piercing—types of ammunition fired from a tank.

IB: International boundary.

Infrared Device: This was a novelty in 1971. The PT-76 had this facility only for the driver. The T-55, however, had an infrared device fitted for the commander and gunner, making acquisition of targets at night possible up to limited ranges.

Khaji: Palm tree.

LD: Lance Dafadar. Rank held by an NCO. Identified by two stripes.

'Loaded': In tank crew drill, this signifies that the loader has completed all actions so that gunner can commence fine laying of the gun before the commander gives the executive order of 'Fire'.

Marrying up: Process of integration between armour/infantry units/sub-units to coordinate the battle plan, etc.

Mechanized: Foot infantry units, when equipped with Armoured Personnel Carriers, on conversion.

MMG/MG: Medium Machine Gun/Machine Gun.

MS Branch: Military Secretary's Branch. Handles all promotions and postings of officers.

Mujahid/Razakar: Paramilitary forces raised by Pakistan.

Mujib-ur Rehman: Father of the Nation of Bangladesh.

Mukti Bahini: Freedom fighters of Bangladesh.

MVC: Mahavir Chakra; the second-highest gallantry award of the country.

Naxalites: Indigenous Communists who first gained notoriety in the early 1970s for the killings in Naxalbari (West Bengal)

Nb/Ris: A Non-Commissioned Officer on promotion to Junior Commissioned Officer in the Armoured Corps attains the rank of Naib Risaldar.

NCO: Non-Commissioned Officer.

NDA, IMA: National Defence Academy; Indian Military Academy.

OIC: Other Indian Classes. An amalgam of all classes that had not found specific representation in the Army.

Omar Khayyam: Persian poet whose literary works have been translated by Fitzgerald.

OP/FOO: Observation Post/Forward Observation Officer.

Generally, a young officer from the artillery who moves with the leading troops to provide fire support of light and medium guns.

Pakhals: Small steel water tank capable of carriage by all known means of military transport, including animals.

Paltan: Unit.

Panchsheel: Policy of friendship adopted with China prior to the 1962 India–China War.

Patiala Peg: Large peg of alcohol. As per one version, the original measure stood for enough alcohol in a glass to cover the four fingers of the hand holding the glass.

Pippa: Colloquial name given to the PT-76 tank when inducted into service with the Indian Army. Pippa means pot or container made of tin.

POW: Prisoner of war.

PRO: Public relations officer.

R&R: Rest and refit relief.

R&S Bn: Reconnaissance and Support Battalion. Usually allotted to an infantry division in the plains. These units have a higher proportion of anti- tank and medium machine guns and recce platoons. Usually sub-allotted to brigades, based on operational requirement.

Ranges: Generally refers to field firing ranges where the main armament is zeroed and firing practice conducted under war simulated conditions.

Rashtrapati: President of India.

RCL: Recoilless Gun. An anti-tank gun generally mounted on a jeep/jonga.

Risalawala: One who serves in the cavalry/armoured unit.

Rocket Launcher: Handheld anti-tank weapon.

RM: Raksha Mantri.

Sabres: F-86 jet aircraft of American origin used by Pakistan.

Scramble: Quick take-off to intercept enemy planes.

Shakarparas: Staple diet of soldiers during combat. Invariably cooked in sub-unit cookhouses, from flour/maida and deep-fried. Salted/sugar coated. Carried as part of emergency rations.

Shilajeet: Aphrodisiacs—there are many varieties.

SOP: Standing Operating Procedures.

T-55 Tank: Tank of Russian origin carrying the 100mm gun.

Tank Troop Leading: The art and science of leading a troop of tanks in all operations of war.

Tankodrome; Tank Directrix: A training facility at the field firing ranges.

TOT: Time on target.

VCOAS: Vice-Chief of the Army Staff.

Veer Bhogya Vasundhra: 'The Earth is for the Brave Only'.

Regimental motto of 45 Cavalry, taken from the Gita.

Walking wounded: Medical categorization for evacuation of a casualty.

Wilco: Used in radio telephony. Implies message understood, will comply.

Woordie Major: The JCO adjutant in an armoured regiment. He works directly under the adjutant and assists in maintaining discipline.

Yahya Khan: Erstwhile President of Pakistan.

Zeroing: Gunnery procedure wherein line of sight and fall of shot are adjusted.

ACKNOWLEDGEMENTS

I assume that if you are reading this book, it is because it carries an unusual battle account or it is radiating some good vibrations that are holding your attention. If I was younger, I would have claimed all the credit for writing it, but, as my mother used to say, kismet, destiny, chance, randomness plays an important role in the lives of mortals. Translated, it implies that a host of friends, relations, comrades-in-arms, course mates, regimental officers, veterans as also the larger fraternity of cavaliers, serving and retired, have singly and collectively contributed their time, knowledge, talent or blessings and participated in the completion of this book, making it better than any which I could have created alone.

My first thanks go to my tank crew Acting Lance Dafadar (ALD) Ramphal, Lance Dafadar Harishchandra and Lance Dafadar Shibe Lal for the many errands they performed unhesitatingly while I was writing the manuscript as also for being my constant companions through the thick and thin of battle. The battle account was written in longhand immediately after the war ended and the unit had moved to the desert sector. Writing acted as a stress buster and released the tension and trauma accumulated during the weeks of intense combat. The first draft was read by a few regimental officers and my brothers Lt Narinder Mehta (5 Garhwal) and Surinder Mehta. The manuscript became my most prized possession, placed in cold storage till 1996, when it was reviewed for press briefings when the country and the Army celebrated the Silver Jubilee of the 1971 War and the independence of Bangladesh. It again went into silent mode as the exigencies of military service gained priority. Talk of publishing would surface periodically due to enquiries from family members and regimental officers. I would review the contents of my prized possession, but the bubble of enthusiasm to publish would burst within days as the compulsions of daily life and military service received priority.

I took premature retirement from the Army in 1998 and moved to Ahmedabad on a contractual assignment with the Government of Gujarat. During this period, I employed Ramesh as my computer operator who painstakingly transferred the manuscript on to the computer and made a hard copy and saved the soft copy on a CD. The dedication and hard work of Ramesh impressed me and I remain indebted to him. In 2003, I came in contact with Mr Anthony Antimuro, my transcendental Meditation Guru, working in the Maharishi Institute of Management at Noida. Anthony studied the text and helped by giving detailed comments on various aspects of writing style, content and language. His suggestions and guidance, along with positive vibes and encouragement that the account was worthy of publication, triggered my resolve. The corrections took considerable time as I remain a one-finger computer key punching liability. Before I could complete the task, Anthony moved back to the USA while I took on the responsibilities of higher education at the Maharishi Shiksha Sansthan in Madhya Pradesh.

By now, the proposed book had developed a life of its own. It existed not only in memory but had found a special place marked 'TBC' on my computer. At home, my wife Jayshree, and children, Brijraj and Nandinii, would tease me about my promise of publishing the war account. Their reminders kept the subject alive and strengthened my resolve that someday soon I would publish the account of the sacrifice, bravery and glory of the regiment into which I was commissioned. At the deeper, subconscious level, the stories I had heard from my parents and uncles during my growing-up years of bloodshed and mayhem during the partition of India in 1947 mingled with memories of being witness to the starving, half-naked refugees streaming into the camps around Calcutta. The common denominator between the accounts of 1947 and what I had witnessed in 1971 made me realize the true meaning of genocide. This war was a humanitarian war and my regiment had played a pivotal role in the restoration of human dignity against the depraved perpetrators of genocide.

Having reached the age of superannuation as Vice Chancellor, I took the blessings of Dr Girish Chander Verma, Chancellor, Maharishi University of Management and Technology, Bilaspur, Chhattisgarh, to retire. I had steeled my mind to complete *The Burning Chaffees*, this long pending commitment. During a lunch meeting of 45 Cavalry officers at New Delhi, hosted by General and Mrs Amit Sharma, Colonel of the Regiment, the subject of the Golden Jubilee Celebrations was under discussion when I volunteered to publish the war account. Over the next few weeks, I kept the TBC file on the computer open to complete the final draft. The late Col Narinder Mehta (5 Garhwal), who was wounded while leading the battalion attack on Hilli in December 1971 had shared his sharp, incisive comments on the original draft. I now shared the finished version with my brothers Maj Gen Raj Mehta (16C, 83AR, 50AR) and Lt Gen Shammi Mehta (63C) and received valuable inputs and advice. Raj not only read the entire book thoroughly but made valuable suggestions, some of which were incorporated to add value for the young readers from the Mechanised Forces. Shammi, who had commanded the 5 Independent Armoured Squadron which entered Dacca with the PT-76 tanks after swimming across River Meghna, provided fresh insights. Additional comments were received on certain sections of the book from Lt Gen Amit Sharma, Colonel of the Regiment 45 Cavalry, Maj Gen Ravi Bhandari, Brig S. K. Gupta, Brig Ravi Bains, Col T. Sidhu, Maj Durga Dass and Maj Anil Sabharwal, all war veterans and Brig S. Jha and Col Mir Ahmed Shah. Strong support came from my Non-Governmental Organization (NGO) friends from Jai Jawan Nagrik Samiti, Surat, particularly Shri Kanjibhai Bhalala, Manoj Godhani and Savji Dolakhia. The constant encouragement and support of serving and retired members of the Fighting Forty-Five finally worked the miracle of TBC reaching the publishers.

We all know how wonderful it is to have on one's side a person who will not only provide unfailing support but also inspiration during the lowest moments of life, wisdom in challenging times, practical advice when confusion reigns and unconditional love. Of course, finding such an extraordinary person is rare unless it is God's will/destiny. In my life, this treasure arrived in the persona of Jayshree. She is my lover, my friend, my partner, and my wife. I am also grateful to her for our two lovely children, Brijraj and

Nandinii, who have individually and as a family brought cheer, hope, fun and happiness to this union. They never got tired of the long discussions I drew them into about the style and content of the book or were too polite to complain. I also owe a debt to the clerical staff, computer operators and other members of 45 Cavalry who helped in providing links to old documents, war diaries and photographs, for their tireless efforts during my recent visit to 45 Cavalry. A special word of thanks to some fine officers, Junior Commissioned Officers (JCOs) and Other Ranks (ORs) who were transferred out to other regiments whose 'intense regimental spirit' during war and peace contributed to the foundation of 45 Cavalry. Finally, a word of thanks to my course mates of the 28 National Defence Academy (NDA) and 37 Indian Military Academy (IMA) course, including the direct and technical batches commissioned on 15 June 1966, with whom I spent some memorable years of my life, preparing for this profession which kept us regimented. Now, as veteran course mates, we will be assembling at Delhi Cantonment to celebrate the Golden Jubilee of victory in the 1971 war.

Kismet, destiny, chance or randomness has played its hand again as far as I am concerned. While most celebrate one Golden Jubilee, I am blessed to celebrate two in 2021: one with the regiment I had the honour of being commissioned into, to learn the finer aspects of cavalry spirit: dash, elan, swagger and readiness to engage the enemy at once, without fear of loss; and, the second, with course mates celebrating over five decades of loyalty, courage and fidelity to the Army and India.

Brigadier B. S. Mehta
Dharamshala, Himachal
7 November 2021